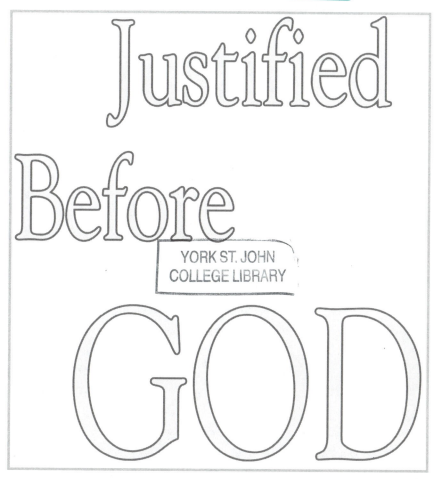

Justified Before GOD

A Contemporary Theology

Walter Klaiber

Abingdon Press
Nashville

JUSTIFIED BEFORE GOD
A CONTEMPORARY THEOLOGY

Copyright © 2006 by Abingdon Press

All rights reserved.

This book is printed on acid-free paper.

Library of Congress Cataloging-in-Publication Data

Klaiber, Walter.
   Justified before God: a contemporary theology/ Walter Klaiber.
      p. cm.
   Includes bibliographical references.
   ISBN 0-687-06316-7 (binding: adhesive perfect: alk. paper)
      1. Justification (Christian theology)   2. Justification (Christian theology)—Biblical teaching.   I.
Title.
   BT764.3.K63 2005
   234'.7—dc22

                                                                                    2005020424

All scripture quotations unless noted otherwise are taken from the *New Revised Standard Version of the Bible*, copyright 1989 by the Division of Christian Education of the National Council of the Churches of Christ in the United States of America. Used by permission. All rights reserved.

06 07 08 09 10 11 12 13 14 15 —10 9 8 7 6 5 4 3 2 1

MANUFACTURED IN THE UNITED STATES OF AMERICA

···r··· ··· t John

JUSTIFIED BEFORE GOD

CONTENTS

FOREWORD

The issue of justification has preoccupied me for many years. Ever since I've tried to reflect theologically on my faith—which has basically been the case since I was sixteen—I've been fascinated by the Pauline doctrine of justification. Through my encounter with my teacher, Ernst Käsemann, this fascination was decisively deepened. Justification was a central theme of my exposition of the New Testament—both in my preaching in the church and also in my seminary teaching. For that reason, the discussion about a possible agreement between the Roman Catholic and Evangelical Lutheran churches in matters of the doctrine of justification met with my particular interest.

However, my impression was that the results of exegetical work were of little interest in the intense discussions on the *Joint Declaration on the Doctrine of Justification*. There was a great deal of proof–texting, but little mention was made of the consensus that had been reached in the last forty years between Protestant and Catholic exegesis about the exposition of the Pauline doctrine of justification. And yet the consensus could have helped to clear up many contentious issues. In ensuing discussions, the inquiry into the biblical basis for the doctrine should present the decisive criterion for judging the results of talks. This discussion can also provide an important impetus for passing on to others the doctrine of justification today.

I hope this book will be a contribution to this discussion. It is meant to help not only clergy and academics but also others interested in theology to understand the breadth and depth of the biblical message of justification and to help them form an opinion regarding the current debate about the doctrine of justification. But above all, I hope this book can convey something of the creative and critical power of the message of justification and make it fruitful for the contemporary transmission of the gospel.

The literature on the subject is vast. Hence, only a selection from it can be mentioned and discussed in this work. Authors and key words in the notes point to the materials in the bibliography. In a few places I have used sections from my recent publications, and I have noted these at the appropriate places.

Since the publication of the German edition of this book, the discussion continued. Especially the debate on the *New Perspective* on Saint Paul's doctrine of justification went on. I did not change my mind on this matter. But I added to the notes of the English translation some referrals to the most important recent publications on this subject.

In the meantime the World Methodist Council has prepared a *Methodist Statement*, which declares its agreement with the *Joint Declaration on the Doctrine of Justification*. This Statement also draws the special image of a Methodist version of the doctrine of justification. Therefore the quest for the common biblical ground of this doctrine at which many look as the core of Christian teaching and preaching is more urgent than ever.

Many people have helped me to write this book and to publish it—first in the German original and now in the English translation. I want to thank them all; they are too many to mention them by name.

Above and beyond all that, this book is meant to be a thank you for all that God's healing justification has done in my life. "My mouth will tell of your righteous acts, of your deeds of salvation all day long, though their number is past my knowledge" (Ps 71:15).

Walter Klaiber

CHAPTER 1

THE CONTEMPORARY QUESTION

Who is God and what is God's relationship to me? Who am I and what value does my life have? Throughout the history of humanity these questions have been posed again and again. They remain timely today, even if they are posed with differing priority in differing religious cultures. In terms of the Bible there is a basic recognition that these questions belong indissolubly together. The response to the one question is mutually dependent on the response to the other.

Within the biblical message, these questions find their most emphatic answer in the Pauline doctrine of justification. It is through the revelation of God's righteousness and through the justification of our lives that we experience who God is and how God relates to us, as well as who we are and what our lives mean. Despite its unique depiction in Paul's writings, this doctrine is not unrelated to the rest of biblical theology. It is rooted in a broad-ranging biblical transmission concerning the justifying action of God and the revelation of God's righteousness.

But what does justification mean and what is the biblical understanding of God's righteousness? And what do these terms have to do with a response to the questions posed above? Isn't the question to which the teaching on justification responds, particularly in its reformation expression, not much more than an expression of a crisis of conscience from the late Middle Ages that still today preoccupies people existentially? It remains instructive to read how this problem was formulated in the fourth world-wide conference of Lutherans in Helsinki in 1963: "Today people no longer ask: How do I find a gracious God? People today ask something much more radical and elementary. They question the very existence of God: Where are you, God? People today no longer suffer from the sense of God's wrath, but from the sense of God's absence. They no longer suffer from their sense of sin, but from the senselessness of their existence. They no longer ask after a gracious God but whether God is real."[1]

But if the question of "whether God is real" is approached not in terms of a distanced philosophical question about the supreme being that we traditionally call God, but rather if the question is existentially asking how the source and supportive ground of all being relates to me personally and can become real to me, and whether my life is kept safe in him, and whether he can be encountered in person; if all this is so, then this question is in the final analysis identical to the question concerning a gracious God.

Anyone who studies the biblical message of justification as a whole will notice that it has been formulated precisely by people who also have endured the experience of the absence of God and through it have encountered God anew. The promise of justification is a response not only to a very specialized question posed to a particular religious consciousness. Rather, this promise makes one encounter the saving God. So says Paul in Romans 1:16ff. And this promise is also the heart of the teaching of the Reformation on the doctrine of justification.

In light of the agreement between the Roman Catholic Church and the Lutheran World Federation on the "consensus in basic truths of the doctrine of justification" in the *Joint Declaration on the Doctrine of Justification*[2] in the course of the execution of which there was once again an intensive discussion on the differing takes on Lutheran and Catholic understandings of the doctrine of justification, it seems important to me that we don't set aside our interest in the question of justification, relieved that the now overcome Reformation conflicts can be left in peace, but rather that we discover and unpack anew the power of the message of justification for our own era as well.

At the conclusion of the "Official Common Statement" by the Lutheran World Federation and the Catholic Church, the dialogue partners expressed their commitment to "continued and deepened study of the biblical foundations of the doctrine of justification."[3] They further promised that "Lutherans and Catholics will continue their efforts ecumenically in their common witness to interpret the message of justification in language relevant for human beings today, and with reference both to individual and social concerns of our times." I am convinced that there is a deep connection between these two concerns. A new understanding of the biblical fundamentals of the message of justification will facilitate its proclamation.

However, in terms of our exegetical work we find ourselves in the strange situation that considerable consensus seems to have been reached between Protestant and Catholic exegetes, and yet more recently, particularly in the Anglo-Saxon arena, completely new questions have arisen of the doctrine of justification. A "new perspective" on Paul has been developed, in the light of which the old "Lutheran" perspective seems to be merely a projection of problems of Late Middle Age theology into Pauline tests.[4] It is at this point that this book hopes to offer a clarifying overview. It asks about the entire biblical depiction of the doctrine of justification: What does justification mean in the Old Testament, and what is the relationship between the event of justification and the basic affirmations concerning the righteousness of God and of humans? What were Paul's particular concerns about the doctrine of justification, and what is the relationship between these and his larger theology and the message of the rest of the New Testament, particularly Jesus' proclamation? What does the message of justification say about God's actions toward humanity, and are there circumstances in which this is expressed differently?

In what follows, a brief overview of the different historical theological emphases leads to contemporary questions in light of the aforementioned ecumenical consensus on the doctrine of justification. The concluding theses in the book intend to highlight the meaning of the message of justification for the advancement of the gospel today.

CHAPTER 2

RIGHTEOUSNESS IS LIFE: THE OLD TESTAMENT

To this day, the concepts of "justice" and "righteousness" are important indicators of what people hope for in a community and need in their lives. The slogan, "No Peace Without Justice," which originates in the fight against apartheid, demonstrates the deep conviction that it is essential for the life of a society in which all the people in that society have the same opportunities for personal development and the protection of their rights.

But what is justice and what means righteousness? The Old Testament legacy is foundational for the biblical answer to this question. An initial look at this legacy does admittedly show very different nuances of the term. Some of it sounds familiar. When Lev 19:15 says, "You shall not render an unjust judgment; you shall not be partial to the poor or defer to the great: with justice you shall judge your neighbor," then this more or less corresponds to our understanding of justice.

Psalm 24:4-5 translates the same Hebrew word differently: "Those who have clean hands and pure hearts, who do not lift up their souls to what is false, and do not swear deceitfully. They will receive blessing from the LORD, and vindication from the God of their salvation." The NRSV renders the Hebrew word for "justice/righteousness" with "vindication" because here it does not describe those who behave appropriately during a legal trial but rather a gift of God that is full of blessing. Salvation and "righteousness" can be seen as being parallel: "The LORD has made known his salvation; he has revealed his righteousness in the sight of the nations" (Ps 98:2 in literal translation).

What aspect of this term is the key to understanding its totality? Whereas Josef Scharbert emphasizes "that the talk of 'Righteousness' has its original *Sitz im Leben* in the administration of justice," Friedrich Horst concludes that "the Old Testament characterizes righteousness on the basis of God's righteousness. But this righteousness is, like the name, holiness, radiance, and majesty of God, an action of God that proceeds from the sphere of God and has its effect in tending to the world's needs."[1] In studying the Old Testament texts more closely, one can establish that both approaches are justified. We will turn first to the use of the term in the sense of the administration of justice.

1. RIGHTEOUSNESS: SOCIAL ELEMENT OF LIFE

The warning "with justice"[2] in legal process is found in almost all layers of the OT tradition. It is part of the basic components of the Book of the Covenant (Exod 23:6), part of the Holiness Code (Lev 19:15), of the Deuteronomic texts (Deut 25:1), and of the Proverbs (Prov 17:15; cf. 18:5; 24:24).

Judging fairly is particularly the task of the king: "May he defend the cause of the poor of the people, give deliverance to the needy, and crush the oppressor" (Ps 72:4). He is told to "speak out for those who cannot speak, for the rights of all the destitute. Speak out, judge righteously, depend the rights of the poor and needy" (Prov 31:8-9). What this means concretely is to "act with justice and righteousness, and deliver from the hand of the oppressor anyone who has been robbed. And do no wrong or violence to the alien, the orphan, and the widow, or shed innocent blood in this place" (Jer 22:3).[3]

These texts lead to a whole series of important observations. Strangely, a norm by which a just court is to act is never named. The measure is exclusively the recognition of who is in the right and who is not, and the expectation that one acts accordingly. Apparently the Old Testament understanding of righteousness is dependent on the person and circumstance. More than one hundred years ago the New Testament scholar Hermann Cremer had already indicated this and characterized biblical "righteousness" as a relational term.[4] It subsequently took until the middle of the twentieth century for this understanding to become established.[5]

In more modern exegesis, the story of Judah and Tamar in Genesis 38 often serves to demonstrate the Old Testament understanding of righteousness.

When Judah recognizes that Tamar, whom he had accused of adultery, has seduced him in order to provide her deceased husband with a legitimate heir, he admits, "She is in the right, not I" (Gen 38:26).[6] The fact that her basically offensive behavior is called "righteous" "can only be explained by understanding that she acted in a way that was appropriate to her spousal relationship in order that the name of her husband would continue.... Tamar acted correctly and appropriately by putting her life at risk and not only her reputation, above and beyond what virtue and custom demand. In this episode, good and evil are not measured against a single norm, a single law; for which law could command such behavior? It's much more a case of heeding the web of community relations in which one finds oneself, and encountering one's fellow humans correspondingly."[7] According to Old Testament understanding, righteousness is conduct that is fair to and furthers community—a community faithfulness.

A second observation follows. Although one is fundamentally called upon to judge impartially and without regard to the person, whether in respect to the lowly and poor or to the distinguished and highly regarded (cf. Exod 23:3; Lev 19:15), the danger of the lowly being shown preference was apparently relatively slight, so that where deplorable states of affairs are criticized, there is a reminder about insufficient advocacy for the poor and the weak.

For this reason, Jerusalem is accused thus: "Your princes are rebels and companions of thieves. Everyone loves a bribe and runs after gifts. They do not defend the orphan, and the widow's cause does not come before them" (Isa 1:23; cf. Isa 1:17). The king and nobility in Jerusalem are supposed to speak up for those who are powerless to make their own voices heard in court.[8] The legal help expected here goes way beyond the verdict and the legal proceedings. Doing right, saving, and helping become synonymous here (cf. Ps 72:4 with vv. 12-14).

Jeremiah's accusation in 22:13-17 shows precisely to what extent corruption and extortion went hand in hand in reality. In his censure, Jeremiah accuses Jehoiakim of having built his glamorous buildings through illegally extorted slave labor, and holds up to him the positive example of his father, Josiah: "Did not your father eat and drink and do justice and righteousness? Then it was well with him. He judged the cause of the poor and needy; then it was well. Is not this to know me? says the LORD. But your eyes and heart are only on your dishonest gain, for shedding innocent blood, and for practicing oppression and violence" (vv. 15-17).

The call to "justice and righteousness" also encompasses the fight against "iniquitous decrees" and "oppressive statutes," which are imposed "to turn aside the needy from justice and to rob the poor of my people of their right, that widows may be your spoil, and that you may make the orphans your prey!" (Isa 10:1-2).[9] The socially weak are to be deprived of a fair wage because of legal subterfuge; rather, they should receive their due. In the Old Testament, "justice" is what a person is due,[10] and what is meant by this is not only what is legally enforceable but rather whatever a person needs in order to live and whatever is necessary in terms of care and help to enable communal life to flourish. Without social responsibility there can be no just society.

The connection between social exploitation and open or concealed perversion of justice is perhaps addressed nowhere more drastically than in Amos's lament over circumstances in Israel:

> Ah, you that turn justice to wormwood, and bring righteousness to the ground! . . . They hate the one who reproves in the gate, and they abhor the one who speaks the truth. Therefore because you trample on the poor and take from them levies of grain, you have built houses of hewn stone, but you shall not live in them; you have planted pleasant vineyards, but you shall not drink their wine. For I know how many are your transgressions, and how great are your sins—you who afflict the righteous, who take a bribe, and push aside the needy in the gate. Therefore the prudent will keep silent in such a time; for it is an evil time. Seek good and not evil, that you may live; and so the LORD, the God of hosts, will be with you, just as you have said. Hate evil and love good, and establish justice in the gate (Amos 5:7, 10-15a).[11]

"Justice and righteousness" describe that which is helpful and needful for life and what builds up community. It describes the good that leads to life.[12] This is an underlying conviction of Israel, and it is emphasized in the Wisdom literature: "Whoever is steadfast in righteousness will live, but whoever pursues evil will die" (Prov 11:19).[13]

To what extent "justice and righteousness" constitute the foundation of life for all Israel's existence is shown by the juxtaposition of eager but superficial worship busyness and what God actually wants and what really makes a difference in life, in Amos 5:21-24:

> I hate, I despise your festivals, and I take no delight in your solemn assemblies. Even though you offer me your burnt offerings and grain offerings, I will not accept them; and the offerings of well-being of your

fatted animals I will not look upon. Take away from me the noise of your songs; I will not listen to the melody of your harps. But let justice roll down like waters, and righteousness like an ever-flowing stream.[14]

Perverted righteousness poisons and embitters life (Amos 5:7; 6:12); lived righteousness is as much an element of life as running water.

This addresses a third characteristic that directly or indirectly shapes these texts. Behind the demand for justice and righteousness stands God and God's actions. God's incorrupt and ameliorating judging is supposed to shape human judging. This is expressed as follows in Deut 10:17-19:

> For the LORD your God is God of gods and Lord of lords, the great God, mighty and awesome, who is not partial and takes no bribe, who executes justice for the orphan and the widow, and who loves the strangers, providing them food and clothing. You shall also love the stranger, for you were strangers in the land of Egypt.

God's concern regarding justice and righteousness is personified in the form of a promised Davidic king of peace, of whom is said: "He shall not judge by what his eyes see, or decide by what his ears hear; but with righteousness he shall judge the poor, and decide with equity for the meek of the earth" (Isa 11:3b-4b).[15]

And in the later prophetic text of Isa 32, beside the promise that in the future day of salvation "a king will reign in righteousness, and princes will rule with justice" (v. 1), we find the affirmation that God will pour out "a spirit from on high": "And the wilderness becomes a fruitful field, and the fruitful field is deemed a forest.... The effect of righteousness will be peace, and the result of righteousness, quietness and trust forever" (vv. 15b-17). Righteousness is the essential condition for peace and prosperous and secure life together. But such righteousness can only be a gift of God and the work of God's spirit.[16] Whoever seeks righteousness must ask for the righteousness of God.

2. GOD'S RIGHTEOUSNESS AND HUMAN SALVATION

We cannot avoid it; one cannot speak of righteousness in the Old Testament without speaking of God's "righteousness." That is, his covenant faithfulness forms the basis and possibility of a righteous human life. "The LORD works vindication and justice for all who are oppressed" (Ps 103:6). He "is righteous; he loves righteous deeds" (Ps 11:7).[17] This is the basis for the hope of righteousness. Whenever earthly practices of justice fail, God is to create justice through God's judgment so that God will "judge your servants, condemning the guilty by bringing their conduct on their own head, and vindicating the righteous by rewarding them according to their righteousness" (1 Kgs 8:32b.) What is requested on behalf of the king is: "Give the king your justice, O God, and your righteousness to a king's son. May he judge your people with righteousness, and your poor with justice" (Ps 72:1-2).

Yet God's sphere of activity is not limited to legal affairs. The oldest Old Testament evidence of this can be found in Deborah's song: "To the sound of musicians at the watering places, there they repeat the triumphs [literally, the righteous acts] of the LORD, the triumphs [literally, the righteous acts] of his peasantry in Israel" (Judg 5:11). Proof of God's righteousness is deliverance from need, liberative triumph over enemies and oppressors.[18]

The appearance of the righteousness of God therefore signifies his liberating presence among God's people and on this earth. Above all, it is at Zion, the mountain of God and the place of the temple, where God abides, that is the principle place of the revelation of God's righteousness: "The LORD is exalted, he dwells on high; he filled Zion with justice and righteousness; he will be the stability of your times, abundance of salvation, wisdom, and knowledge; the fear of the LORD is Zion's treasure" (Isa 33:5-6; cf. Ps 48:11). Righteousness and justice are integral parts of theophany, of God's appearing in power and majesty; Ps 97:1-6 expresses it particularly emphatically: "The LORD is king! Let the earth rejoice; let the many coastlands be glad! Clouds and thick darkness are all around him; righteousness and justice are the foundation of his throne. Fire goes before him, and consumes his adversaries on every side.... The heavens proclaim his righteousness; and all the peoples behold his glory."[19]

God's creation and sustaining of the world are also expressions of God's righteousness. That which gives the community of persons order and security also gives the natural world constancy and prosperity. Psalm 33:4-6 substantiates its call to praise God in this way: "For the word of the LORD is upright, and all his work is done in faithfulness. He loves righteousness and justice; the earth is full of the steadfast love of the LORD. By the word of the LORD the heavens were made, and all their host by the breath of his mouth."

So righteousness also means the salvific "world order" that "unites cosmic, political, religious, social, and ethical aspects."[20] This idiom embraces elements of ancient Middle Eastern presuppositions, particularly characteristics of "Ma'at," the Egyptian goddess of wisdom and order, but gives them a new biblical cast of belief in God. Here, "righteousness [appears], rather like peace or faithfulness or grace, as an almost separate entity and yet at the same time is still completely integrated into the picture of the one God of Israel."[21]

The best example of this is Ps 85:9-13:

> Surely his salvation is at hand for those who fear him, that his glory may dwell in our land. Steadfast love and faithfulness will meet; righteousness and peace will kiss each other. Faithfulness will spring up from the ground, and righteousness will look down from the sky. The LORD will give what is good, and our land will yield its increase. Righteousness will go before him, and will make a path for his steps.

Here not only are the creation and preservation of the world expressions of the righteous actions of God but so also are fruitfulness and prosperity (cf. also Pss 65:5-13; 72:2ff.; Hos 2:18-22). The dependability of God's righteousness and justice and the richness of his goodness and truth are the basis and fulfillment of human life:

> Your steadfast love, O LORD, extends to the heavens, your faithfulness to the clouds. Your righteousness is like the mighty mountains, your judgments are like the great deep; you save humans and animals alike, O LORD. How precious is your steadfast love, O God! All people may take refuge in the shadow of your wings. They feast on the abundance of your house, and you give them drink from the river of your delights. For with you is the fountain of life; in your light we see light. O continue your steadfast love to those who know you, and your salvation to the upright of heart! (Ps 36:5-10)

The Appeal to God's Righteousness

This trust in God's righteousness is not only expressed in the thanksgiving of the people. In the individuals' lamentations it is precisely those individuals who find themselves in distress who refer to it. The cry, "In you, O LORD, I seek refuge; do not let me ever be put to shame; in your righteousness deliver me" (Ps 31:1), or even more pointedly, "Wake up!

Bestir yourself for my defense, for my cause, my God and my Lord! Vindicate me, O LORD, my God, according to your righteousness, and do not let them rejoice over me" (Ps 35:23-24).[22] This accords in many psalms with the song of praise on the occasion of the giving of desired help: "Then my tongue shall tell of your righteousness and of your praise all day long" (Ps 35:28).[23] Apparently here God is being called upon and praised as the guardian of justice, and therefore it is no surprise that these themes appear particularly in the lament of those who feel themselves to be unjustly persecuted.[24]

But the remarkable thing is that the appeal to God's righteousness also occurs in those psalms in which the ones praying confess their failings and plead for forgiveness of their sins.[25] The appeal to God's righteousness is not tied to the question of guilt and innocence—although it plays an important role in threatening a person's existence—but rather refers to the need of the prayer as a whole. Help is expected from God's righteousness whenever there is sickness, an enemy threat, or an unjustified accusation.[26]

The right to life, for which God's intervention can assure new meaning and security, encompasses more than God's acquittal of specific guilt: God's righteousness is an expression of his salvific affirmation of the prayer's threatened existence. Yahweh's *tsedaqah* (righteousness) in the Psalms is "the denotation for the deliverance of the individual Israelite from the trouble which separates him from Yahweh and other persons, and hence also the denotation for his reincorporation into this community." Through it, "the person who has become isolated and estranged from his surroundings through suffering, transgressions, and accusations receives restitution and is reincorporated into [the community]. Promise, healing, and once again being accepted are fundamentally a process, a process that applies wholistically, bodily, and above all socially."[27] But all of this is "justification" in the Old Testament sense of the word, through which a person who is afflicted and whose existence is threatened receives encouragement from God about his dignity and right to life.[28]

It is for this reason that the at first surprising fact can also be explained, namely, that it is precisely in this context that the reference to God's righteousness runs parallel to the appeal to his goodness and faithfulness, his pardon and mercy.[29]

But it is surely confusing for the contemporary reader that the one praying such a psalm can in the same context also refer to his own righteousness, as, for example, in Ps 7:8: "judge me, O LORD, according to my righteousness and according to the integrity that is in me," which closes by saying, "I will give to the LORD the thanks due to his righteousness, and sing praise to the name of the LORD, the Most High" (v. 17).[30] Obviously we have here a similarly complex situation as the one just noted: A sinner's confession does not rule out an appeal to God's righteousness as surely as calling upon God's righteousness does not make unnecessary the affirmation of one's own innocence. Even those who enter in to the gate of the temple with "clean hands and pure hearts" are told that they will "receive blessing from the LORD, and vindication from the God of their salvation" (Ps 24:5). Declaration of integrity only receives "positive content through the justifying intervention of Jahweh. It is only through God's turning God's countenance toward the one praying that divine righteousness is bestowed on the supplicant, and that he becomes properly justified."[31] The "justification of the righteous one" is a deep and serious concern of the psalm, precisely because it cannot be taken for granted. It's not a matter of self-justification, but of "God bring[ing] to light the righteousness of the righteous against all questioning and temptation."[32] Psalm 37, which follows the wisdom style in accentuating the difference between "the righteous one" and "the wicked one," encapsulates this difference: "Commit your way to the LORD; trust in him, and he will act. He will make your vindication shine like the light, and the justice of your cause like the noonday" (vv. 5-6).

Even the "righteousness" that people prove by their behavior and deeds is never their "own" but remains a part of that which God's righteousness works in a person. "In the final analysis, this is why the morally good human deed lacks the character of personal achievement and works righteousness."[33] Despite the emphatic way in which the Old Testament seeks behavior that corresponds to the will of God and his righteousness, nonetheless it holds true that "the relationship to God is not determined by human behavior."[34]

Salvation for the People, Salvation for the World

Whether the people confess their sins or whether they gratefully boast of God's salvific help, they always see in God's dependable, relational faithfulness the basis for their own actions of salvation (cf. Ps 65:1-5). The effects of this faithfulness are not limited to the people who gather for worship at the temple in Zion. God is "the hope of all the ends of the earth and of the farthest seas" (v. 5b). For he created this earth and preserves it and bestows on it overflowing fruitfulness (vv. 6-8). Forgiveness of sins and worshipful communion with God, God's salvific actions in history, and God's presence in the creation and flourishing of the earth—all these are capsulated as God acting "in righteousness."

This universal scope of God's action, for which the terms "righteousness" and "salvation" are almost synonymous characteristics, is also found in a series of psalms that praise Yahweh as King.[35] In a literal translation, this is most poignantly formulated in Ps 98:1-3: "O sing to the LORD a new song, for he has done marvelous things. His right hand and his holy arm helped him. The LORD has made known his salvation; he has revealed his righteousness in the sight of the nations. He has remembered his steadfast love and faithfulness to the house of Israel. All the ends of the earth have seen the salvation of our God."

The revelation of God's righteousness makes visible his acts of salvation toward Israel and is an expression of God's fidelity to God's people. If the human world at first seems to be only a spectator to allow this process to be highlighted, then the continuation of the psalm shows that the whole world is included in this event and should therefore rejoice before Yahweh's face: "For he is coming to judge the earth. He will judge the world with righteousness, and the peoples with equity" (98:9). Here, what is apparently meant by "judge" is not the punishment of an evil world but a helpful setting to rights of the world according to the standards and order of God's salvific righteousness.[36]

It has long been recognized that the message of these psalms is linked to the proclamation and theology of Second Isaiah. To this people in exile, which was bemoaning its distance from God and its godforsakenness, this prophet could say, "Here is your God! See, the Lord GOD comes with might, and his arm rules for him" (Isa 40:9b-10a). The fact that God will make visible his reign totally anew will mean peace and salvation for God's people (Isa 52:7-10a).

God's reign will lead people in a new exodus out of exile.[37] The whole creation is included into this revelation of God's salvific righteousness: "Shower, O heavens, from above, and let the skies rain down righteousness; let the earth open, that salvation may spring up, and let it cause righteousness to sprout up also; I the LORD have created it" (Isa 45:8). It is not nature's fertility that is being discussed here; "the striking picture of the imparting of the coming salvation through heaven and earth shows that salvation is meant to encompass the whole world and all its regions. What's spoken of here is not 'a new heaven and a new earth' but rather a healed world."[38] Here righteousness and salvation are obviously almost synonyms. The doubting people, shaped by reproachful resignation, are told: "Listen to me, you stubborn of heart, you who are far from righteousness: I bring near my righteousness, it is not far off, and my salvation will not tarry; I will put salvation in Zion, for Israel my glory" (Isa 46:12-13; NRSV has deliverance instead of "righteousness"). And the "survivors of the nations" are told: "Turn to me and be saved, all the ends of the earth! For I am God, and there is no other. By myself I have sworn, from my mouth has gone forth in righteousness a word that shall not return: 'To me every knee shall bow, every tongue shall swear.' Only in the LORD, it shall be said of me, are righteousness and strength" (Isa 45:23b-24a).[39]

"Righteousness" and "salvation" are concepts that interpret one another (cf. Isa 51:6, 8b). "What is meant is the salvation established through God's righteousness; not just liberation and deliverance but much more all encompassing the new condition of all things in which God's righteousness rules."[40]

Viewing the promise of salvation together with the conduct of the people then determines the message of Third Isaiah.[41] He intensifies Second Isaiah's direct promise of salvation, but contrasts it with the religious and social situation in postexilic Judah. In summary, what he says is, "Thus says the LORD: Maintain justice, and do what is right, for soon my salvation will come, and my deliverance [righteousness] be revealed" (Isa 56:1). The demands put to Israel to "maintain justice and do what is right" are based on the announcement of the proximate presence of God's salvific righ-teousness. "Because Yahweh's *tsedaqah* [righteousness] is coming, *tsedaqah* must now be practiced."[42]

For this reason, chapter 58 turns against the self-analysis of the people "as if they were a nation that practiced righteousness and did not forsake the ordinance of their God." This chapter also challenges their "delight to draw near God" (Isa 58:2). For the people's fasting, to which they refer, is superficial and without consequence for social life together. As God sees it:

> Is not this the fast that I choose: to loose the bonds of injustice, to undo the thongs of the yoke, to let the oppressed go free, and to break every yoke? Is it not to share your bread with the hungry, and bring the homeless poor into your house; when you see the naked, to cover them, and not to hide yourself from your own kin? Then your light shall break forth like the dawn, and your healing shall spring up quickly; your vindicator [righteousness] shall go before you, the glory of the LORD

shall be your rear guard. Then you shall call, and the LORD will answer; you shall cry for help, and he will say, Here I am. (Isa 58:6-9a)

The righteousness of the people continues to be a gift of God in Third Isaiah, albeit a gift that must be lived out in active and practical behavior in order to remain effective. Isaiah 64:5 shows the deep tension that the people inhabit: "You meet those who gladly do right, those who remember you in your ways....We have all become like one who is unclean, and all our righteous deeds are like a filthy cloth. We all fade like a leaf, and our iniquities, like the wind, take us away." All that remains for one is to find refuge in God himself: "Yet, O LORD, you are our Father; we are the clay, and you are our potter; we are all the work of your hand. Do not be exceedingly angry, O LORD, and do not remember iniquity forever. Now consider, we are all your people" (Isa 64:8ff.).

God's righteousness must become the righteousness of the people; their "righteousness" resides solely in the fact that God speaks his salvific "Yes" to them. The fact that this people finds its source of life in this Yes and allows its doings to be formed by him makes present God's Yes to this world before all peoples.[43]

3. JUSTIFICATION: WORD OF DELIVERANCE AND RECOGNITION

That God shows his righteousness is equally Israel's hope in a hopeless situation and the hope of many people who turn to God in prayer seeking help and justice from him. The fact that God in his righteousness brings justice to the oppressed is their "justification"; it is the very reason for their new way of being before God and before other people. In order to understand what the Old and New Testaments mean by "justification," it is important to know how legal processes were handled in Israel and how judgments were reached.[44]

Ancient Israel had no system of justice through which crimes were pursued in society and brought to trial. In those cases where the communal life of society was damaged by the behavior of a citizen, one of the other citizens had to bring charges. The offense was decided by an ad hoc court of local citizens in good standing gathered "at the gate."[45] The object of the decision was not only the facts of the accusation; the criminal act as a whole burdened the community. Therefore, the community had been harmed either through the accused's wrongful behavior or by the accuser's wrongful accusation. The Old Testament judicial process does not serve to impose a righteousness measured against a preconceived norm; rather it serves to mediate between accuser and accused. What must be publicly established is who is in the right and who is not.[46] Deuteronomy 25:1 offers a short and succinct description of the process: "Suppose two persons have a dispute and enter into litigation, and the judges decide between them, declaring one to be in the right and the other to be in the wrong."

The positive verdict is: "You are in the right" or better translated as "You have behaved rightly," and therefore: "You are righteous." This judgment was pronounced by either the judges or by a participant in the legal proceedings, though of course it was understood that the person speaking would be the guilty party. "She is more in the right than I," says Judah about Tamar (Gen 38:26), and Saul, convinced by David's magnanimity, says, "You are more righteous than I" (1 Sam 24:17).

What this means for the accused is, first of all, "to be freed in all ways, in the sight and hearing of all, of the stigma heaped upon him."[47] Through this, innocence is shown, and in some places, such as for example in 2 Kgs 10:9, the respective formula can only be translated as "You are innocent."[48] But that is the exception, and the judgment "You are right(eous)" fundamentally means more than a declaration of innocence. It is not a double negative ("You are not guilty") that determines the judgment, but rather a positive statement: "You have behaved rightly. You are in the right." The declaration of innocence is at one and the same time justification of the accused and also more than that: "By it, the accused is recognized as a *bona fide* member of the community."[49] For the ancient Near Eastern person, "this public recognition of his rightful place in society is indispensable."[50] The very existence of anyone who becomes enmeshed in a legal process is threatened. The task of the judge is to "establish a person who is not guilty of transgressing community norms as being faithful to the community and [to] once again publicly grant him his rightful place in the community."[51]

This is also the reason why society is so endangered if a guilty person is pronounced innocent. For by so doing one has not only mistakenly allowed a criminal to go free but has also integrated someone into society who at the same time endangers the very core of the community by his antisocial behavior. The reverse is also true: a person who is judged guilty has not only lost the case but stands outside of the law-abiding community, which is the basis of all social existence. Persons without legal standing, those legally represented by no one (e.g., widows, orphans, and aliens), and persons held in little esteem very easily found themselves in danger of living outside the community.

Since the legal proceedings happened in a relatively unstructured way, other clashes between conflicted parties were described using the same legal categories. We have already mentioned the example of Saul in 1 Sam 24:17. But after the seventh plague, the king in the conflict between God and the Pharaoh in Exod 9 makes his confession using precisely the formula of a defeated legal opponent: "This time I have sinned; the LORD is in the right, and I and my people are in the wrong" (Exod 9:27b).

With reference to the destruction of Jerusalem and the deportation of its ruling class to Babylon, the exilic and postexilic community also wrestles with the question of whether Yahweh acted justly toward the community in allowing Jerusalem to be destroyed. The response given in Lamentations is "Jerusalem sinned grievously" (Lam 1:8a), and therefore Zion confesses, "The LORD is in the right, for I have rebelled against his word" (1:18a).[52]

This situation is also the background against which one begins to search the Old Testament to understand justification of the individual. The conception that all will have to answer before God in a final judgment is basically alien to the Old Testament.[53] But there is one place in the text where an Israelite had to repeatedly prove to God that he was able to live as part of the community. Exegetes have recognized for some time that Ps 15 presents a kind of liturgy for admission to the temple.[54] The pilgrims come to the temple and at the gate ask: "O LORD, who may abide in your tent? Who may dwell on your holy hill?" (v. 1). To which the priest responds: "Those who walk blamelessly, and do what is right, and speak the truth from their heart; who do not slander with their tongue, and do no evil to their friends, nor take up a reproach against their neighbors; in whose eyes the wicked are despised, but who honor those who fear the LORD; who stand by their oath even to their hurt; who do not lend money at interest, and do not take a bribe against the innocent. Those who do these things shall never be moved" (Ps 15:2-5).[55] Or, as Ps 24:5 formulates the consequence, whoever does this "will receive blessing from the LORD, and vindication [righteousness] from the God of their salvation."[56]

It appears that there was no individual test of whether these conditions had been met. Questions and answers were intended as a self-examination, a kind of confessional. The entrance liturgy fundamentally assumed the "unquestioned uprightness" of the pilgrims.[57] This collective certainty was questioned by the prophetic writings and was destroyed by the events of the destruction of the temple and the exile. It is precisely in the context of the understanding of a collective responsibility that the question arises of whether God is really being fair to individuals with his court of justice. This question is taken up systematically in Ezek 18 and 33. The prophet quotes slogans circulating among the populace. There are people who say, "The way of the Lord is unfair" (18:25, 29; see also 33:17, 20). Others say, "The parents have eaten sour grapes, and the children's teeth are set on edge" (18:2b). And yet others complain, "Our transgressions and our sins weigh upon us, and we waste away because of them; how then can we live?" (33:10). Apparently rebellion and resignation spill over into each other.

The response that the prophet gives to this on behalf of God is a passionate appeal for life: "As I live, says the Lord God, I have no pleasure in the death of the wicked, but that the wicked turn from their ways and live; turn back, turn back from your evil ways; for why will you die, O house of Israel?" (Ezek 33:11; cf. 18:23-24, 31).

But at the same time what is accentuated is that deeds of "justice and righteousness" and affirmation of life are tightly bound together. After recounting a series of basic social and cultic laws, comparable to the list in Ps 15, the prophet says of those who follow these laws: "Such a one is righteous; he shall surely live, says the Lord GOD" (Ezek 18:9). In this respect, each person is accountable to God for his or her own behavior (vv. 10-18). Not only is the liability of one generation to another abolished as an unavoidable fate,[58] even in his own lifetime a person should have the opportunity to repent and find the path to life.

A whole series of observations on this text is important for our context. What is particularly notable is once again the connection between righteousness and life. The affirmation of life does not describe a divine reward, and the threat of death is not a punishment from outside; rather, both expound upon what is already included in the living out of righteousness, or conversely, of injustice. This has been repeatedly established in Proverbs: "Whoever is steadfast in righteousness will live, but whoever pursues evil will die" (Prov 11:19), or, "In the path of righteousness there is life, in walking its path there is no death" (Prov 12:28).

In asking about the contents of this promise of life one must remember that to this point nothing explicit has yet been said in the Old

Testament about eternal life. "Life," which corresponds to righteousness, is a fulfilled and preserved life, a life given by God, a life lived under God's blessing and in his proximity.[59] But since God is "the fountain of life" (Ps 36:9), for whoever holds to God, even death can no longer be a final frontier (Ps 73:26; cf. Ps 63:3).

Through the connection between actions and consequences presumed in the Old Testament,[60] the promise of life is actually already based in doing righteousness. And yet of necessity it remains a promise, something beyond a crude automatism. This connection between actions and consequences is not simply a neutral doctrine, but rather "the expression of a hope whose realization is tied at one and the same time to the righteousness and the love of God."[61] In Ezek 18, the righteousness also remains "inferred" righteousness. Ezekiel 18:9 is a typical "declaration formula," the kind proclaimed by temple priests: "Such a one is righteous; he shall surely live." Neither in the courts at the gate nor on admittance to the temple can one declare oneself to be righteous. "The nature of righteousness, and who the righteous man is, is determined by Yahweh alone, and a man lives as he acknowledges this."[62] Justification as (re)acceptance into the community and admission into the place of the presence of God is "grace," not in the Western sense of grace preceding law, but rather in the biblical sense of a person's justification, affirmation, and fulfillment being found in God's and others' turning to them.[63] For that reason, in the Old Testament, righteousness is at one and the same time the condition and the gift in the encounter with God.[64]

Righteousness is thus "reckoned to a person" (see Gen 15:6). This term derives not from accounting practices but from cultic life, and describes the process of a priest declaring a sacrificial animal to be fit for cultic use.[65] Precisely because the people's "fitness for cultic life" and hence also their fitness for community with God depended not only on the fulfillment of individual commands but also on the ceremonial "declaration of righteousness" at the entrance to the temple, this word of the priestly declaration can also be used where a particular explicit behavior is declared as being "righteousness" before God. So, for example, with reference to the intercession of Phineas (Ps 106:30ff.), but above all with reference to Abraham in Gen 15:6 in the famous words "[Abram] believed the LORD; and the LORD reckoned it to him as righteousness." Admittedly this seems to take a step in a completely different direction: Although Abraham's faith could be described as human behavior that is recognized by God, nevertheless "all the emphasis . . . is on God and his promise. The only possible way a person can behave in response to this promise is to believe, to welcome, to accept the promise."[66] Thus, Abraham's faith is understood here not as an achievement. Within the context of the Israelite faith story, the text assumes "that basing righteousness on human behavior has every time proved itself impossible. For this reason, it is through an unmediated act of declaration that Abraham is addressed by God himself."[67]

This declaratory act precisely does not establish "that Abraham finds himself in a condition of righteousness because of his ethical uprightness" and that because his relationship "to Jahweh is in every respect a good one ... he lives in a condition of godly well-being."[68] The comparison with Ezek 18:9 shows that reckoning faith as righteousness puts a new dimension on this godly affirmation of life, affirming its sole basis to be the relationship to God.[69] What results is a recognition that is singular in the whole ancient Near East: "that righteousness and the life possible as a result of it must be accepted as a gift of God, and that not human behavior but the divine gift of righteousness becomes the basis of life."[70] Therefore, in this sense "justification" means not that someone is in the right and is therefore a part of the community but rather refers to the freely given promise of fellowship with God, through which God says of a person, "You're all right" and which first establishes this fellowship.

4. GOD'S JUSTIFICATION AND A SINNER'S JUSTIFICATION

In order to understand what justification means in the Old Testament, we have to consider yet another dimension of this question. Wherever people in Israel question the meaning of their lives before God, wherever they wrestle with the question in the face of trials, suffering, or misfortune, in all these situations the question about God and his justification arises. This questioning of humans is also the questioning of their God and their relationship to him. "Where is your God?" ask the adversaries (Ps 42:3-10).[71] The justification of the one praying is therefore also the justification of God, whom he confesses. The plea for retribution toward the enemies corresponds not only to the desire for personal revenge but also to the necessity of clarifying on whose side God is and whether he has the power to accomplish his justice.[72]

23

The Question of Guilt

This question is posed particularly poignantly in the aftermath of the destruction of Jerusalem during the exile. Although the preexilic prophets' message about legal proceedings offered a way to explain the catastrophe and "to give positive meaning to the experience of downfall," "it was not the God who had failed; indeed, in contrast he had shown himself to be Lord of history by himself taking steps against the faithfulness of his people."[73]

But this realization did not go uncontested. For, after all, the catastrophe affected not only the people; the Temple had been destroyed, many had been expelled to a country whose gods seemed more powerful, despite the fact that shortly before the catastrophe recognition had begun to catch on that Yahweh was the only God and was to be worshipped exclusively in Jerusalem. Thus the question of "the righteousness" of God, of his faithfulness to himself and his people, began to be brought into extrasharp focus.[74]

This is particularly reflected in the proclamation of the exilic prophets. Particular idioms common among the people crop up in the exilic prophets that the prophet picks up and contradicts.[75] For example, the accusation is made, "The Lord does not act justly,"[76] or the slogan recited, "The parents have eaten sour grapes, and the children's teeth are set on edge,"[77] or as the complaint of Israel, "My way is hidden from the LORD, and my right is disregarded by God,"[78] or "The LORD has forsaken me, my Lord has forgotten me" (Isa 49:14).

The responses to these questions and complaints are multifaceted. We have discussed Ezek 18 and 33 above. In Deutero-Isaiah the entire emphasis is on the promise of the boundless creative power of God, which is directed specifically to the faint and weary (Isa 40:28-31). God no more gives up on his people than a mother forgets her child (Isa 49:15-17). The promise of the unbreakable faithfulness of God is intended to conquer all resignation.

Wherever this faithfulness is contested, the prophet picks up a form of legal language in which God is clashing with the people's complaints and allegations (cf. Isa 42:18-25; 43:22-28; 50:1-3). In this context we must mention Isa 45:18-25 once more, a passage that belongs to these courtroom speeches. Those of the people who have gone astray are called upon to recognize that Yahweh is "a righteous [= salvific] God and a Savior" the like of which there is no other. Therefore they are challenged with great urgency to turn to this God and allow themselves to be saved, to recognize him openly as God and in so doing to confess that "only in the LORD...are righteousness [literal plural = acts of salvation] and strength." As the people ascribe righteousness to God, so too will Israel receive justice.[79] God's justification is also the justification of his people—but this occurs under the condition that God's salvation is for all.[80]

In the process of reformulating this message what moves center stage is the question about guilt, which is what separates the people from their God and excludes them from fellowship with him. After all, in a "regular" court case the innocent party would be declared innocent and the guilty judged. This is likewise what is expected of God (1 Kgs 8:33-34). And although the judgment itself is not the chief goal of the Old Testament legal process, but rather that which "sets things right,"[81] part of the judgment of God is also the act of punishing. In choosing between right and wrong, between the innocent one and the sinner, God is bringing to light true righteousness (Jer 51:9ff.; Ps 37:6). And yet the Old Testament does not speak at all of a punishing righteousness, or at most peripherally.[82] God's wrath turns against injustice and guilt; his innermost revulsion against everything that is contrary to his being.[83] It is those, however, who open themselves to his words and actions, for whom his righteousness is intended. But what happens to guilt then, whose unmitigated reality prevents a deadly danger to the people?[84]

There are a variety of responses to this question—even within the prophetic writings of Deutero-Isaiah. Thus in the long introductory words of comfort, the city of Jerusalem is to be told "that she has served her term, that her penalty is paid, that she has received from the LORD's hand double for all her sins" (40:2).[85] In exile, the people had emptied "the cup of his wrath...to the dregs" (51:17)—but not "to satisfy a higher righteousness"[86] but rather because the people had poured the cup themselves. But all this must now be at an end, because God has said "It is enough!"

At the same time, in Isa 43:22-28, in the name of Yahweh the prophet defends the people against the accusation that the people went to great effort and trouble with their sin offerings and sacrificial offerings but God did not honor these. To this Yahweh responds, "I have not burdened you with offerings.... But you have burdened me with your sins; you have wearied me with your iniquities. I, I am He who blots out your transgressions for my own sake, and I will not remember your sins" (Isa 43:23b,

24b, 25). The execution of justice among the people (v. 28) belongs to this "treating" of Israel's sins.[87]

A completely new perspective appears when Isa 43:3b, 4 speaks about God, in his love, giving other nations to his people as a ransom in order to ransom Israel from their captivity to sin and their fall into death and decay.[88] Can guilt be overcome by someone taking it on by proxy? This is the message in the fourth song of God's servant in Isa 52:13–53:12. What is at first an incomprehensible fate of God's servant is recognized through its interpretation in the prophetic word as a deputized suffering for the people: "Surely he has borne our infirmities and carried our diseases; yet we accounted him stricken, struck down by God, and afflicted. But he was wounded for our transgressions, crushed for our iniquities; upon him was the punishment that made us whole, and by his bruises we are healed" (53:4-5).

Verses 10-12 explain the meaning and goal of this event: Because the servant gave his life as "payment for sin,"[89] "Jahweh's plan" can succeed, a plan he had with his servant for the salvation of Israel and of the peoples. For because the servant bore the sins of many, because he gave his life even unto death and allowed himself to be reckoned among the sinners who had fallen away from God, because of all this he "shall make many righteous" (v. 11ff.). It is not "to satisfy a higher righteousness that his giving of his life is necessary. It is to break the ever-renewing cycle of effectiveness of the denial of guilt, the displacing of guilt, and the unconquered grip of sin. In taking the guilt of many on himself, the servant manages to do what otherwise the sentencing of the guilty does: he make sin known and renders it impotent."[90] For this reason, both are important: the actual working out of real guilt in the life of the one, and the recognition from afar by the many of one's own guilt being taken on.[91] Through taking on their guilt (and punishment; in the Hebrew, the word means both!) the servant puts "the many" in the right and frees them from the bondage of guilt into a renewed salvific relationship with God.[92]

No Righteousness of One's Own

Postexilic Judaism did not pursue this conception of the processing of guilt any further than this.[93] One was searching for a way to a renewed relationship with God, acknowledging one's own guilt and recognizing that God acted justly toward his people, even in his judgment. In a so-called "judgment doxology"[94] the people confess: "The LORD is in the right, for I have rebelled against his word" (Lam 1:18). It is precisely out of this confession that the confidence grows to dare to trust oneself to the unwavering faithfulness of God and his inexhaustible mercy, even in the face of judgment (cf. Lam 3:22). This motif can be found repeatedly in the long prayers of confession of the exilic writings, which, in reflecting on the history of the people, say, "You have been just in all that has come upon us, for you have dealt faithfully and we have acted wickedly" (Neh 9:33; cf. Ezra 9:15). But this does not preclude the simultaneous confession, "Nevertheless, in your great mercies you did not make an end of them or forsake them, for you are a gracious and merciful God" (Neh 9:31). These motifs are most poignantly interwoven in Dan 9:

> And now, O Lord our God, who brought your people out of the land of Egypt with a mighty hand and made your name renowned even to this day—we have sinned, we have done wickedly. O Lord, in view of all your righteous acts, let your anger and wrath, we pray, turn away from your city Jerusalem, your holy mountain; because of our sins and the iniquities of our ancestors, Jerusalem and your people have become a disgrace among all our neighbors. Now therefore, O our God, listen to the prayer of your servant and to his supplication, and for your own sake, Lord, let your face shine upon your desolated sanctuary. Incline your ear, O my God, and hear. Open your eyes and look at our desolation and the city that bears your name. We do not present our supplication before you on the ground of our righteousness, but on the ground of your great mercies (vv. 15-18).[95]

As a result of God's justification and the lack of claim to any righteousness of one's own, the hope increases that even the sinful people can once again participate in God's righteousness. The reliance on God's righteousness and the reliance on mercy not only don't stand in opposition to each other, they belong together because they express the hope in God's continuing and graceful care.

This development can also be traced in the later layers of Deuteronomy. Whereas in 6:25, right after the basic laws of Yahweh have again been reinforced, it is said, "If we diligently observe this entire commandment before the LORD our God, as he has commanded us, we will be in the right," in 9:4-6 in light of the expulsion of the other peoples from the promised land, the Israelites are warned not to say, "It is because of my righteousness that the LORD has brought me in to occupy this land" (v. 4).[96] In discarding any reliance on "personal" righteousness in a book that so emphatically lifts up the meaning of God's commandments and their pursuit for God's covenant with Israel, motifs of the Pauline doctrine of justification are hinted at.[97]

The positive counterpart to this rejection of a call to a "personal" righteousness is found in Jer 33:14-18, where the Messiah-name, "The LORD is our righteousness" (Jer 23:6), is taken over thereby making clear that God and his actions alone can be the basis of salvation for his people.

Similar thoughts can be found where individuals wrestle to find the right relationship with God. The prayer in Ps 143 pleads to be heard and saved from need "for the sake of your righteousness" (in vv. 1 and 11: "in your righteousness") and immediately adds, "Do not enter into judgment with your servant; for no one living is righteous before you" (v. 2).[98] Knowing about oneself being a sinner of course doesn't preclude the one praying from clearly differentiating his relationship to God from that of his enemy (cf. Ps. 143:11ff.). Justification of the sinner does not yet mean justification of the wicked or ungodly—in the Old Testament there is obviously a quite special variation of *simul iustus et peccator*![99]

In this context, Ps 51 seems to be more radical. Here too the one praying can expect help only through God's gracious care: "Have mercy on me, O God, according to your steadfast love; according to your abundant mercy blot out my transgressions" (v. 1). But at the same time the one praying knows that his whole being is pervaded by sin and that his existence has been determined by it from the beginning.[100] Verse 12 clarifies: "Only God's free, creative act can renew the innermost being of persons."[101] In response, the one praying with his sense of guilt can only abandon himself totally to the judgment of God and acknowledge his sovereignty.

The radicality of this confession of sin and the knowledge of one's total dependence on God's help serves to establish this Psalm as being in the orbit of what the New Testament calls "the justification of the ungodly."[102] But to call this hope by this name would take the prayer of Ps 51 one step further than he intended to go. His assurance rests solely in the fact that he entrusts himself to that particular God to whom he attributes right and whose righteousness he chooses to praise (Ps 51:15). This way of being then also determines his relationship to others: "Restore to me the joy of your salvation, and sustain in me a willing spirit. Then I will teach transgressors your ways, and sinners will return to you" (vv. 12-13).[103]

This exegetical tradition is impressively extended in the "Songs of Praise" (1QH) and in the final hymn of the Community Rule (1QS) of the Qumran community. Here, the motifs of judgment and lowliness doxologies and the confession of the utter sinfulness of all people are linked with the hope for justification through God's righteousness.[104] Thus, in 1QH 12:29ff. (Vermes 265-66) it says: "What is a creature of clay for such great marvels to be done, whereas he is in iniquity from the womb and in guilty unfaithfulness until his old age and suffers from the guilt of unfaithfulness until old age? Righteousness, I know, is not of man, nor is perfection of way of the son of man, to the Most High God belong all righteous deeds." What is put in contrast to this is the confession that "for thine, O God of knowledge, are all righteous deeds and the counsel of truth; but to the sons of men is the work of iniquity and deeds of deceit" (1QH 9, 26ff., Vermes 255).[105] The one praying then immediately follows up by giving voice to his hope: "For Thou wilt pardon iniquity, and through Thy righteousness [Thou] wilt purify man of his sin" (1QH 12:37, Vermes 266). He can indeed confess: "Thou hast cleansed a perverse spirit of great sin" (1QH 11:21).

All these motifs are then emphatically linked in the closing psalm of the *Community Rule*: "As for me, my justification[106] remains with God and in his hand is the completeness of my transformation together with the uprightness of my heart, and through his righteousness my sin is wiped out" (1QS 11:2ff.). The one praying then praises the participation of God's chosen people in the heavenly council gathering and contrasts with this: "But I number myself among dastardly humanity, among the mass of wanton flesh. My sins, my overstepping, my transgressions, together with the corruptness of my heart belong to the mass of worms and to those who walk in the darkness" (11:9ff.). And yet he places his hope totally in God and God's righteousness: "But I, when I waver, then God's signs of grace are my help forever. And when I stumble on account of the wickedness of my flesh, nevertheless my justification is found in God's righteousness for ever. And when he frees me from my distress, then he draws my soul up from the pit and leads my feet on the path again. Through his mercy he has brought me near, and through the signs of his grace comes my justification. He has judged me with the righteousness of his truth, and with the riches of his goodness he expiates all my sins, and through his righteousness he cleanses me from all the human impurity and from the sins of the sons of men, in order that I might praise God for his righteousness and the Most High for his majesty" (1QS

11:12-15). It is appropriate that interpreters have seen in this thought the expression of the line of a deep conviction of salvation *sola gratia*, of a grace that was certainly known in the way of life of the Qumran community and was part and parcel of the eschatological election of this group and their obedience regarding their interpretation of the Law.[107]

The Question Concerning the Righteousness of God

The judgment of theological exegetes about this exegetical tradition is as diverse as the tradition is impressive. Whereas some already see in Ps 51 the New Testament recognition "of the *total* and *radical* degradation by sin of *all people*" and in so doing see a glimmer of the beginnings of justification as new creation,[108] others see in it a problematic attempt of God's justification. "In situations of need and despair [one] takes all the guilt upon oneself, in order not to lay any foolishness at God's feet, and in order to recognize his righteousness; one exaggerates the general sinfulness of humanity in order to save the principle."[109]

The book of Job shows that these questions are not just issues of concern to contemporary skeptics. Using the example of Job, the righteous one (cf. Job 1:1; Ezek 14:14), the whole problematic of the connection between suffering, guilt, human justification, and the justification of God is explored toward the end of the Old Testament tradition history. The Job question is not the question about the meaning of life or the question of theodicy, the justification of God in light of the world's suffering. It is the question about the meaning of a person's life when he is afflicted with sickness and excluded from human fellowship and seems to be cut off from communion with God, a person "who cannot see the way, whom God has fenced in" (Job 3:23).[110] Such a life seems so utterly senseless that Job not only wishes for death but also curses the day he was born (Job 3:1-19). His conversations with his friends show that in his frustration he is not concerned with his lost wealth or his health. Their arguments, which are primarily intended as either encouragement or basic considerations—"Is not your fear of God your confidence, and the integrity of your ways your hope? Think now, who that was innocent ever perished? Or where were the upright cut off?" (Job 4:6-7); "Can mortals be righteous before God? Can human beings be pure before their Maker?" (4:17)—burrow into Job's heart like a hook and bring forth his real need in outbursts characterized by deep pain: the question of his life being recognized and accepted by God, the longing for a healed relationship to God.

The friends remain under the misapprehension of the old action-reaction connection. "Of a truth, God will not do wickedly, and the Almighty will not pervert justice. . . . For according to their deeds he will repay them, and according to their ways he will make it befall them."[111]

What is also true at the same time is that in the final analysis no person is righteous before God and therefore no person can insist on his righteousness before God.[112] It is for that reason that the friends point to the educative power of suffering and to the fact that where God wounds, God also binds up and heals (5:17ff.). Above all, the text points repeatedly to the possibility of turning oneself to God and laying one's case before him (5:8-16; 8:5-7), reconciling oneself with God and returning to him (22:21-23). In chapter 33 Elihu describes how God speaks to a person through serious illness, so that he no longer, like Job, appeals to God as someone who is innocent and without sin. Whoever is so led by God "prays to God, and is accepted by him, he comes into his presence with joy, and God repays him for his righteousness. That person sings to others and says, 'I sinned and perverted what was right, and it was not paid back to me. He has redeemed my soul from going down to the Pit, and my life shall see the light'" (33:26-28).

So what Job's friends are teaching is no systematic theory of retribution; there is much that is true and pastorally noteworthy in what they say. But for Job it is not the truth that encounters him and helps him.[113] He wrestles to find valid recognition of his life by God, an encounter with him that is not filtered through particular dogmatic premises. If somewhere in the Old Testament justification is wrestled for, then it is in the book of Job.[114] Job insists more and more impetuously on a real legal argument with God and thinks he recognizes that he has no chance of a fair trial against God.[115] He thinks that if he could only get a hearing or at least an indictment written by his adversary, he would already have half-won his case (Job 31:35-37).

It is not as if Job totally renounces the possibility of having sinned.[116] But he cannot admit that he has renounced God in deed or attitude.[117] And so he says to his friends who have become his opponents: "Far be it from me to say that you are right; until I die I will not put away my integrity [literally: "completeness, perfection"] from me. I hold fast my righteousness, and will not let it go" (27:5-6a).[118] And as much as Job despairs that he will at least receive justice from God, and in despairing, he almost becomes blasphemous: "As God lives, who has taken away my right" (27:2) so it becomes clear to him that in the final resort he can only find justice from God. And so, despite everything he says, "even now, in fact, my witness is in heaven, and he that vouches for me is on high...my eye pours out tears to God, that he would maintain the right of a mortal with God, as one does for a neighbor" (16:19-21). No one can be a witness before God on Job's behalf, no one can vouch for Job against God, no one can decide between him and God except God alone.[119] And in this bold belief, challenging God to justification against God, even Job's hope lies in God as his "savior," the attorney and legal advisor who intercedes for him as does one who ransoms an impoverished relative (Ruth 3:12; 4:1ff.) and the one he will once again take notice of in order thereby to be in a healed relationship with God.[120]

So Job is not searching for a "gracious" God in the run-of-the-mill sense; in fact, he almost defiantly rejects this God.[121] He is looking for the God who will do him justice.

He encounters this God—albeit in a totally unexpected manner—in the Lord's two speeches from the thunder. These "speeches point up neither the reason nor the purpose nor the necessity for Job's suffering. But they do put Job's fate in a new perspective, which denotes the border of the questioning about the reason purpose, and necessity of that fate."[122] It is a perspective that goes beyond Job's anthropocentric questioning and spectacularly draws into the question God's reign in the world of humans and in the battle with the forces of chaos. For the purposes of our theme, a question at the beginning of God's second speech is important, the one where Yahweh asks Job: "Will you condemn me that you may be justified [literally: may stand here as someone who is just]?" (40:8). The question is almost a mirror image of the confession to God in Ps 51:4, "Against you, you alone, have I sinned,...so that you are justified in your sentence." Job has hesitated to allow himself to be forced against his will through confession of his own guilt into the logic of a system of God's justification. Now God warns him against simply turning this logic on its head and justifying himself through God's declaration of guilt. The truth of the justification of God and the justification of Job, of course, rightly is to be found on either side of such theological machinations (this of course also holds true for an original understanding of Ps 51!). When Job, confessing that "I had heard of you by the hearing of the ear, but now my eye sees you" (42:5) recants his accusations against God (v. 6, according to Fohrer and Ebach) and repents and then is silent, "it is no longer simply a matter of the silence of a person who has become conscious of his triviality before God, but also a matter of the silence of a person who has turned to God, a God who gives himself totally and completely to that person and finds peace with him."[123]

The justification that Job experiences therefore oversteps the legal categories within which he has argued up until now. This justification is made complete in "recognizing acceptance by God" and is the basis for "a personal relationship to God [...] which succeeds in connecting the eternal God with the trivial person through the idea of justification [...] independent of all external realities of life," perhaps even above and beyond death.[124] The fact that this narrative of Job nonetheless tells of Job's justification in such an earthly way in God's recognition of the friends (42:7-10*a*) and in the restoration of his earthly fortunes—notably beginning with his social reintegration (42:11-17)—is part of the continuing important "worldliness" of the Old Testament.[125]

Job's justification is not the "justification of the ungodly," but neither is it the "justification of the righteous," as Job appeared to expect; it is the acceptance and recognition of a person who remained steadfast in his attachment to God amidst all his gifts and possibilities but also amidst his final despair.[126] Beyond any and all formulas, a person encounters God and experiences that his or her life and suffering are not "for nothing,"[127] but rather are hidden in God—even when God seems to hide himself—and that life gains meaning and perspective from this.

Habakkuk 2:4 concisely summarizes in a brief phrase what is going on here: "The righteous live by their faith." Behind this saying is the question of why sinners succeed and why the righteous must suffer. The prophet's response is this: "The person who pays no heed to God's order and oversteps God's bounds may perhaps have success now, but in the final analysis will actually lose their life. In contrast, the righteous person—the one who is already righteous because she lives according to the ways of right order!—will keep her life because of her faith despite repression and suffering."[128] At the same time, this describes what is meant by faith in the Old Testament: "So faith is trusting in the life-giving goodness of God, in the face of the converse, in the face of the impression of God's absence. Belief and trust are something active; they are an attitude of life. They constitute the desire to remain constant to a way of life desired by God even when daily life mocks this way of life, even when it mocks, doubts, and tempts it. Life is about believing, trusting, and persevering in one's relationship to God."[129]

5. GOD'S YES TO CREATION AND TO ISRAEL: THE MESSAGE OF JUSTIFICATION IN THE HEBREW BIBLE

The word *righteousness* refers to diverse spheres and dimensions of the relationship between God and humanity in the Hebrew Bible.[130] Nonetheless, the word always expresses affirmation, care, loyalty, and concern. God's righteousness is his unbreakable Yes to his counterpart. In this Yes lies the reason for the creation of the world and its preservation in the face of threatening destruction; in this Yes lies the basis for his holding fast to his people in spite of their lack of faith and their disobedience; this Yes is the basis for his care toward each and every person who needs help in his or her life. This Yes of God seeks for the Yes of humanity; righteousness seeks righteousness. Righteousness creates a life-serving and life-affirming cooperation among people, one in which the weak are protected and given the room they need for the development of their lives. Hence, righteousness is the sustaining force of society, the yeast as a result of which peace, prosperous life, and the common good flourish. It is through its social aspects that righteousness links God and humanity, and wherever righteousness is lacking or becomes embittered, the fellowship between God and his people breaks down.

In this way, the No that God's people establish for themselves through their behavior stands opposed to the basic Yes of God. In the destruction of Jerusalem and in being led into exile, Israel experienced in an exemplary and painful way how God allows his No to run its course and at the same time fights against its antipathy to life. And yet the people in this situation could hear the renewed affirmation that God's Yes is stronger than the self-inflicted No. From this grew the conviction that God in God's righteousness desired to encounter his people anew. God's righteousness signifies salvation for his people. Thus, the expression of God's unconditional acceptance is an expression of his desire to create and shape his fellowship with Israel in a new way. It is intended that precisely as a result of establishing new relations with God as a result of God's own righteousness, a fellowship of righteousness is intended to grow in the community of the people, a fellowship in which exploitation and oppression no longer have a place. Righteousness is the all-pervasive quality of life that gives freedom and space to live—and does so from God, toward God, and thus also between persons.

It is with this background that we are to understand what in the Old Testament is called "justification." The basic structure of this event is exemplified in the positive verdict in a legal case. The innocent party is not only acquitted of the charge but is also given justice and is once again taken back and integrated into the fellowship.

For this reason, "justification" occurs most broadly on the social level, where persons are supposed to receive justice in society. In the Old Testament this isn't restricted to the formal aspects of an aboveboard court case. It means that we encounter those who are easily robbed of their means of life—in other words, the poor, the widows and orphans, or the alien—in such a way in our social life together that they can live in dignity. To recognize the other's value and dignity of life means to encounter one another with righteousness.

"Justification" happens in the temple, where people who seek fellowship with God are told on the basis of their behavior that is fitting for such fellowship: "You are justified, you are among those who God takes up into his fellowship." However, a deepening of understanding was necessary here. The prophets insist that these "entry qualifications" be understood not just as liturgical formalities but that they be adopted as personal responsibilities and as measures by which to organize life together and with God. At the same time, it becomes increasingly clear in the course of the Old Testament story of faith that the final decision concerning the righteousness of a person, and thus about his justification, rests with God, who first and foremost asks each individual about his commitment, in other words, about his faithful trust.

The whole depth and complexity of the question about justification is most clearly to be discerned in the laments of individuals. Those persons whose existence is threatened through illness or hostility, and the associated ostracism they experience, call to God to be reminded of their right to life. Some call to God in honest awareness of their own guilt, others knowing that they cannot stand before God. In either case they know that they are dependent on his judgment and they await his gracious affirmation of them. Such a "judgment" is therefore no verdict from on high but rather a personal recognition and acceptance into fellowship with God. To be lifted up by God and to "behold his face" is the most profound expression of God's justification and acceptance. Even Job, who doesn't get the trial he so urgently thinks he must undergo with God, rediscovers meaning in his life by having his eyes opened to the all-transcending power and wisdom of God. It is a God who does not defeat him in the legal battle as he feared would happen, but it is a God in whom even Job with his fate can feel safe.

The justification of God is not the humiliatingly wily detour through which a person can nevertheless find his own righteousness; rather, it is the gate to a relationship with God, the way by which a person entrusts himself entirely to God and knows himself to be equally safe in his times of strength as in his times of weakness, in times of guilt as in times of responsible and socially faithful behavior. It is precisely in those situations of an individual's life or a people's history when, as a result of their guilty failure they have no claim to anything and people stand before God with empty hands, that calling upon God's righteousness is finally an act of trust in God's divinity, a trust that God's faithfulness to himself and his affirmation of those who have alienated themselves from him do not contradict each other.

Since it is at only a very few places that the Old Testament articulates a hope for life with God after death, what is hoped for from justification by God is mostly thought of as this-worldly.[131] Righteousness and life are closely interrelated. To be declared free of accusations and deathly hostilities and be once again taken up anew into the community is like recovering from a deadly sickness and receiving life anew; it can mean escaping social death and being able to lead a liberated life. It also opens up the possibility of a certain quality of life that can only in a limited way be measured by the standards of earthly welfare, a quality of life determined and borne by the certainty of being accepted by God, and of steadfastly belonging to God. It is at this point in the history of Old Testament belief in God that perspectives of a certain transcendence have arisen, perspectives that open one to a life with God, a life for which even death can no longer be a barrier (Ps 73:24-26).

What is so manifest here is that "justification" and its related terms are terms that denote a relationship, an event that has to do with community. Even though "righteousness" in many places seems to represent an almost natural dimension, a sphere or a condition of wholistic well-being, nonetheless the connection to the legal realm and to the shaping of community does remain central. Granted that the prophets speak of "righteousness" raining down or springing up (Hos 10:12; Isa 45:8), nonetheless righteousness doesn't come over people like an inevitable natural occurrence. Rather, righteousness asks for a response and for responsibility by wanting to establish and shape fitting human behavior and action.[132] This is true both of the individual's encounter with God and of the healing revelation of God's righteousness to his entire people. Precisely at this point where God's righteousness means nothing other than the salvation that God promises his people unconditionally, precisely in the encounter with this salvation can be found the possibility and the duty to live honorably with one another.[133]

As clear as it is at many points in the Old Testament proclamation that this salvation is from God, that it is nothing but a gift that a person can only receive with gratitude knowing that one's own hands are empty, it was nonetheless undoubtedly difficult for a person with an Old Testament faith to understand that salvation could only be accepted completely passively. Such an Old Testament person is too convinced that God's righteousness and salvation motivate and enable a person to do God's will. Perhaps the whole question of whether a person can contribute to his own salvation would appear too individualistic and analytical to him. The person who opens himself to God's grace is taken in to the working of God in his life and in the community; anything that is done about righteousness in this process is never only about the individual's righteousness, but about the reality of a healing and life-giving communal existence before God. Therefore, the concretization of what is righteousness in the Old Testament always remains connected to what God's commandments say and what is presented in the Law. But righteousness is not for this reason righteousness in the Law. What is absolutely central to "righteousness" is the gracious gift of God, concretized both in God's promises and also in God's commandments.

Having said this, however, none of this is systematically sorted out in the Old Testament; indeed, references to both at times occur alongside each other, though yet quite unconnected in the same writings. The words of comfort in Deut 6:25 that "if we diligently observe this entire commandment before the LORD our God…we will be in the right" is not rescinded, even when (probably in a later textual addition) the people are warned not to consider their own righteousness as the reason for God's salvific actions during the taking of the land (Deut 9). Whereas God's wonderful deeds and his salvific actions toward his people are lauded in Ps 111, in the very next psalm (112) the righteous, their faithfulness, and their mercy are praised, and of both God and the faithful is said: "His [or Their] righteousness endures forever" (Ps 111:3; 112:9).[134]

This might be one of the reasons why the implications of the Old Testament sayings on justification are so contested in biblical interpretation. While K. Koch has repeatedly emphasized that "in the Old Testament it is only ever the person who is faithful to the community, and never the ungodly person [...] who is justified" and "that justifying action of Jahweh is clearly distinguished from his unconditionally gracious deeds,"[135] others do not consider this sharp distinction to be factual.[136] In the first instance, this may be a terminological problem; for in the Old Testament the "justification of the wicked" in a legal trial is repeatedly forbidden.[137] What is, however, true is that even where, like in Ps 51 or 143, the justification of a sinner is hoped and pleaded for, the sinner is nonetheless equated with the transgressor, in other words, with the "ungodly one" who has separated himself completely from God, although the mightily tempted prayer does still depend on a final connection to God. He is at one and the same time a sinner and righteous.[138]

So it is not surprising that those works that speak of a "justification of the ungodly" in the Old Testament do not in fact tackle the Old Testament expressions of righteousness and justification but rather what they consider to be the matter of the overall biblical message of justification.[139]

Hosea 11:1-9 is cited again and again in this connection. After a brief survey of the history of Israel that is shown to have had to end in judgment (vv. 1-7), suddenly and with unexpected boldness a new word of Jahweh's comes to the fore: "How can I give you up, Ephraim? How can I hand you over, O Israel? How can I make you like Admah? How can I treat you like Zeboiim? My heart recoils within me; my compassion grows warm and tender. I will not execute my fierce anger; I will not again destroy Ephraim; for I am God and no mortal, the Holy One in your midst, and I will not come in wrath" (vv. 8-9).

This signifies a profound change in God's relationship to Israel: "Jahweh himself overcomes his people's turning away, and the resulting decline into self-chosen evil. He does so by freely, out of grace, giving what Israel by itself cannot achieve: a new beginning, yes, a completely new start through the renewing act of 'healing,' which encompasses forgiveness of sin."[140] What no legal process and no threat of judgment could effect is made possible through the unquenchable love of God. The fact that despite everything God changes his mind is explained to be a result of his divinity and holiness, just as in another place people who can only hope in God call upon his righteousness. It is important to recognize that this essential trait of Old Testament theology did not first develop after the catastrophe of the exile but rather already surfaces in the middle of a preexilic prophet's announcement of judgment. It is echoed in Jeremiah (cf. 31:20) and becomes the heart of Deutero-Isaiah's message.

Along the same lines is the development of the conviction in the prophesying of Ezekiel that only a totally new creation of the people can form a new community with God. Even if Ezek 18:31 demands, "Cast away from you all the transgressions that you have committed against me, and give yourselves a new heart and a new spirit!" Ezekiel 36:26-27. (cf. 11:19) by contrast declares in the face of the history of the people's transgressions: "A new heart I will give you, and a new spirit I will put within you; and I will remove from your body the heart of stone and give you a heart of flesh. I will put my spirit within you, and make you follow my statutes and be careful to observe my ordinances." New life with God is only possible where God creates something totally new. This is presented quite emphatically in the vision in Ezek 37:1-14 with regard to the people of Israel who say, "Our bones are dried up, and our hope is lost; we are cut off completely" (v. 11), in order to make clear that God's power can even awaken a dead people to life again. Because this text is not about "a physical resurrection from bodily death," "but rather about an image of the new beginning of the existence of God's people," it becomes clear that God must and can create the existence and salvation of his people without any preconditions and without any prerequisites from his side.[141] "A continuity of existence is not available to this people; God alone enjoys such continuity, for he remains faithful to himself."[142] The Pauline equation of the "justification of the ungodly" with the power of God to bring the dead to life (Rom 4:5, 17) here finds an emphatic Old Testament anticipation.

The acknowledgment that God "has revealed his righteousness to the peoples" is the basis for the hope in the eschatological accomplishment of God's salvific power. What this will mean for the wicked and for the Gentiles remains an open question. Will it be that on that day "the arrogant and the evildoers" will becomes stubble that will burn in the judgment fire, while the righteous are told, "But for you who revere my name the sun of righteousness shall rise, with healing in its wings" (Mal 4:2)? Will the Gentiles be the spectators, those who will be amazed at what God does to Israel, as seems to be indicated in the Psalms? Or will the revelation of the righteousness of God awaken totally new perspectives on salvation that will overcome these old limitations?[143]

In the final analysis, this question remains open in the Old Testament. It will receive a new answer wherever the revelation of God's righteousness "as witnessed to by the Law and the prophets" is experienced and believed through the good news of Jesus Christ. However, what can be clearly discerned are the workings out of the message of justification that the Old Testament passes on as its inheritance:

- It is the hope in the final revelation of God's righteousness, in which his Yes to his people and to this world will be revealed and come into effect and through which God will set right this earth.
- It is the trust that whenever a person says God is right, his own life will be put to rights and God will give him community and life.
- And it is the certainty that God's love is so powerful and has so much creative strength that it can retrieve people from the deepest alienation from God and give them life when they had fallen into death. Whenever that happens, "justification" happens—whether the word is used or not.

6. JUSTIFICATION AND JUDGMENT: THE ESCHATOLOGICAL PERSPECTIVE

In the first instance the Old Testament does not speak of justification from the perspective of a final judgment in which God pronounces judgment over the lives of people and decides between eternal life or eternal damnation. This conception first arises in Dan 12:3, in other words in a writing that, timewise, appears at the end of the Old Testament tradition history. The fact that this new possibility for an encounter with God opens up is not only the result of the influences of the religious context in which such otherworldly scenarios existed. The decisive reason for this is the newly given conviction that the reality and validity of God's Yes to a person did not end with the boundary of death.[144]

Incidentally, if one researches early Jewish writings on this question, one is in for a surprise. The conception of an end-time judgment in which—comparable to the Egyptian judgment of the dead—a judgment is made and spoken concerning whether each individual is justified or not, is by no means the dominant conception.[145] Within the tradition of Old Testament testimony, the fact that God intends to reveal his righteousness and judge the peoples fairly is portrayed primarily in the depictions of the judgment of the earth in how the sinners and ungodly are punished and the righteousness of the righteous is brought to light.[146] This depiction is found both in the description of the Final Judgment in the book of Wisdom (4:20–5:23) as well as throughout early apocalyptic writings. Thus, we find in what is probably the oldest apocalyptic writings, the Ten Week Apocalypse, this text: "But after this there will be another (week), the eighth week, the one of righteousness, and a sword will be given her, so that a fair judgment can be made of those who do injustice, and sinners will be delivered into the hands of the righteous."[147] Jubilees 23:30 similarly says: "And the righteous ones will see and give praise, and rejoice forever and ever with joy; and they will see all of their judgments and all of their curses among their enemies."[148]

It is obvious that it is not by chance that "the righteous and the elect" in early apocalyptic writings are almost synonyms. Rather than being a matter of the individuals' balance sheet of life, it's about belonging to the true Israel. And yet it's not just about election, for righteousness also includes obedience to the Law.[149]

The texts of Qumran offer a profound insight into the theology and piety of such a distinctive group that understood themselves as the holy and chosen ones, the representatives of the true Israel. One of their hymns of praise declares:

> Thou wilt destroy in Judgement all men of lies, and there shall be no more seers of error; for in Thy works is no folly, no guile in the design of Thy heart. But those who please Thee shall stand before Thee for ever; those who walk in the way of Thy heart shall be established for evermore. (1QH 12:20ff., Vermes 264)

Of those who have found each other in the covenant of the teacher of righteousness, it could be said:

> They ... array themselves for Thee in the Council of the Holy. Thou wilt cause their law to endure for ever and truth to go forward unhindered, and Thou wilt not allow them to be led astray by the hand of the damned when they plot against them. Thou wilt put the fear of them into Thy people and (wilt make of them) a hammer to all the peoples of the lands, that at the Judgement they may cut off all those who transgress Thy word. (1QH 12, 24-27, Vermes 265)

But it is extraordinarily moving to then read in the next song of the Songs of Praise these phrases:

> Righteousness, I know, is not of man, nor is perfection of way of the
> son of man: to the Most High God belong all righteous deeds. The way
> of man is not established except by the spirit which God created for
> him to make perfect a way for the children of men, that all His crea-
> tures may know the might of His power, and the abundance of His mer-
> cies towards all the sons of His grace....I said in my sinfulness, 'I am
> forsaken by Thy Covenant.' But calling to mind the might of Thy hand
> and the greatness of Thy compassion, I rose and stood, and my spirit
> was established in face of the scourge. (1QH 12, 30-38, Vermes 265-66)

Here we encounter a theology of justification in which recognition of an
individual's sin and a group's consciousness of choice, faithfulness to the
Law, and knowledge of *simul iustus et peccator* go together hand in hand.
What happens now regarding justification will be made public at the
judgment.[150]

We encounter a completely different line of argumentation in 2 Esdras
toward the end of the first century. Now it is true that here also it says,
"For after death the judgment will come, when we shall live again; and
then the names of the righteous shall become manifest, and the deeds of
the ungodly shall be disclosed" (2 Esd 14:35). But the question of who are
the righteous and who are the sinners remains completely unresolved.
There is no collective of the chosen ones and no possibility of taking
responsibility for someone else's action. At the judgment, "no one shall
ever pray for another on that day, neither shall anyone lay a burden on
another; for then all shall bear their own righteousness and unrighteousness" (2 Esd 7:105). The prophet does not attempt to represent a theology of grace, following the Old Testament witness: "But it is because of
us sinners that you are called merciful. For if you have desired to have
pity on us, who have no works of righteousness, then you will be called
merciful.... For in this, O Lord, your righteousness and goodness will be
declared, when you are merciful to those who have no store of good
works" (2 Esd 8:31b, 32, 36). But this is refuted as "cheap grace" by the
angel speaking on God's behalf: "Let many perish who are now living,
rather than that the law of God that is set before them be disregarded!"
(2 Esd 7:20). Just as when ore is purified the most valuable metals are the
most rare and therefore most precious, so it is at the judgment: "I will
rejoice over the few who shall be saved, because it is they who have made
my glory to prevail now, and through them my name has now been hon-
ored. I will not grieve over the great number of those who perish; for it is

they who are now like a mist, and are similar to flame and smoke—they are set on fire and burn hotly, and are extinguished" (2 Esd 7:60b-61).[151] Here, the individual's obedience to the Law becomes the sole measure at the judgment. Though 2 Esdras says that a person "will be able to escape on account of their works, or on account of the faith by which they have believed" (2 Esd 9:7), but by "faith" he obviously means loyalty to God's leading, so to speak, the inner aspect of obedience to the Law.[152] But even with 2 Esdras the decision of whether someone is "righteous or a sinner" seems to be determined before the judgment, in that the "righteous" or the "remnant" are saved (6:25; 9:13). The prophet is now already "justified" and for that reason deemed worthy to behold the end of the times (12:7ff.).[153] And he recounts all this to warn others about stupidly relying on God's mercy at the judgment. The decision about death or life is now a matter of obedience in the face of the Law.

So in Judaism both before and during the New Testament time, especially among those who take God's direction seriously, we find the ardent expectation that God wants to establish his sovereignty and reveal his righteousness. Then the differences between the righteous and sinners will also be revealed in their lives; and it will become clear that God sides with those who cleave to him. But this is a process not simply of calculating "merits" through works, but rather of perfecting fellowship with God, a fellowship that is already being experienced during the lifetime of the righteous one.[154] The Old Testament message of justification is "translated" into the eschatological without losing the dimension of justification that is related to the present.

7. An Excursus on the Difficulty of Translation

When the Hebrew Bible was being translated into Greek, a serious shift of emphasis in the meaning of the word cluster "righteousness/law/to justify" emerged. One might imagine that the translator would see no huge problems at this point. Translating *tsedeq/tsedaqah* (righteousness) with *dikaiosyne* and *tsadiq* (righteous) with *dikaios*, and *hitsdiq* (to justify) with *diakaiō* seemed pretty close and for this reason was almost comprehensively carried out.[155] There were certainly word fields where this was much more difficult.

And yet it was precisely through translation into Greek (and then similarly also into Latin and German or English) that the understanding of righteousness and justification was exposed to significant changes. Some peculiarities in the Hebrew understanding of law and righteousness can only be partly expressed by the corresponding Greek (and German or English) terms. To understand what's intended, an expansive "retranslation" back into Hebrew is often required.

I wish to lift up for consideration three aspects in which Greek usage differs from Hebrew usage.

1. Translating *tsedeq/tsedaqah* (*Gerechtigkeit*, righteousness) with the word *dikaiosyne* hides the subtle differentiation between the two closely related Hebrew terms. It could only be translated more accurately into German through artificial sounding. Interestingly, with the words *justice* and *righteousness*, English has two different terms at its disposal in this case. But even they don't reveal the nuances of the two Hebrew terms, though they do help to differentiate between justice-derived and salvific righteousness/justice.[156]

2. In Greek philosophy, the term *dikaiosyne* (righteousness) designates one of the four cardinal virtues.[157] It describes the behavior that makes peaceful coexistence of many within a community possible. It is the Greek standard term for "social justice."[158] In the area of justice, the definition of the late Roman legal expert Ulpian is characteristic: "Righteousness is the firm and long-lasting desire to give someone the justice due him," or, in short: *suum cuique*.[159] In Greek, the term *dikaiosyne* generally describes neither the relationship to God nor a divine characteristic or behavior. In Greek literature, the juxtaposition of "righteousness and holiness" characterizes the relationship of the appropriate behavior toward humans and gods, whereas biblical tradition uses both terms to describe the relationship with God.[160]

So talk about God's helping and saving righteousness is therefore quite alien to Greek usage. That might be one reason why the Septuagint, wherever it does not render *tsedaqah* as *dikaiosyne*, likes to use the Greek equivalent for mercy.[161] On the other hand, that *hesed* (grace) can also be translated with the word *dikaiosyne* shows that the Greek word could by all means be a suitable vessel for the translator to name the corresponding Old Testament idea of righteousness as God's gracious care.[162]

The linguistic usage in the Apocrypha shows very nicely the malleability of language use. In Wis 8:7 righteousness, as it was for the Greeks, is shown to be one of the cardinal virtues. But in 5:18 it is said of God's helping of the righteous that God "will put on righteousness as a breastplate, and wear impartial justice as a helmet," and in 12:16 God's strength is seen as the source of his forgiving and sparing righteousness. Following the tradition of Third Isaiah, in Bar 5:2 we read: "Put on the robe of the righteousness that comes from God; put on your head the diadem of the glory of the Everlasting." If this sounded strange even to the Greeks, nonetheless they had a sense of what was meant.

3. Translating the Hebrew "to justify" with the Greek *diakaiō* is likewise shown to be problematic. In the Greek, the word actually means "to put in the right" or "to be set right."[163] But the de facto meaning of "justifying the guilty one" is punishing him. So, expressed in Greek, the warning not to "justify" the guilty one (Exod 23:7; Isa 5:23) was, in the first instance, incomprehensible. Why shouldn't "justice be done to him" in his punishment? For this reason, the Septuagint translates Prov 17:15 differently: "One who pronounces the wicked just and the righteous guilty...." However, in Exod 23:7 or Isa 5:23 the reader had to notice, without such an aid, that apparently exactly the opposite was intended than he or she at first supposed.[164]

Yet this difference demonstrates the elasticity of the language that eventuates in the Greek terminology, on account of its contextual use, coming very close to the meaning of the Hebrew.[165] This is also the assumption for its usage in the New Testament. A Greek reader, for example, would presumably have quickly noticed that by this phrase, "justification of the ungodly" in Rom 4:5 Paul does not mean to signify a person's punishment but rather the remarkable fact that God declares him or her righteous.

JUSTIFICATION IS FREEDOM: THE NEW TESTAMENT

New Testament pronouncements on justification are found almost exclusively in the Pauline writings. Above all, the fact that they rarely occur in Jesus' proclamations has led to the critical question of whether the gospel of Jesus even could and should "be expressed in the form of teaching about justification."[1] The question therefore arises: Even if it is not so designated terminologically, but only in its contents, is there such a thing as a message of justification from Jesus?

1. THE RIGHTEOUS AND SINNERS: JESUS' MESSAGE OF JUSTIFICATION

Jesus seldom spoke of righteousness and justification.[2] In describing to people how God encounters them, he always talks about "God's kingdom" being near to them.[3] The roots of these statements can be found in the Old Testament, particularly in the Yahweh-King Psalms (47, 93, 96–99), which proclaim Yahweh's royal reign and his righteous rule over the entire earth, and in Deutero-Isaiah, who proclaims that God will establish anew, visible to all, his saving reign over his people and over all the peoples of the world (cf. Isa 52:7-11). This is part of the same tradition circle in which the hope in the revelation of God's salvific righteousness is based (cf. Ps 98:2; Isa 51:5).

In the early Judaic literature and particularly in the apocalyptic literature, one speaks of the "kingly rule of God" when one wants to express faith in God's present rule, but most particularly when wanting to describe the hope in God's final victory over the power antithetical to God and God's judgment over all his enemies. Similar to its use in the New Testament, the term describes the *completion* of his reign, in other words, the "kingdom" of God. And yet nowhere is it the central theme of the proclamation.[4]

So those who heard Jesus must have been struck by how central this theme was for Jesus, but presumably even more by how Jesus was imbued with the immediate presence of God's sovereignty and to what extent he lived and acted out of this sense of presence. And yet, without it disappearing altogether, the judgment aspect of this theme took a back seat with Jesus.[5] In Jesus' words and works people encounter God and his reign precisely in its goodness that overcomes all sense of the absence of God or distance from God. It is also this goodness that takes over people's lives for God and that thus leads them to be under the rule of God. The promise that God accepts people without condition and the expectation of a love that knows no bounds belong undividedly together in Jesus' proclamation of God's kingdom.

The first Beatitude offers a pithy summary of this message: "Blessed are you who are poor, for yours is the kingdom of God" (Luke 6:20).[6]

At first, the fact that Jesus calls the poor blessed seems to be an indecipherable paradox. For the parallel sayings in the second and third Beatitudes show that he really is talking about material poverty. Jesus addresses people in need: those who don't have enough to earn their living and therefore suffer from hunger; those who suffer through having lost important relationships and therefore weep; and those whose lives are characterized by lack and whose lives are therefore deemed of no value. Despite its obvious connection to an Old Testament spirituality of the poor, Jesus' promise of salvation must not be spiritualized.[7]

But while Jesus promises those who are weeping that they will once again laugh and the hungry that God will fill them, the poor are not simply told that God will make them rich. The reasoning that God's kingdom belongs to them goes far beyond this. The promise applies already to the present and its content encompasses far more than the prospect of future riches. To those who have nothing is promised what no one person can possess and yet will be God's incomparable gift to them: the fullness of the all-encompassing kingdom of God!

The context in which this promise reappears in the New Testament is significant. In Mark 10:14 Jesus says, "Let the little children come to me; do not stop them; for it is to such as these that the kingdom of God belongs." "Such as these" means first of all the children themselves, those often pushed aside, overlooked, and not taken seriously—and yet people longing to be cared for and accepted, those ones who are dependent on the care of others and yet at the same time always ready to allow themselves to be gifted. "Such as these" therefore also means those who receive God's kingdom "as a little child" (Mark 10:15), those who know that they are alive because of his gifts, who do not hesitate to accept with open hands what he gives.

Children and the poor depend on God's giving, and for this reason God's kingdom belongs to them; the kingdom is the epitome of his powerful closeness and on it depends the worth and richness of their lives.[8]

The concept of "the poor" no doubt takes on a meaning because of this text that goes beyond economic statistics. It continues to be true: what is meant are "the poor in the flesh, the have-nots, the oppressed, those without rights, the dependent."[9] Jesus' promise applies to them absolutely—without any preconditions or caveats. Yet at the same time the reality of this promise is found in the relationship to God made possible through it. It is for this reason that the original stated function of the first Beatitude seems so important to me: its contents are no neutral declaration about the relationship between God and people in situations of economic deprivation but rather the promise of God's care of the affected people.[10] They are "poor before God."

Such "poverty before God" can then also be understood in an applied sense (cf. Matt 5:3, "the poor in spirit" like "becoming as children"). Yet those whose lives are characterized by want and need and who doubt the worth of their lives always remain the point of connection and the goal of such care. They are told that God stands by them, filling and enriching their lives with his presence.

The gospel traditions repeatedly emphasize that the poor are being particularly addressed by Jesus' proclamation. Thus, according to Luke 4:16-21, his appearance is the fulfillment of the salvific action through the one anointed by God's spirit announced in Isa 61:1ff., in the center of which is the task of "bringing good news to the poor." And with this and other Old Testament promises as a backdrop, Jesus summarizes his actions and their meaning with the words "the blind receive their sight, the lame walk, the lepers are cleansed, the deaf hear, the dead are raised, and the poor have the good news brought to them. And blessed is anyone who takes no offense at me" (Luke 7:22ff.; cf Matt 11:5ff).[11]

The announcement of the good news to the poor is apparently the summary and meaning of the healing action of Jesus.[12] The miracles are a sign of the beginning of the end times in which God will establish his salvific reign.[13] God creates new life where people have reached the end of their abilities. The fact that this holds true for all who, through deprivation and social ostracism, seem cut off and excluded from life, that is the good news, that is the gospel for the poor.

The stories of Jesus casting out demons show most clearly of all how, entirely without prerequisites, the salvific and liberating proximity of God's reign helps those who are alienated from God and from their calling as his creatures. It is at those times when people are quite clearly no longer master of themselves but rather destroy themselves in some divided existence; it is when they isolate themselves from others and dwell in graves while yet still alive that Jesus most clearly sees the lordship of Satan and his demons at work in the people of his time. Yet to Jesus this lordship is fundamentally broken: "I watched Satan fall from heaven like a flash of lightning" (Luke 10:18). From God's perspective Satan is already fundamentally disempowered,[14] and it is to this that the saying refers: "But if it is by the finger of God that I cast out the demons, then the kingdom of God has come to you" (Luke 11:20, cf. Matt 12:28). "The finger of God," his saving and liberating hand, can reach into the deepest alienation from God, an alienation in which a person cannot even turn to God anymore and stay with him in faith, an alienation into which only defensive voices penetrate, an alienation from which a person can only find himself again thanks to contact with the all-powerful words of Jesus.[15]

Many of the healing stories can be understood in this context. The fact that Jesus touches lepers (Mark 1:41), that he allows an unclean woman to touch him (Mark 5:25-34), and that he allows himself to be persuaded by the motherly logic of a Gentile woman to help even her child (Mark 7:24-30), all these show by whom he was sent. This mission is on behalf of the excluded and the untouchable in society who, through him, are reached by God's helping and healing hand. Healing always aims also at integration into society.[16]

That healing is an important goal of Jesus' ministry is made clear again and again. Just as Jesus liked to use the image of a large celebratory meal as a symbol of fulfilled fellowship with God (e.g., Luke 14:16-24), he likewise understood his fellowship with people of very disparate origins as a sign of their acceptance by God. Luke 15:2 is cited as an accusation of the scribes and Pharisees: "This fellow welcomes sinners and eats with them." Whoever offers hospitality to others, accepts them. This is why those contemporaries of Jesus who took the law seriously separated themselves from him over table fellowship. Jesus' contrary behavior was therefore all the more offensive to them.[17] Jesus himself cites a current defamatory remark about himself: "For John came neither eating nor drinking, and they say, 'He has a demon'; the Son of Man came eating and drinking, and they say, 'Look, a glutton and a drunkard, a friend of tax collectors and sinners!'" (Matt 11:18f.; Luke 7:33f.).

Even in the story told in brief strokes in Mark 2:15-17 of Jesus eating with tax collectors and sinners cites the scribes and the Pharisees asking Jesus the indignant accusatory question, "Why does he eat with tax collectors and sinners?" Jesus replies, "Those who are well have no need of a physician, but those who are sick; I have come to call not the righteous but sinners."[18]

In these passages, the term "sinners" seems to have not only a theological but also a sociological significance. For apparently notorious sinners known throughout the town are meant, i.e., people who are called "sinners" on account of their offensive lifestyle or their affiliation with a particular social class. Just how such a circle of people came to be composed in a small Galilean town cannot be said for sure. Women who led an immoral lifestyle were certainly part of such a group (cf. Luke 7:37-39;) as too, no doubt, were the group of persons from which the Pharisee distances himself in Luke 18:11: thieves, rogues, adulterers, and tax collectors. It is likely that the reason tax collectors were included in this ranking was their frequent interactions with Gentiles, but especially their reputations as deceivers.[19] It is possible that the circle was even larger and encompassed "the disreputable, the *'amme ha-'aräç* [i.e., the "rabble"], the uneducated, the ignorant, whose *religious* ignorance and *moral* behavior stood in the way of their access to salvation, according to the convictions of the time."[20]

Obviously the term "sinner" here also has a social component to it. As in every society, so in Judaism it was those who belonged to the lowest levels of society who were in real danger of adopting deviant forms of behavior under the pressure of the circumstances, and then, so branded, of not finding a way back to social integration. Whereas it is typical of Old Testament spirituality of poverty to treat the poor and the righteous equally, in the Jesus tradition the terms "poor" and "sinner" come close to meaning the same without them being unequivocally considered parallel or equivalent.[21] In any case, the stereotypical idiom of "tax collectors and sinners" shows that the economic situation is not the dominant concern. For, financially speaking, these people surely more likely belong to the upper-middle or upper class.[22] Anyone who only wants us to take seriously the oppressed and exploited tax collectors[23] in Jesus' company has not yet grasped how nonconformist Jesus' behavior really was. He turned his attention toward the shunned of all kinds and allowed them to experience the healing reign of God. His mission to the entire people of God was intended to exclude no one (cf. Luke 19:10).

The images of the sick who need the doctor and especially the parables about the lost sheep and the lost coin (Luke 15:4-10) solicit understanding for the fact that this makes necessary the special efforts on behalf of those pushed to the edges of society or those who have fallen away from the community of the people of God. Using these metaphors, the critical hearers of Jesus' words are taken up into the solicitous search for the lost and the overwhelming joy when a person is found. And in Jesus' fellowship with tax collectors and sinners, they are invited to discover God's seeking and finding of the neglected and to rejoice with God in them. Jesus thus interprets "his table fellowship as a way of being found again, by which he means the reestablishment of fellowship with God that had been lost through sin. This is an incredible claim. For by it Jesus insists that God has here and now taken the initiative to break through to the sinner without waiting for the sinner to achieve what at that time was still considered to be the necessary disposition for regaining such fellowship."[24]

In Luke 19:1-10 we have a story as an example to show how this being found can be carried out and how it quite naturally results in particular consequence. The fact that Jesus "has gone to be the guest of one who is a sinner" (v. 7) means that "salvation has come to [his] house" (v. 9). The closing comment of this story, "For the Son of Man came to seek out and to save the lost" (v. 10), impressively connects a vivid description of Jesus' actions of seeking and rescuing those who have lost their way and themselves in life[25] with his theological significance as the salvation of those who are threatened with the final loss of their lives before God.[26]

But what happens to the "righteous"? As those who are well, do they have no need for the doctor (Mark 2:17) and do they really not need to repent (Luke 15:7)? To begin with, the question certainly remains unanswered in the Jesus tradition. Although Jesus, like John the Baptist, fundamentally assumes that all Israel is ripe for judgment (cf. Luke 13:1-5),[27] his mission sends him first to those who most obviously have fallen out of fellowship with God and must therefore be sought out and brought back into fellowship. The question of the righteousness of the righteous is decided not by a more intensive illumination of their lives before God but by their stance regarding God's mercy toward sinners.

Jesus discussed the matter most deeply in his parable about the father and his two sons (Luke 15:11-32). In the form of the younger son we meet a person who gets lost because he claims for himself and loses his rights, a person who, moved by a last spark of hope to begin afresh, opens himself up to his father once more.[28] And we encounter a father who, before his son even arrives at home and has a chance to say anything about his behavior, hurries toward him, motivated by a deep sense of mercy, so that the son utters his confession of sin in the father's arms. What happens next in the narrative is "justification" in its real sense: The one who has squandered his rights as a son and therefore declares, "Father, I have sinned against heaven and before you; I am no longer worthy to be called your son" (v. 21), is accepted as a son and, bedecked in festal garb, signet ring, and the shoes of a free man, is restored to the rightful place of a legitimate son.[29] Then, of the one who has once again found his way home it is said, in deep consonance between the narrated and implied world, "This son of mine was dead and is alive again" (v. 24).

Alongside them stands the older son; in light of the unconditional acceptance of his brother and the joy of his return, he suddenly feels disadvantaged and neglected. The father approaches him also and invites him not to desire compensation for the supposedly lost opportunities through going astray by demanding sanctions for his brother, but rather to discover for himself the freedom to be found in living in fellowship with his father, and to join the father in rejoicing over the brother who has been found again.

The narrative distinguishes very carefully between the two brothers. And yet troubling parallels arise. Even the one who stayed at home did not really experience "fellowship with the father as father; he lives as a servant, not as a son."[30] And it is precisely the father's approach that shows that the older brother is also in the wrong place: "outside, not at the feast, in denial. The father's goodness makes evident that the son's life is an estranged existence. It does so by showing the brothers' behavior toward each other."[31] Thus, in using the example of the two sons, Jesus portrays "two forms of estranged existence without caricaturing either; in the story, one son is reconciled, the other is offered a new and reconciled way of life."[32]

The outcome of the story is left open. This open outcome is at one and the same time an invitation to the listener to ask himself where he stands. Standing on God's side and living in fellowship with God is not decided by external characteristics of distance from or proximity to God, but rather by whether one shares God's love with others. Though the path of repentance may look very difference for both brothers, the decisive step is the same for both: returning to the father who has already taken the initiative of taking the first important step toward his sons. For both, the experience of renewed acceptance, of a renewed sense of freedom and empowerment in the fellowship of the father is the same.

Although the question of the justification of the "righteous" remains open in this parable, in other parables the question has already been answered. Jesus addresses the story of the Pharisee and the tax collector who were both praying in the temple (Luke 18:9-14) to people who self-confidently understood themselves to be righteous and therefore despised others. While the Pharisee, full of pride, prays, "God, I thank you that I am not like other people: thieves, rogues, adulterers, or even like this tax collector," the tax collector is standing far off, not daring to look heavenward, but rather beating his breast and saying only, "God, be merciful to me, a sinner!"[33] And Jesus comments, "I tell you, this man went down to his home justified rather than the other."[34] Evidently, the Pharisee is being criticized not for what he does but rather for the fact that he thinks he can attain his position with God by comparing himself to others. The tax collector is not only concerned about his relationship to God; he knows that he can expect help and acceptance for his life only because of God's gracious willingness to be reconciled. But exactly this is the attitude appropriate for fellowship with God, and for this reason Jesus can say of him: He left the temple justified; God absolved him from his guilt and has taken him up into fellowship with him.[35]

One further observation about this: In contrast to similar pleas in the Psalms (cp. 41:4; 79:9; 143:2), the tax collector expressly identified himself as a "sinner." Yet "sinner" (*hamartolos*), along with "ungodly one" (*asebes*), is one of the concepts that the Septuagint translates from the

Hebrew rš' (wicked). When Jesus promises a sinner justification through God, he dares to speak of the justification of the "ungodly." At the same time it is the justification of those who trust God unconditionally. In contrast to this, the Pharisee's relationship to God is shown to be unviable. The reason for this is not primarily that he also is not free of sin. Jesus does not spy into his life to show him that he is no better than the tax collector, just as the father in the parable does not do so in the encounters with his two sons. Instead of depending totally on God's mercy and faithfulness, he trusts in himself and his comparative merit compared to others.

The expression, "Before God, all are sinners," which Pesch cites at the conclusion of the parable of the two sons, for this reason seems to me to be too leveling to apply to Jesus' message. Nevertheless, it is true for all people that they can only then live in fellowship with God (and thus be "righteous") if they "turn around, and truly recognize God as God, as the merciful, good, forgiving, accommodating father, and recognize him practically in accepting one's brother, in joy over his new life, over new life together."[36] Jesus' point of departure is not a soteriological theory about the proper attitude of humans before God. His point of departure is the inbreaking of God's healing reign in people's lives, a reign that wants to draw them into the working of his love, whoever they might be and from wherever they might come.

Hans Weder expressed this most fittingly in his exposition of the "Parable of the Prodigal Son": "The love of God supersedes humans' pasts *as forgiveness* and it supersedes humans' righteousness as a *plea* to come and celebrate [...] The aim of God's love is to unite *both* the lost at the love feast."[37] The "justification of the sinner" means as little with regard to the justification of his sin as the "justification of the righteous" means with regard to the justification of his righteousness. In each case it's about the unconditional acceptance of one particular person through God's unconditional Yes. "God's eschatological Yes to humanity" is declared in Jesus' announcement of God's reign just as it is also in Paul's teaching about justification.[38] It is a Yes that at one and the same time liberates and empowers a person to celebrate and to live God's love.[39]

Jesus has given his life for this Yes of God's. He saw the resistance with which his message met as the expression of the fundamental No that people say to God's Yes. He wanted to take this No upon himself, and so Mark 10:45 is absolutely the right summary of his way.[40] For its part, the Christian community then recognized in Jesus' resurrection God's Yes to his way and denoted it as the "justification" of Jesus (1 Tim 3:16). In this lies the empowerment to pass on Jesus' "message of justification" about God's definitive Yes to people. The liberating power of the inbreaking reign of God that Jesus announces and the acceptance of the lost that he exemplified in his life are the objective bases of the New Testament message of justification.

2. CHRIST OUR RIGHTEOUSNESS: THE FOUNDATIONS OF THE PAULINE MESSAGE OF JUSTIFICATION

Anyone wishing to talk of the doctrine of justification must discuss Paul's theology. It has single-handedly caused the doctrine of justification to become the central expression of reformation theology. For this, Paul has been greatly praised but also heavily criticized. To describe God's salvific action toward humans as justification was not Paul's invention. Rather, he was able to draw on the legacies of the Old Testament and of early Judaism, and probably also on the formulations he found to hand in the Christian community.[41] What is new to Paul is that the event of justification becomes the defining description of God's salvific action.

And yet even for Paul the significance of the doctrine of justification is contested. Is it really the center of his theology or only a situation-specific battle cry, a subsidiary theme of his Christian piety that is limited in its significance to the question of the missive to the Gentiles, whose central message was freedom from the law?[42] Isn't the theological interpretation since Augustine, in fact, based on a big misunderstanding of Jewish theology of the law that Paul is trying to understand?[43]

An important argument in this discussion is the observation that the doctrine of justification only appears in the later letters of Paul.[44] Is it a result of a development in Paul's theological thinking[45] or the destination of a path "that leads from infantile to oedipal identification to mature identity"?[46] Does it bring up what Paul had always already thought but had not voiced because of the contemporary situation?[47] Does it expound in a new way what had already been laid out in the Pauline theology of the cross?[48] Or is it a special topic that does not go beyond the contemporary posing of the question?[49]

So we must try to establish how Paul's theological thinking developed and what priority the terminology and subject of the message of justification attain in this process.

Paul's Call

The key to Paul's theology is his call.[50] In this single experience can be found all of the most important core decisions that Paul will make in his later theological work.

He never speaks of this experience without mentioning that he used to persecute the Christian community. That a persecutor can be called to be an apostle in Paul's mind demonstrates in exemplary fashion what effect God's grace has (1 Cor 15:9ff.). In Gal 1:13ff. Paul depicts the background to these events: "You have heard, no doubt, of my earlier life in Judaism. I was violently persecuting the church of God and was trying to destroy it. I advanced in Judaism beyond many among my people of the same age, for I was far more zealous for the traditions of my ancestors."[51]

Evidently, zeal for the law and persecution of the Christian community are connected. Two reasons were definitive for this. The group in the early church that came out of Hellenistic Judaism and historically can be equated with the circle of Stephen presumably drew consequences from the message of Jesus that were critical of the temple and the law and may perhaps as a result of this have made early forays in mission work among the Gentiles.[52] Yet Paul was also offended by the Christian assertion that God had established a crucified person as Messiah. After all, Deut 21:23 said quite unequivocally that "anyone hung on a tree is under God's curse," a statement that, according to the Qumran texts, in Judaism quite clearly referred to the crucifixion.[53]

One particular conclusion from the self-portrayals of Paul is especially important for our context. Paul was "not converted . . . to faith in Christ as a contrite sinner or a desperate seeker after God." Rather, he considered himself "strong and secure in his life, a life that . . . was directed by the instructions of the Law."[54]

Although it has happened so often in the history of interpretation, Rom 7 must not be allowed to be read as evidence of a deep-seated uncertainty of Paul's, regarding his inability to keep the law.[55] Before Jesus Christ encountered him as the resurrected one (cf. 1 Cor 9:1; 15:8), Paul was sure of his identity and integrity on account of his active membership in the salvific realm of the transmitted law (Phil 3:5ff.). Yet this encounter was apparently so unambiguous and urgent that Paul could no longer doubt that God himself had resurrected Jesus from the dead and confirmed him as his son and the Messiah. And yet by this, the exclusive opposition between law and crucified Christ was radically reversed. Now that the law could no longer call into question the affirmation of Jesus as Messiah, the news of the salvific actions of God in the cross of Christ called into question the law as the way of salvation and realm of salvation.[56]

For Paul, this experience is at one and the same time conversion and call. In Gal 1:15 he reports how "God, who had set me apart before I was born and called me through his grace, was pleased to reveal his Son to me, so that I might proclaim him among the Gentiles." Paul becomes open to the good news through his encounter with the resurrected one.[57] The appearance of the resurrected one is a revelation of the "Son" because it makes clear "that in Jesus, God himself comes to men, and that the risen Christ is fully bound up with God."[58] Because of this, the curse of the law cannot be the last word about him, and the question of why God allowed him to be struck by this curse was answered by the recognition that Christ took it on himself on our behalf (Gal 3:13).

For Paul, the task of proclaiming to the "Gentiles" Jesus and God's actions in him as gospel was linked to this, i.e., as good news calling them to fellowship with God and into his salvation. Where, from the perspective of the law, he had previously seen only an insurmountable barrier, now a door had been opened through which he himself had to go. It seems that for Paul this call had been clear from the outset of his Christian existence, quite apart from the question of when to began his missionary activity.[59]

Paul did not convert himself. He "was converted" in that the encounter with the risen Christ also fundamentally changed his self-perception. Philippians 3:4b-11 describes this. Paul had made clear that what he had earlier counted as "gain" in his life was, in reality, loss, or at least some kind of detriment that prevented him from really living from a place of fellowship with God. He recognized that instead of living from his "own" righteousness granted by the law, he could depend totally on the righteousness that God gave him through Christ.

Even if Paul only in retrospect describes this experience using terms of the doctrine of justification, nevertheless his experience showed him from the beginning that his understanding of life to that point was not tenable. His zeal for God was revealed as zeal for himself because he set himself up in opposition to God's salvific action in Jesus Christ. And yet at the same time Paul discovered that despite his misguided understanding of life, he was being called by God to proclaim Christ to those who were not Jews and to find the goal and fulfillment of his life in doing so. Paul saw his call from persecutor to apostle as the form of justification of the ungodly that applied to him personally. For him, this experience was not the response to a subjectively perceived need; he was instead overwhelmed by the reality of God's salvific actions in Jesus Christ. Only through this did he finally recognize the misguidedness of his life to that point. His personal situation did not become the hermeneutical key to the formulation of the question to which the message of justification is the response. Yet his life remains a witness to the all-embracing call of God, which calls to his service the persecutor in the same way that it calls the Gentiles to salvation.

The Message of the Early Letters

It is the early letters of the apostle that develop this conviction. First Thessalonians is completely dedicated to accompanying and counseling a young congregation. Gratitude for the effects of the apostle's message pervades the first two chapters. Paul repeatedly lifts up the power of the gospel to lead people to salvation even in contrary circumstances and amidst persecution. He continues to be gratefully amazed at the miracle that the Word is accepted as God's effective Word despite the maltreatment of its messengers (cf. 1:6ff.; 2:1ff.).

The pivotal reason for the encouragement and exhortation of the congregation is its calling to salvation through the death and resurrection of Jesus (cf. 1:9ff.; 5:9ff., 23ff.) This is also true for life lived under salvation, which is described as a consequence of this calling and not as a condition for salvation.[60] The law it not mentioned; Paul proclaims a "lawless" gospel for the Gentiles.[61] And when he speaks of the Thessalonian Christians' "work of faith and labor of love and steadfastness of hope in our Lord Jesus Christ" (v. 3), this is absolutely not a contradiction to the message of justification. For the fact that the congregation lives out its faith, its love, and its hope in everyday life is the effect of the working of the Holy Spirit that gives power to the human words of the message.

At first it seems as if the epistolary conversation of the First Letter to the Corinthians proceeds along similar lines. Here too Paul expresses thanks for the grace of God, through which the congregation has been generously gifted, and for the strengthening and consolidation of their testimony to Christ. Here too God's call is the basis of the certainty of their keeping the faith, for "God is faithful; by him you were called into the fellowship of his Son, Jesus Christ our Lord" (1:9).

But this fellowship is endangered. There are divisions in the congregation, cliques being formed that call on various early Christian authorities, and, connected to this, significant theological differences of opinion, so much so that Paul considers not only the fellowship between members to be endangered but also the fellowship with Christ. He sees the main source for this as being a striving for a "wisdom of the word" that threatens to empty the message of the cross of its significance.

To this day, it is still not quite clear to what kind of "wisdom" he was referring. What is plain is that, despite the reference to the "Greeks," this was not a controversy about Greek philosophy. Rather, it was about forms of religious wisdom that promised, through speculative or rhetorical penetration of the Christ event, to lead people into the "depths of God" (cf. 2:10) in order to be made certain of and to be empowered by the revelation of God, as it were, from the inside.[62] For Paul, what is in danger of happening here is that the message of the cross will be robbed of its power and emptied of its meaning.

Paul argues using clear antitheses in 1:18-25. "For the message about the cross is foolishness to those who are perishing,[63] but to us who are being saved it is the power of God" (v. 18). In order to understand at least a little how objectionable and absurd Paul's contention that God wanted to lead this world to salvation through a person who ended up on the cross must have seemed to Paul's contemporaries, one has to be aware of how scandalous death on a cross was for people who lived in the Roman Empire.

But for Paul the deepest wisdom and power of this message lies precisely in this: "For since, in the wisdom of God, the world [as, for example, could be seen in the creation] did not know God through wisdom, God decided, through the foolishness of our proclamation, to save those who believe" (v. 21). This sounds like stubbornness, and yet it is the holy crisis of a kind of wisdom that has again and again led people to place in the position of God themselves or whatever was within reach of their own knowledge.[64] The "believers" who make the message of the cross the foundation of their lives are contrasted with the world that is in danger of being lost. Paul quite consciously contrasts the striving for wisdom with the attitude of receiving and trusting, such as in Gal 3:22 where he identifies believers as recipients of the promise in contrast to those who trust in the works of the law. The believers are also the "called" whom God has chosen from among the weak and despised of this world (1 Cor 1:24, 27ff.) in order through them to make clear the nature of his salvific actions.

Paul puts all this in a universal context by naming the Jews and Greeks[65] as representatives of the religious world and characterizes them according to their religious longings and claims.

In so doing, the Jews are identified not on account of their relationship to the law but rather as representatives of the question of "signs," that is, of unequivocal proofs of the revelation of God's might.[66] It's not about belonging to the people of God but instead about the revelation of God in Christ. In the one case the revelation of God in Jesus Christ has to be identified by messianic signs (thus the "Jews'" claims); in the other (thus the striving of the "Greeks"), this revelation is to be made comprehensible through the presentation of Christ as the manifestation of divine wisdom. The fact that these characteristics are tied neither to the religio-historical paradigms of "Jew" or "Greek," but rather are foundational encapsulations of people's religious questioning is as clear as the fact that these questions are fundamentally not illegitimate and can, in fact, quite easily be given a biblical legitimation. But at the same time these questions are dangerous projections of human ideations of God that displace encounter with him and lead to a deification of human conceptions of power and speculations about wisdom. The fact that God breaks through these projections by way of the cross of Christ and instead, and to some degree in contrast to this, shows his true strength and wisdom by way of profound human weakness and futility, is precisely what constitutes salvation for the weak and despairing.

Paul highlights this point by looking at the composition of the Corinthian church. Of them he says, "Not many of you were wise by human standards, not many were powerful, not many were of noble birth" (1 Cor 1:26).[67] Paul bases this not on the fact of the congregation's lack of appeal to people from higher social levels but on the fact of God's call. "But God chose what is foolish in the world to shame the wise; God chose what is weak in the world to shame the strong; God chose what is low and despised in the world, things that are not, to reduce to nothing things that are" (vv. 27-28.)

This sounds destructive. And yet the criticism unmasking human wisdom and power found in the message of the cross and in the elective actions of God is in service to the radical grace of God that reaches precisely those who are worth nothing and are nothing. "The fact that God chooses the have-nots is, like the justification of the ungodly, an act of resurrection of the dead and creating from nothing."[68] The healing destruction of people's self-glory is done in service to the first commandment ("Let the one who boasts, boast in the Lord" [v. 31]), and at the same time makes space for those to be accepted who know they can't point to anything of which they might be proud, for the poor, the weak, and for those who have reached rock bottom.

For God gives them a new existence: "He is the source of your life in Christ Jesus" (v. 30). Christ, and what God has done in him, is the basis for existence, the basis of faith, and the space for life for the faithful and the called, no matter their origin. "He is the source of your life in Christ Jesus, who became for us wisdom from God, and righteousness and sanctification and redemption" (v. 30). Christ's becoming wisdom for us is shown not by a speculative wisdom christology but by his death on the cross and by what he does through his death for those he reaches in the depths of their "worthless" lives. Three further concepts clarify what Christ is for those who belong to him and what "in him" is true for them: righteousness, sanctification, and redemption. One mustn't be too quick to explain away this unusual formulation by saying "through Christ we were justified, sanctified, and redeemed."[69] The righteousness is not "*our* righteousness, but rather God's righteousness for us, which was realized in Christ."[70] This reality is what supports and determines the life of the Christian; it describes the element of life named "righteousness," its new relationship to God that is founded in Christ. Thus Christ is also sanctification for them, the basis of such a life's belonging to God (cf. 1 Cor 1:2: "sanctified in Christ Jesus"), and "redemption," the medium and guarantor of liberation out of bondage to guilt through sin and death.

Even if the key word *righteousness* were not to appear in this context, one could not overlook the proximity of Paul's argumentation to his teaching on justification. Anticipating the discussion of its significance in the Letter to the Galatians we can say, for Paul, the decisive question concerning the enduring foundation of our existence before God is not only posed where it's a question of whether the Gentiles will be able to be taken up into the people of God without circumcision. Even where he writes about inter-Christian arguments concerning the right understanding of Christ's significance, this question always surfaces when he has the impression that people are suggesting that something other than God's salvific act in Christ should be made the basis of Christian existence.

Here and elsewhere the key word for this problematic is the term "to boast." I boast about that on which I build my life. Yet this can and must be God alone, and what God has done.[71] And this not only for God's sake—whose glory would otherwise be compromised—but also for people's sake, who would otherwise build their lives on shifting sands. By what do I live and what bears me up? It is this question that Paul passes on to the Christians as the enduringly important and decisive one. His answer, even in different contexts, is always the same: I live by that which God has done for this world in Jesus Christ through the cross and resurrection.

Last of all, we should note that in 1 Corinthians, Paul draws also on earlier formulations of the message of justification. First Corinthians 1:30 is not an isolated example. We encounter a very similar formula in 1 Cor 6:11 that apparently describes what happened when a person became a Christian—particularly what happened in baptism: "But you were washed, you were sanctified, you were justified in the name of the Lord Jesus Christ and in the Spirit of our God." The context shows that what is being outlined is the foundational turning point in life that happens in baptism: cleansing from sin, being welcomed into the realm of God's holiness,[72] and acceptance by God, which establishes the new existence before him. Once and for all, God has caused something to happen in the life of the Christian, something that, of course, must then be lived out and treasured.[73]

What is important is that along with such individual references, the basic meaning of the link between a theology of the cross and a theology of justification remains conscious. In the final analysis, the question about salvation is the question about God and about how and where we can truly encounter God. If this occurs at the cross, at the sign of the deepest humiliation and greatest weakness, then this means that no person's life can be so unworthy, so unuseful, or so far from God that it cannot be reached by God's love.[74] It does not matter whether the theology of the cross found in 1 Corinthians is supposed to develop the teaching on justification that quietly lies at its core and is "available also for former Gentiles,"[75] or whether the word from the cross represents only "the nucleus of the theology of justification's antithesis," which Paul first formulated in Galatians and Romans.[76] No matter what the case, both are deeply entwined theologically. Though it may be uncertain whether the *theme* of justification was determined from the get-go,[77] what was always determinative for Paul was the fundamental conviction that formed the basis of his message of justification.

3. ONLY POLEMICS? ON THE DEVELOPMENT OF THE PAULINE TEACHING ON JUSTIFICATION

Both friend and foe of the doctrine of justification are of one mind about this: the trenchant outworking of the Letter to the Galatians and the situation in which it arose had a particularly poignant significance. Even those not inclined to agree to there being an evolution in Pauline theology will admit that the Letter to the Galatians offered Paul an important opportunity to more systematically formulate and develop his message of justification. What was it that led to this?

Paul had heard that people had come to Galatia who confronted the local Gentile Christians with the demand that they allow themselves to be circumcised in order to belong fully to the salvation community of the people of God (5:2ff.; 6:12ff.). Faith in Jesus Christ, they said, was only the beginning of the way to God. It is only obedience to the law that will bring you to the goal (cf. 3:2, 3). In so doing they presumably didn't argue, as was earlier often assumed, that it was necessary to attain salvation through fulfilling the law. They wanted to answer the question, "Who belongs to the covenant people and what demands are to be fulfilled in regard to this membership?"[78] Their response was, "Whoever takes on circumcision as a sign of the covenant with Abraham and keeps the food laws and holy day rules belongs to the people of the promise" (cf. 4:9ff.; 5:2ff.). For them it was not a matter of fulfilling the whole law; Paul was the one who first pointed to this consequence (5:3). It was a matter of "identity markers" that had become important to New Testament Judaism.[79]

This analysis of the opposing position finds significant consensus with the research. It also meshes well with the recognition represented emphatically by a series of exegetes that there is no evidence from New Testament Judaism that one could or should, so to speak, earn salvation through following the law. God's covenant with his people was the gracious context that formed the foundation for Israel's salvation and life.

Obedience in response to the commandments was the consequence and form in which the covenant was lived out.[80]

Paul was extremely alarmed by this development. To him, what was at stake in this was the freedom from the law of the whole mission to the Gentiles and the "truth of the gospel" (Gal 2:5, 14). The fact that his authority as an apostle was disputed and that he was reproached for preaching a "diluted" gospel in order to please people (1:10) made the situation more poignant for him. It is for this reason that in his letter he first of all points to the origins of his authorization of his gospel in a call from God (1:11-24). At the same time he also names the agreement made with him in Jerusalem about the Gentile mission freed from the constraints of the law (2:1-10).

Yet in this connection he also mentions an episode in Antioch that led to a conflict with Peter, who had given up the table fellowship that he, along with other Jewish Christians in Antioch, had had with the Gentile Christians. James's people and subsequently Peter and Barnabas had good grounds for their behavior. What was important to them was not to endanger their ties with Judaism through table fellowship with Gentiles. The community of Jesus could only keep its identity by also maintaining its continuity with Israel. But Paul doesn't allow this line of argumentation to prevail. The essence of the congregation is its inclusivity, the social counterpart to the universality of the Gospel, and this is expressed precisely by eating with one another.[81]

So Paul tried to make clear to Peter that his change of behavior put the Gentile Christians into a difficult position (2:14). For now the question arises as to what will in future be decisive for their identity as Christians: Taking on the Jewish religious culture or faith in Jesus Christ? The form of life together in the congregation and the question about the salvation that God gives through Christ are intimately connected. Paul makes this quite clear in the continuation of his report on the conflict with Peter.[82] Next Paul makes a concession to Peter: "We ourselves are Jews by birth and not Gentile sinners" (2:15). Even Paul must not annihilate the difference between those who have God's law and live according to it and other people. And yet one deciding realization links both Jewish and Gentile Christian: "We know that a person is justified not by the works of the law but through faith in Jesus Christ. And we have come to believe in Christ Jesus, so that we might be justified by faith in Christ, and not by doing the works of the law, because no one will be justified by the works of the law" (2:16).

This carefully worded phrase, which has become the central phrase of Pauline teaching on justification (cf. Rom 3:20, 28), is at first rather strange in its context. Why does Paul suddenly speak of "being justified"? Why does he place justification "through faith in Christ Jesus" in opposition to a(n impossible) justification "by the works of the law" when, according to the testimony of many present-day exegetes, neither the Jewish Christian agitators in Galatia nor anyone in the time of New Testament Judaism had so much as thought of basing salvation before God on the fulfillment of the law?

The answer at first seems simple. After 1 Cor 6:11, "being justified" characterizes becoming a Christian, being accepted into the congregation by baptism.[83] What seems to fit well with this idea is that according to some exegetes' opinions, what is meant by the "works of the law" is not the effort to do everything possible to fulfill all the commands of the law but rather the "prescriptions of the law" with which Jews traditionally distanced themselves from the Gentiles, in particular circumcision, Sabbath observance, and purity and food laws.[84] If this were correct, then in the debate about justification, the question of how one enters into the salvific fellowship of the people of God and how one demonstrates one's loyalty to God would be the key questions.[85] And indeed more recent research points to the fact that Gal 2:16 was a kind of "canon of mission theology" of the Antiochean congregation to which Paul points. He says, "We must not insist on circumcision as the *condition sine qua non* of Gentile converts' acceptance into the fellowship of the holy; their confession of Christ suffices."[86]

But Paul does not stop at the declaration of Gal 2:15ff. The phrase is important to him because he bases being a Christian in "faith in Jesus Christ" and contrasts this faith with "works of the law." The prepositions "out of" (= because of) or "through" qualify this contrast as a criterion for the question of out of what or through what a person is justified, i.e., on what he bases his existence before God.[87] It is not only a matter of the "identity markers" or "badges," it's a matter of the question of from what a person lives.[88]

This makes the continuation of the argumentation clear. Although the Jews, in seeking justification through faith alone, show themselves in the deepest sense to be "sinners," this does not make Christ the "servant of sin" as Paul was accused of making him.[89] It's more like the opposite: Anyone who, like Peter, rebuilds the wall that he has already torn down, necessarily makes himself a transgressor of the law (v. 18).

Yet it is the personal consequence that Paul names in vv. 19-21 that is decisive. He does this using the first-person form, which on the one hand is meant to be typical for the "I" of every Christian, yet at the same time appears "as an existential presentation of his understanding of the Gospel."[90] "Through the law [Paul] died to the law" because he has "been crucified with Christ," that is, through baptism he has been included in Christ's death, Christ who bore the curse of the law and so brought to an end its judgmental power (cf. 3:13). Yet this happened so that he "might live to God." The law that to Jews is the God-given way to life has become an obstacle to Paul to really live for God. It became clear to him through his encounter with the risen Christ that his fight for the law was a fight against God. Yet it is Christ, and no longer the "I" imprisoned and led astray by the law, that is now the center of his life. "It is no longer I who live, but it is Christ who lives in me" (2:20), says Paul—which might have been quite an enthusiastic declaration if Paul had not immediately qualified it by saying, "The life I now live in the flesh [i.e., under the condition of my earthly existence] I live by faith in the Son of God, who loved me and gave himself for me" (v. 20). Extinguishing the "I" is not the goal, rather anchoring it in the sacrificial love of Christ who from now on determines my life. Faith in Jesus Christ is not one form of identification alongside others but rather the way of life that links one's own life with God's love in Jesus Christ. And so the inference for Paul is: "if justification comes through the law, then Christ died for nothing" (v. 21). And to draw such a conclusion would mean to disempower God's grace!

Paul achieves this final sense of certainty about the path to salvation not through a critical analysis of the theory and praxis of the fulfillment of the law in contemporary Judaism but rather through his encounter with Christ.[91] In other words, he argues from the perspective of a Christian. In what follows, he, for that reason in the first instance addresses the Galatian Christians with respect to their experience. He reminds them of their encounter with the crucified one in Paul's proclamation and of the gift of the Holy Spirit, God's gift to the end-time people of God, which they have received not because of "works of the law" but "by believing what [they] heard" (3:1-5).

But then Paul also goes on to argue on the basis of the witness of the Scripture by showing that the promise to Abraham of his faith being reckoned to him as righteousness (Gen 15:6) at the same time holds within it the promise that in him "all peoples will be blessed."[92] For this presages what now occurs in the law-free mission to the Gentiles: like Abraham, God justifies the Gentiles on the basis of their faith and thus includes them in the blessing of Abraham. By the same token, the opposite is also true: that all who live according to the works of the law, i.e., those who rely on the works of the Law, are under the curse. Paul proves this by a quotation from Deut 27:26 that places under the curse all who do not keep all that is written in the book of the law (3:6-12).

This line of argumentation seems to lead to two possible conclusions: (1) If Paul's opponents indeed understand "works of the law" to mean the most important distinguishing features particularly of Jewish identity, then Paul shows the Galatian Christians that these features, in fact, lead them right past the real intentions of the law; and (2) the problem to which justification by faith responds is, for Paul, the lack of fulfillment of the law and not the misled effort in trying to be justified by the doing of the law.[93] But Paul's further reasoning demonstrates that Paul is arguing at a more fundamental level. For in Hab 2:4 it says: "The righteous live by their faith."[94] But law "does not rest on faith," i.e., it does not point to faith as the final and decisive basis of life before God. The law is oriented to doing: "Whoever does the works of the law will live by them" (Lev 18:5).

Given this argument, a person almost unavoidably finds himself under the curse of the law: on the one hand, because he never totally fulfills the law, and on the other, because this fulfillment is not at all the path to fellowship with God. By taking it upon himself, Christ has freed humanity from this curse. This opens the way for those Gentiles to benefit from the blessing promised to Abraham, who through faith receive the promised Spirit of God and thus also his living presence (3:13ff.).[95]

Chapter 3:26-29 shows how this occurs and also thereby illuminates a new ecclesiological perspective. All who belong to Christ have become "sons of God" through faith, i.e., his legally responsible children. For all who are baptized "into Christ" "have clothed [themselves] with Christ" (v. 27). No doubt the background to these statements is the idea of the body of Christ into which the faithful are incorporated through baptism and at the same become partakers in being children of God.[96] The consequence of this is that all dividing differences are erased: "There is no longer Jew or Greek, there is no longer slave or free, there is no longer male and female; for all of you are one in Christ Jesus" (v. 28).

The fact that Paul changes the symbolization at this point is not arbitrary. Christ is more than a mediator of restitution for the people of God.

In some way he remains determinative of what happens in his community, something Paul can describe only with spatial categories. By showing Christians their place "in Christ," he makes clear what part of the eschatological fellowship with God is valid now. The common status of Jews and Gentiles before God shown soteriologically in the justification of the sinner (Gal 2:16) finds its counterpart in the equality of all in Christ, in which all societal differences of rank and worth are eliminated. In Gal 4:1-7 Paul describes the liberation effect of the Christ event in a further image. By God's Son being placed as a human under the rule of the law, he freed those who had lived as slaves under the guardianship of the law to real life as children of God, made them mature heirs of the promise, and placed them in a personal father-child relationship through the working of the Spirit.

Two things are worth noting at this point: By perceiving the laws together with the *stoicheia tou kosmou* (the "elemental spirits of the world") as enslaving powers in 4:3, which Paul later identifies with the heathen gods in 4:8ff., he places the law into the world of religion and hints at a phenomenological parallel between law and religion.[97] Each person finds himself or herself faced with demands that are based in the cosmic order or in the will of God transmitted through salvation history (by the angels) but which "can give neither life nor identity nor meaning"[98] because they cannot really communicate fellowship with God.

But God's spirit does communicate such fellowship. It is received by faith and becomes a life-determining force in this new existence before God. It inspires love that helps to fulfill what the law prescribes as God's will. And so there is no ethical vacuum when people are set free from the enslaving power of the law (5:13ff.).

How does the Letter to the Galatians speak of justification? We will try to achieve an even-handed portrayal.

   1. In the controversy described by the Letter to the Galatians, justification, first of all, means acceptance into the people of God and the community of salvation. The ecclesiological aspect is important even for Paul. Acceptance into the people of God is a continuing foundation for a way of living together that does not discriminate against others and thus befits acceptance by God. God's justifying action that makes all who believe into his beloved children at the same time creates the fond community "in Christ" that overcomes all human differences.[99]

2. Justification is a person's acceptance by God; *dikaiosyne* (righteousness) signifies what gives life form and content and thus salvation and life. The forensic aspect of this, meaning the implied judgment situation in which God vindicates and accepts, is in the background but is not described in any great detail.

3. Paul sees a mutually exclusive contrast between being justified by the law (*en nomō*) and being justified by Christ (*en Christō*), and likewise being justified "by the works of the law" and being justified "by faith in Jesus Christ." What this makes clear is that Paul's repudiation of the law as the way to salvation is not simply about distinguishing between the Jewish privilege and the Gentile misuse of the law and its prescriptions. It's about a decision between two ways of living before God: a life determined by Christ or by the law. It's a matter of whether a sense of identity and a foundation for life is derived from the "works of the law," from "doing," or out of a sense of trust about what God has done in Jesus Christ and how this places us in relationship to God.

4. Justification is liberation from the deathly domination from our own anxious ego (what Paul terms "the flesh"). But at the same time justification means finding oneself. Wherever the enthroned ego dies (2:19; 6:14), God's beloved "thou" comes to life and an "I" is created whose nature is determined by the relationship to God. The fact that in Galatians Paul writes in the first person in such a multilayered way "occurs as a result of the meaning of the revelation of God in Christ for the individual's self-understanding. The discovery of subjectivity is [...] the consequence of the christological-soteriological universalism." For justification of a person through faith "unconditionally assumes the differentiation between his unmistakable person and the characteristics that he can gain, have, and lose."[100] This constitutes not only new self-understanding but also a new way of being with others in community: "Each person is recognized as an individual and subject with equal rights."[101]

5. Justification is therefore liberation to love (5:1, 13), through which persons, freed from anxiety about themselves, can live out what God's spirit effects for others through them (5:22ff.).

With this message of liberation of Galatians, Paul has established new emphases that arise, on the one hand, from contemporary demands, and, on the other, follow logically from the basis of his theology of the cross. This raises the question of what significance this new emphasis in his message of justification, which now appears as a full-fledged doctrine of justification, takes on in his theology as a whole. This will be researched in what follows using the Letter to the Romans. Relevant sections of 2 Corinthians and Philippians will be included in the discussion.

4. THE EXPOSITION OF THE PAULINE DOCTRINE OF JUSTIFICATION

The question of the significance of the doctrine of justification for Pauline theology is intricately connected to the question of the character of the Letter to the Romans. Is it, like the other letters of Paul, an occasional writing that addresses the problems of the Christian congregation in Rome or discusses the still-current argument about the law-free mission to the Gentiles? Or is it a systematic summary of Paul's theology, which gives the doctrine of justification its due place at the center of this theology?[102]

Much has been written on this, and no doubt the truth lies somewhere between such simple alternatives. For the Letter to the Romans is also a letter that was written in response to current events. Underlying it is Paul's desire to come to Rome, preach the gospel there, and travel on to Spain with the support of the congregation (1:8-15; 15:14-24). Yet first Paul must go to Jerusalem in order to pass along the Gentile Christian church's collection as a sign of its solidarity with the mother church in Jerusalem, and he is unsure whether this token will be accepted (15:25-33). Thus the argument about the law-free Gentile mission and the unresolved tensions between Jewish and Gentile Christians are once again at the forefront of his mind; all the other conflicts to be solved during his missionary activity in Asia Minor and Greece are not to be forgotten either.

It is this contemporary situation that has led to the Letter to the Romans becoming a kind of Pauline "theological report."[103] The letter basically wants to effect something of what the announced visit is hoped to do, namely to make the Roman Christians feel a part of the Pauline proclamation of the gospel (1:1-15; 15:16).[104] So this piece of occasional writing becomes a basic exposition of the Pauline gospel, certainly shaped by a particular situation but by no means written with the intention of only wanting to solve time-sensitive problems.

Just how serious Paul is about this can be seen by a glance at the prescript, the letterhead of his epistle. Here Paul expands the salutation beyond all formal conventions in order to present his mission as an apostle and the basis of his gospel of Jesus Christ (1:1-6).[105] Paul underscores his willingness also to proclaim the gospel in Rome with another "definition" of the gospel, which describes its effectiveness and goal and at the same time forms the underlying thesis of the entire letter: "For I am not ashamed of the gospel; it is the power of God for salvation to everyone who has faith, to the Jew first and also the Greek. For in it the righteousness of God is revealed through faith for faith; as it is written, 'The one who is righteous will live by faith'" (1:16-17).

This gospel is like the "word from the cross," and in the end is identical with it. It is the power of God because it saves people. In the New Testament, the word *sōtēria* (salvation, deliverance) has an important and encompassing meaning, embracing not only help in concrete situations of need and political good deeds but also the gift of eternal life. To Paul himself, in the first instance the term means being saved from the threatening annihilation of the Final Judgment (cf. 13:11; but also 5:9; 1 Cor 3:15; 5:5; Phil 1:19). In the Old Testament the term means, among other things, God's salvific help (often paralleled with righteousness, cf. Ps 98:2ff.; Isa 56:1ff., etc). It was held in high esteem even in Hellenistic society and was linked with the hope of being saved from and helped in very diverse existential and social needs. "In taking up this expression, the primitive church's message promises a response to the weight of the suffering of human existence and thereby gets into competition with other 'ways of salvation.'"[106] This had a very weighty religious aspect to it: "By and large [...] people lived with the sense of being totally lost in earthly reality as a death-bearing deception. Salvation therefore only seemed possible as a heaven-sent initiative whose purpose was to partake in a heavenly reality. It was for this reason that there was an extraordinarily great openness to any kind of announcement of salvation."[107] At the same time, this general mood of openness to diverse expectations and promises of salvation also was the reason for the necessity for Paul being so specific about the promises of the gospel.

Paul's first effort at specificity occurs in naming the individuals he is addressing. Salvation is meant for every person who believes, first the

Jew, but then also the Greek. The duo "Jew and Greek" once again is intended to describe the entirety of a religiously and culturally divided society, and once again Paul attempts the balancing act that he began in Gal 2:15ff. and continues in various ways in the Letter to the Romans. He does this, on the one hand, by holding tight to the preferential status of the Jewish people and, on the other hand, by relinquishing that status's exclusive character. The target group of the gospel is not determined by old marks of identity such as membership in religious or social groups. "Each one who has faith" is intended here. It is very consciously formulated in the singular to signal the separation from any kind of group that promotes either well-being or the lack of it. It is also clear from this that the term "believers" is being used here, not as is sometimes the case elsewhere simply as a synonym for "Christians" (cf. 1 Thess 1:6–2:10; 1 Cor 14:22), but rather very precisely to describe the act of accepting the gospel. Yet it is equally clear that Paul does not intend this description of the acceptance of salvation to draw new lines between people. Rather, he aims to describe the universality and inclusivity of the message of salvation that knows of no other "condition" of its effectiveness than that it be trustingly accepted.[108]

The second reason for Paul's specificity lies in the more precise description of what happens when the gospel is proclaimed: "In it the righteousness of God is revealed" (Rom 1:17). Paul thus places his announcement of the good news in the tradition of the expectation of the eschatological revelation of God's righteousness, of God's salvific help for his people and for the entire earth.[109] According to Ps 98:2ff., this revelation occurs before all peoples and announces to the whole world God's faithfulness to his people; it will also set to rights all the people and world (v. 9).

Influenced by Mal 3:16–4:3, in the further history of this tradition, the divisive effect of the revelation of God's righteousness comes to the fore: "Then once more you shall see the difference between the righteous and the wicked, between one who serves God and one who does not serve him" (v. 18).[110]

Paul contrasts this with the universal and potentially all-embracing goal of faith. Not that he would overlook the reality of wickedness and sin. They will be highlighted in their entirety in 1:18–3:20. Yet in contrast to this is the totality of grace, whose effectiveness is characterized by the formulation "from faith to faith." It may be that this formulation is simply a rhetorical paraphrase of "through faith alone."[111] But with reference to Hab 2:4, it is probably describing how the revelation of God's righteousness becomes effective by faith and aims to evoke faith.[112]

By using this fundamental thesis at the beginning of the Letter to the Romans, Paul makes it clear in what theological framework he sees the doctrine of justification. It is not just a matter of the entry requirements into the community of the people of God. It is a matter of God's revelation in the gospel. What Paul formulates in a relatively compact and abstract manner takes on concrete form in light of its Old Testament background. In his righteousness, God himself encounters persons, and does so with his powerful claim on them, but all with his all-embracing goodness. He encounters a person with his salvific and rectifying "Yes." What God's people have come to expect for themselves, namely, that despite all their failings, God in his faithfulness confesses his allegiance to them, and it is this that is promised to each and every person through the proclamation of the gospel. Anyone who trustingly and with faith accepts this as the basis for his or her life receives the certainty that his or her life is not passing by without worth or meaning but rather is safe in God and will attain its goal. Paul cites Hab 2:4 to encapsulate this certainty: "the one who is righteous will live by faith."[113]

The Missionary Context

The connection between justification and faith therefore has a dual function in Romans. It makes clear that the revelation of God's righteousness in the gospel expects absolutely nothing from people in terms of their origins or demands they must achieve. Rather, God's righteousness hopes exclusively and solely for the trusting acceptance of the message. It is precisely through this that the range of effectiveness of the message is broadened and universalized. Wherever Paul speaks of God's righteousness being valid for the faithful, he does it by adding, "everyone [each one] who believes" (1:16; 10:4) or "all who believe" (3:22; 4:11). This shows how much Romans and the teaching on justification developed in it is written from a missionary perspective.

This is pertinent not just for Paul's already completed missionary work in the East or in anticipation of the mission to distant Spain (15:23ff.) Although he does not articulate this very clearly, it is evident that Paul wants to evangelize in Rome.[114] In Rome he sees gathered in one place the diversity of peoples found in the Roman Empire and thus envisages himself called to be "the apostle to the Gentiles," i.e., of the non-Jewish peoples. "I am a debtor both to Greeks and to barbarians, both to the wise and to the foolish" (1:14). Here, within the world of the "heathens" new areas of well-being and doom, worth and worthlessness appear. Cultural and educational barriers exclude people. But it is precisely in this situation that the border-crossing power of the gospel manifests itself, and the apostle, as the messenger of this gospel, feels himself to be challenged to carry the message of God's salvation, which applies to all, across these very borders. The universal power of the gospel—which Paul demonstrates in exemplary fashion in 1:16 by the overcoming of the exclusion of the "Greeks" from the promise made to the Jews—is valid also for those, such as the uneducated non-Greek-speaking "barbarians" or those always considered the "foolish," who are often excluded.

To what extent Paul maintains this perspective is shown by the conclusion of the letter. Paul turns our attention away from the treatment of the tension that has sprung up in the Roman church between "the weak" and "the strong" and toward Christ who has accepted all (15:7) and thus once more to the universal context of the Christ event that his mission serves (15:8-13). Forming a brotherly/sisterly community and the missionary task of the church are obviously closely connected with each other and deeply formed by the message of justification. Christ's unconditional acceptance of all has an effect both inside and externally.[115]

It is precisely the basis of the doctrine of justification that "a person is justified by faith apart from works prescribed by the law" (3:28) that is made serious for Paul through the recognition that God is not only the God of the Jews but also the God of the Gentiles. Israel's foundational confession that "God is one" leads it to the consequence that this God justified circumcision on the grounds of faith and equally justifies uncircumcision through that same faith (3:30).

Even the Jewish theologians of Paul's time knew that the God of Israel was also the God of the peoples; indeed, it was in this that they saw the significance of Israel's election and its being set apart as a sign for the peoples.[116] It is within this context that the radicality of Paul's contention is shown, as is the risk inherent in it. For even Paul's universalism could work exclusively, for example, in excluding unbelieving members of Israel.[117] Paul tried to respond to this danger with the theological perspective of Rom 11. Yet grasping, living, and holding on to the connection between justification and faith in its missionary dynamic so that these terms are more than just a new kind of identity or "boundary marker" remains an important challenge to the church.

This must not be a signal to us to give up the question about faith in Jesus Christ. But it is important always to see in faith the goal of the gospel—what proclamation hopes to call forth from people. Only under these circumstances is faith then also a sign of identity and a boundary marker for membership in the church of Jesus Christ.

The Anthropological Rationale

How does Paul view the people to whom he proclaims the gospel? What human situation does the message of justification assume? A thorough diagnosis of this situation demonstrates that the message really is for all. Its conclusion is, "For there is no distinction, since all have sinned and fall short of the glory of God" (3:22ff.). That is the conclusion of the exposition from 1:18–3:20, a section that follows immediately on the basic thesis about the effect of the gospel, in 1:16ff. It also begins with a thesis: "For the wrath of God is revealed from heaven against all ungodliness and wickedness of those who by their wickedness suppress the truth" (1:18).

As in the Old Testament, "God's wrath" is the counterpart to "God's righteousness." The parallelism between the two terms shows that in both genitive constructions the concern is with God's own actions with which he encounters humans. If *God's righteousness* means his salvific fidelity to the community and his gracious justice that he employs to gather back humanity under his rule, and thus his merciful Yes to all, whoever they may be, then *God's wrath* means his reaction against everything that disrespects him and his saving justice, everything that disrupts life and community, and thus his No to everything that separates humans from him. As much as God's No presents a strong response to everything antigodly, it is in the final analysis nothing more than the unavoidable echo to the life-denying action of people and the No of sin. Unlike righteousness, wrath does not turn directly against people but rather "against all people's despising of God and ignoring of justice."[118]

How Paul thinks God's wrath is revealed is still an open question. The phrasing "from heaven" excludes the possibility that this does occur or should occur in the gospel. Paul sees the wrath of God at work in the reality of the world in which people live and suffer.[119] The task of proclaiming the gospel is not to invoke or reveal the wrath of God, but rather to point to its undeniable and passionate reality.[120]

The fact that people "suppress [and oppress] truth through injustice" is shown by the way that people treat the reality of God. Although God is recognizable in his creation, people have turned away from God's glory; they have turned away from his everlasting and incomparable being as creator and instead idolize the creation in images of people or animals. But in so doing, they are in the final analysis idolizing themselves.[121] Therefore, as Paul thrice lays out, God gave them up to themselves and their lusts. Everything that Paul lists as social improprieties in vv. 24-31 is to him a result of a distorted relationship to God from which results a destructive relationship to others and oneself. Here "immorality is the punishment, not the guilt."[122]

Although, technically speaking, throughout the section Paul simply refers to "people," we can't overlook that he really means non-Jews, the Gentiles, and that in so doing he takes over many motifs of traditional Old Testament idol and heathen polemic.[123] But this is not intended to lead the Jewish readers astray into believing that they can participate in God's judgment as impartial observers. Paul vehemently opposes any such reasoning: "Therefore you have no excuse, whoever you are, when you judge others; for in passing judgment on another you condemn yourself, because you, the judge, are doing the very same things" (2:1). Paul here is critiquing an attitude that gladly accepts for oneself God's goodness and forbearance at the same time as judging the outsiders on the basis of their obvious faults. Such an attitude is, for example, found in Wis 15:1ff. where, after some harsh polemic, we read, "But you, our God, are kind and true, patient, and ruling all things in mercy. For even if we sin we are yours, knowing your power." Although 15:2 continues with, "but we will not sin, because we know that you acknowledge us as yours," Paul sees in this attitude a great danger that a Jewish person will be satisfied with having the law and belonging to God's people. It is in opposition to such covenantal nomism that Paul clearly puts the thesis: "It is not the hearers of the law who are righteous in God's sight, but the doers of the law who will be justified."[124] By the same token, he also considers it (at least hypothetically) possible that Gentiles who do not have the law can find the demands of the law written on their hearts and act according to them (2:14ff.). Circumcision as a sign of the covenant is only worth something if the Law is also being fulfilled; likewise, there can be such a thing as "a circumcision of the heart" of those who, led by God's spirit, fulfill the law.[125]

Despite all of this, Paul does not simply want to do away with the privileged place of the Jews and put in question God's faithfulness to his people. But God's faithfulness is manifest precisely in this argument about justice because God continues to be just in the face of human failure, as Paul makes clear by drawing on Ps 51:5. And yet the possible conclusion from this is that only with his unrighteousness can a person put "God's righteousness"[126] in the right light, and therefore really ought not to be punished (3:5). This sort of bargaining with God is as deluded and devious as the suggestion that the Pauline doctrine of justification leads a person astray to do evil in order to effect the good, namely to make yet more impressive God's righteousness and grace through one's own unrighteousness (cf. also Rom 6:1; Gal 2:17).

For Paul, all this is like fighting thin air and unworthy of both Israel's calling and the seriousness of people's situation. Jews and Greeks alike are under the rule of sin (3:9). What is needed is not a listing of individual failings but a recognition of the basic human situation. As is almost always the case with Paul, here sin appears as power that determines persons' behavior and alienates them from God. A series of quotations from the Old Testament is intended to show that no one can stand before God, for neither their bearing toward God nor their practical behavior toward others corresponds with God's will (3:9-18).

Paul refutes the objection that all this was, after all, meant in regard to sinners, especially Gentiles, by pointing out that the law (here meaning the Holy Scripture) speaks to those who live in its jurisdiction and that therefore all the world is guilty before God.[127] This leads to the fundamental conclusion in 1:18–3:20 that "'no human being [literally: no flesh] will be justified in his sight' by deeds prescribed by the law, for through the law comes the knowledge of sin" (3:20).

What does this saying mean in connection with Paul's doctrine of justification?

> 1. Judgment follows because no one really does God's will as it is written down in the law. It is not stated that the doing of the law could in itself be sin.[128]
>
> 2. Like in Galatians, the question of circumcision as a sign of the covenant and as a distinction from being a Gentile does play a role in Rom 2 as well (cf. 2:25; 3:1). Trust in the law and this form of praising the law are fought similarly hard. And yet the entire context of Rom 1:18–3:20 speaks against limiting the

"works of the law" in 3:20 to the "cultic-ritual demands of the law" that would need to be fulfilled in a conversion to Judaism and that presented the exterior signs of identity of Jewish life.[129] Regarding Rom 1:18–3:20, there is much more to it than the question of the requirements for the covenant people to enter into the community of salvation. In Rom 2:14, *ergon tou nomou* means what the law requires and what the Gentiles can, at least theoretically, fulfill.

3. But because no on fulfills these demands, the law is excluded as a path to salvation. Its task is quite different. It highlights sin and makes it clear to people where they stand with God. In so doing, the law does indirectly serve people's salvation. Romans 3:20 is inconclusive about whether this is only true *de facto* because no on really does the will of God, or whether it is fundamentally true because the law is not given to "make alive" (Gal 3:21) and therefore, despite Lev 18:5, keeping the law never leads to life; only faith in Jesus Christ does so.[130]

4. Even though Paul beginning at 2:1ff. primarily speaks of the guilt of Jews, his argument continues to be focused on proving the commonality of sin. In 3:19ff., the verses that sum up both parts of the section, Paul twice highlights "the whole world may be held accountable to God" and "no human being" will be justified on the basis of the works of the law. Likewise, in 2:14-16 the demands of the Torah, the Jewish law, are paralleled with what even a Gentile can sense in his heart as a demand on his life. The struggle in his conscience is an indicator of how every person knows deep down about the necessity for justification of his life, even if the full extent of this is only revealed on the day of judgment.[131]

But for the time being Paul continues to address those people within the jurisdiction of Jewish law. And though this discussion in 2:1–3:20 is striking and bold in nature, it reoccurs in a different place in a much more pastoral and subtle way.

In Rom 7:7-25 Paul describes the dilemma faced by a person under the law. Although he does so in the first-person singular, he is not describing a subjective experience of his conversion (as opposed to the accounts in Gal 1:14 and Phil 3:6) but rather is to some extent retrospectively analyzing what the fight against sin was like for him under the law.

Sin as power now comes into play much more emphatically, the sin that overpowers a person, and the sin that misuses the law that in and of itself is "holy, righteous, and good" in order to lead a person astray into overstepping particular laws, and has led him into the deep irreconcilable conflict of wanting to do the good that the law prescribes and yet always failing to carry out this desire.

Perhaps a deeper problem lies behind this conflict. The "good" that a person wants to do is the "life" that the law promises. But this life is not to be attained through "doing." And this leads to an irreconcilable dilemma. "What a person wants is salvation. What he creates is disaster."[132] That text does not say this.[133] But the sayings in 7:4-7 cast it in this light. "Fruit for God" only grows with those who have died to the law through Christ, because otherwise through the sinful passions aroused by the law they only produce "fruit for death" (v. 5). Therefore what is true for Christians is that "now we are discharged from the law, dead to that which held us captive, so that we are slaves not under the old written code but in the new life of the Spirit" (v. 6; cf. 2 Cor 3:6). This is basically the theme for 7:7–8:17 and because of it the law is fundamentally excluded as a way of salvation.[134] Apparently what is behind the "antinomian" conflict, in other words behind the failure because of the demands of the law, is the "nomian" conflict, i.e., the fundamental failure of the law to be a way to salvation.[135] But Paul is not describing this through the caricature of a Pharisee, proud of the law, as an example of human self-assertion, but rather as a story of someone's failure exemplified by his self. Without Christ, this "I," this self, is nothing but "a marionette of the sin that lives in him and that totally rules him."[136]

Approaching it from a different perspective, a person's situation under the law is depicted once again, in Rom 9 and 10. Though Rom 7 spoke quite deliberately about the individual, in Rom 9–11 the discussion is about Israel as a whole and about those who are part of the covenant people, and yet cut themselves off from faith in Christ. Paul at first tackles this question by citing the choice of God's free grace. What is remarkable about this is that he mentions that Jacob's election is "not by works but by his call" (9:12). Clearly, Paul is here trying to show the contrast between deeds and God's call!

Paul once again takes up this motif in 9:30–10:4 when he talks about Israel having taken the wrong path to God. The calling of the Gentiles promised in Scripture (9:24-29) does, after all, lead to the paradox that those who did not participate in the intensive striving for righteousness, as Israel understands it, nonetheless received righteousness, namely "righteousness that comes from faith" (10:6). By contrast, those who followed the law and its promises of righteousness did not attain the real goal of the law.[137] The reason for it is that they did it not "on the basis of faith" but "as if it were based on works" (9:32). Yet this leads to their downfall, as Paul shows using a Scripture citation from Isa 8:14; 28:16.

Why? Paul responds to this in 10:3 after he has again expressed his urgent wish for salvation for his people and his respect for their zeal for God: "For, being ignorant of the righteousness that comes from God, and seeking to establish their own, they have not submitted to God's righteousness" (10:3). The parallels to Phil 3:6-9 are striking. In Philippians, Paul also speaks of the zeal with which he persecuted the church and of his blamelessness regarding righteousness under the law. This zeal is not to be limited to the fight for "boundary markers."[138] It is a zeal for God that is manifested in labors on behalf of his law and the righteousness represented by it. But it is precisely in this that the zeal is misplaced because it underestimates God and his righteousness. So for Paul the basis for new being in Christ is therefore no longer "a righteousness of my own that comes from the law, but one that comes through faith in Christ, the righteousness from God based on faith" (Phil 3:9). In Phil 3:9 as in Rom 9:31 personal righteousness "based on the law" or "based on works" is contrasted with God's righteousness. In Phil 3:9 where he discusses an existential life conversion, Paul speaks of "the righteousness from God" that God gives to believers; in Rom 10:3 where he is discussing the new order of salvation, "God's righteousness" appears as a salvific power with which God himself encounters persons and asks them about the obedience of their lives, their obedience of faith.[139] In all this, Israel and the Jew are not being described as those who fail in their attempts to fulfill the law, but rather as those who are on the wrong path if they think they can find righteousness through their own doings and instead only find a righteousness by their own efforts that is "no righteousness at all, because God is no longer to be found in the law as a bringer of salvation."[140]

Even here, the final certainty about the truth of these statements is not to be found in a critical analysis of a legalistic piety of achievement but in the encounter with Christ: "Christ is the end of the law so that there may be righteousness for everyone who believes" (Rom 10:4). "In Christ we are encountered by the previously given victorious power of the righteousness of God, which is not brought to realization by our testing it but which makes this possible. Christ according to 2 Cor 1:19 is God's Yes to us. This Yes is unequivocal and irrevocable."[141]

And so it is not by chance that everywhere that Paul tries to portray the vulnerability of a person for whom righteousness and liberation through Christ are intended, that precisely at those points something must be said about the Christ event.[142] The person to whom the message of justification must be announced is the person who has failed God and hence life. That this is true for everyone is shown by various factors. Paul names people's self-idolization, which leads to people being given over to themselves in an egomaniacal society. He describes the failure of the earnest attempt to do God's will, a failure that results from a person's getting embroiled in himself and thus failing to reach his goal of God and God's righteousness. These situational analyses do not have to grasp all possible signs of problems. For the definitive and most convincing insight into his problem is not afforded a person through the appropriate analysis but rather through the encounter with God in the gospel of Jesus Christ.

The Christological Center

"Christ Jesus ... became for us ... righteousness" (1 Cor 1:30). This is the basis of Paul's message of justification. Therefore justifying faith is "faith in Jesus Christ."[143] Righteousness "by works" and "by faith" do not simply give rise to two different ways of life or ways of behaving religiously.[144] With faith, it's not just a matter of the appropriate inner attitude toward God in place of faith in one's own achievements in life or even of some deed done in recompense for a person's failure in the face of the law's demands. The key issues in humanity's new situation before God are not a person's turning to faith as a more appropriate stance toward God; the key issues are God's turning to humanity in Christ, which a person in faith gratefully allows to be true for him.

Romans 3:21-26 makes this absolutely clear. Paul once again takes up the basic thesis from 1:16ff.: "But now, apart from the law, the righteousness of God has been disclosed,[145] and is attested by the law and the prophets, the righteousness of God through faith in Jesus Christ for all who believe" (vv. 21-22). Paul refers to the witness of the Old Testament Scriptures, in which God's righteousness is depicted as his unconditional and unreserved Yes to his people and to his creation, and applies their promise of the appearing of God's salvation to the Christ event.

Paul once again explains why this is meant to apply to "all who believe" (v. 22): "For there is no distinction [between Jews and Gentiles], since all have sinned and fall short of the glory of God; they are now justified by his grace as a gift, through the redemption that is in Christ Jesus" (3:22b-24). Alongside the fact that all people have actively overstepped God's commandments comes the realization of the complete lack of the real presence of God that surrounds and fulfills the lives of persons.[146]

Without any limitation or any hesitation, the fact that God justifies all is added to this description of people's failure toward God and their lack of faith.[147] This occurs without cost through God's grace, thanks to the redemption that happened in Christ Jesus. These are expressions that, on the one hand, underscore the total graciousness of the event and, on the other, elementally tie it to the Christ event. The term "redemption," or literally "ransom" (cf. Heb 11:35), bears elements of the message of redemption of Deutero-Isaiah and—as v. 25 shows—of the idea of representative atonement.[148]

So here Paul hints at what he will expand on in v. 25ff.: justification of the sinner depends not only on the judge's sovereign pronouncement of innocence but also on the sinner being set free from his imprisonment by guilt that God effects for him through the Christ event. Verse 25 describes this through an extraordinarily complicated sentence structure that only becomes transparent when we acknowledge that Paul is here using a stock piece of Jewish-Christian tradition.[149] The original piece of tradition probably read, "God openly set him up for atonement through his blood as a sign of his righteousness for the sake of the forgiveness of sins that had occurred previously in the context of God's patience."

This has often been misunderstood in the history of interpretation. What is central to the correct understanding is the recognition that even here there is no talk of a "neutral" or "higher" righteousness of God that he somehow had to prove by punishing an alternative subject in place of the guilty party. Here too, righteousness is an expression of God's salvation-bringing faithfulness, which, by effecting atonement, transforms everything that is destructive of life that has come between God and God's people. It's a matter of disempowering sin by getting rid of its consequences.

The key term, *hilastērion* (place of atonement), points to the symbolism of the Great Day of Atonement (Lev 16), which is then transposed to Jesus' death. "God allowed Jesus to take the place of *hakkepporet* [Greek: *hilastērion*; Luther: throne of grace] hidden in the Temple and that of the rite of atonement associated with it. Through 'his blood,' i.e., through the giving of his life, Jesus effected atonement. Thus the crucified became the locus at which God himself, openly and visibly to all, let redemption become a reality. Good Friday thus became the eschatologically Great Day of Atonement."[150]

Paul picks up this tradition and expands upon it. He adds the phrase "through faith" to make it clear how what happened on the cross has an effect on each individual's life. And he removes the restriction on understanding the atonement event as being limited to forgiving sins that were committed before Jesus' death and adds the pivotal phrase: "As proof of his righteousness now, in our time, so that he himself is righteous and justifies the one who lives by faith in Jesus."

The event of the cross is valid once and for all time and is made present in the proclamation of the gospel. Paul links the saying about the revelation of God's righteousness in the gospel (1:16) with the saying about its revelation in the Christ event (3:21-26). And he links the proof of the righteousness of God in the Christ event with the justification of the one who believes in Jesus. In the death of Jesus, the justification of God, i.e., the proof of his unfailing faithfulness and his salvific intention for his creation, and the justification of the sinner, i.e., his liberation from guilt and its bondage and his being taken up into fellowship with God are indissolubly linked. Through God in Christ's death carrying the entire No that holds sway over humanity because of the life-negating power of sin, his Yes to their lives shows itself to be at one and the same time the most profound expression of his own being, his creative and saving love, and the foundation of a new, liberated, and redeemed way of being before God.[151]

Paul again and again returns to this christological reason for justification. We find it, for example in Rom 5:1-11, where the he explains the certainty of the love of God that the Holy Spirit has poured into our hearts. The certainty lies in the fact that Christ died for the ungodly while we were still weak—and could do absolutely nothing by our own strength.

This anticipatory love of God is linked with justification and salvation in a particularly poignant and persuasive passage:

> But God proves his love for us in that while we still were sinners Christ died for us. Much more surely then, now that we have been justified by his blood, will we be saved through him from the wrath of God. For if while we were enemies, we were reconciled to God through

the death of his Son, much more surely, having been reconciled, will we be saved by his life. (5:8-10)

These sentences say some extremely important things about the justification event. They point to the totally unconditional concern of God's love in the cross of Jesus: It is the weak, the sinners, the ungodly, the enemies to whom God turns. Furthermore, these sentences describe the way of God's love toward people: from the crucifixion where God gave himself up for those who were still quite distant, the path leads to justification "through his blood," or rather, to reconciliation "through his death." What happened on the cross becomes their lived reality through faith and baptism. And that, in turn, leads to final salvation in perfected fellowship with God, which was made possible through the resurrection of Jesus ("his life").

This path is not so much a path of human endurance—although this aspect is not excluded in v. 3—but rather a path showing the endurance of God's faithfulness, which is made known to us through the death of Christ and his justifying actions.

One final significant point is relevant here: Verse 9 equates the event of justification with that of reconciliation. Both terms derive from the arena of human interaction and describe how a broken relationship is reestablished anew.[152] *Justification* occurs where accusation and guilt are resolved and a person is once again granted integrity and allowed to become integrated into the community. *Reconciliation* occurs where animosity is overcome and peace is once again afforded room. And both of these become possible in situations where God in his love through Jesus' death takes upon himself the deadly consequences of guilt and enmity and through doing so opens up the way into his saving fellowship and peace.[153]

Paul had already presented this connection rather impressively in 2 Cor 5:18-21. In the first instance, this text concerns the contested nature of his apostolic life and the content of his message that Paul must defend. Paul very fundamentally grounds his service and his proclamation by mentioning the compelling power of the love of Christ (14ff.), the new way of life given us "in Christ" (v. 17), and the task given him to carry out the "ministry of reconciliation" (v. 18). This task is embedded in God's reconciling action to the whole world: "In Christ God was reconciling the world to himself, not counting their trespasses against them, and entrusting the message of reconciliation to us" (v. 19).[154]

Verse 21 describes how God accomplishes reconciliation and how the power of sin that arose as enmity between God and humanity was broken and removed. God made him who knew no sin from his personal experience into the bearer of sin, in fact made him "sin itself"[155] so that we, the apostles and congregations, become "representatives of the righteousness of God." Paul does not simply say that Jesus became a sinner so that we might become righteous. Wherever sin and righteousness are in opposition to each other they are seen first and foremost as forces that determine our lives (cf. Rom 6:18ff.). That Christ became sin means that Jesus subordinated himself to the complete power and guilt of sin (cf. Rom 8:3). That in him we become the righteousness of God means that the characteristics of Christ (1 Cor. 1:30) are transferred to Christians when Christ becomes the center of our existence. We became representatives of God's righteousness that is revealed in the gospel. We live through God's faithfulness and salvation and are at one and the same time formed and shaped by them and called to communicate them as the arenas of peace and communion with God. Through the phrase "in Christ," Paul denotes the "place" of our fellowship with God. It is the place in which justification and reconciliation are given and lived, the place where God's righteousness becomes the foundation of our lives, and the lifeblood in it, and yet remains *God's* righteousness (Phil 3:9ff.).[156]

Following on from Rom 7, this same central thought is also found in Rom 8. The promise, which continues from 7:6, is in response to the presentation of the agonizing battle against sin that, on account of the law, becomes not easier but rather bleaker: "But now we are discharged from the law, dead to that which held us captive, so that we are slaves not under the old written code but in the new life of the Spirit." The reason for this is given in a particularly sparse summary of the salvific meaning of the Christ event:

> For God has done what the law, weakened by the flesh, could not do: by sending his own Son in the likeness of sinful flesh, and to deal with sin, he condemned sin in the flesh, so that the just requirement of the law might be fulfilled in us, who walk not according to the flesh but according to the Spirit. (Rom 8:3-4)

Paul's argument is so compressed that it is hard for us to understand. It combines two sayings into one. (1) By letting his son go into the realm of sin and allowing him to be judged although sin has no right to him, God judges and conquers sin—to a certain extent on its own turf, that of the "flesh." Just at that point where people fall prey to sin because they cannot bear the limits of their creatureliness, just at that point Christ withstood them and broke their power; and (2) In the disempowering of sin, the vicious cycle of the duel between sin and law that was so impressively portrayed in Rom 7:7-25 was ended. Now that they are no longer under the power of sin but in God's spirit's sphere of influence, people can finally fulfill the demands of the law, what the law really wants of people.[157] A life so led and fulfilled by God's spirit and so shaped by life-giving righteousness (cf. 8:10) leads to the freedom of the children of God and holds true even in extreme situations and in the temptations of an as yet unredeemed world (8:9-30).

Chapter 8 and with it the entire first part of the Letter to the Romans closes with yet another christological explanation of justification and salvation. This is perhaps the densest text that Paul has written on this matter.

> What then are we to say about these things? If God is for us, who is against us? He who did not withhold his own Son, but gave him up for all of us, will he not with him also give us everything else? Who will bring any charge against God's elect? It is God who justifies. Who is to condemn? It is Christ Jesus, who died, yes, who was raised, who is at the right hand of God, who indeed intercedes for us. Who will separate us from the love of Christ? Will hardship, or distress, or persecution, or famine, or nakedness, or peril, or sword?... No, in all these things we are more than conquerors through him who loved us. For I am convinced that neither death, nor life, nor angels, nor rulers, nor things present, nor things to come, nor powers, nor height, nor depth, nor anything else in all creation, will be able to separate us from the love of God in Christ Jesus our Lord. (8:31-35, 37-39)[158]

Nowhere that Paul speaks of justification is this situation of a court scene so vividly presented as it is here. There's someone who wants to accuse or judge, but someone else who declares one innocent or intervenes as an intercessor.[159] But right away things are said that far outstep what is handled or decided by a court of law. Who can separate us from the love of God? It's a question that is no longer concerned with accusations or declarations of innocence but about proximity and fellowship with everything that might separate or distance oneself from God.

This is also shown by the way the salvific meaning of Jesus' death is described. The fact that God gives up his own son points to the event of substitutionary sacrifice of life.[160] But there are no further indications of whether this is a subtitutionary assumption of punishment or an expiatory sacrifice. The heart of this section that is subsequently developed further in vv. 35-39 is the deep conviction that in Jesus' death God's love has drawn near to us right to the depths of our existence and unequivocally guarantees his fellowship.[161] To this, Paul links the certainty that through Jesus' death, resurrection, and ascension, the power of God's love, which overcomes all division and alienation from God, is made effective and valid.

No other text in Paul makes it as clear as this one that for him the question of whether justification means declaring someone righteous or making him righteous offers a false option. It is right here, where v. 33 first presents the legal significance of "it is God who justifies," that we see that with justification it's not a matter of ascribing or recognizing or proposing righteousness to be a trait of the individual person but rather of establishing a relationship to God in which unconditional acceptance and creative renewal are combined.

"God is for us," is the most concise summary of the salvific meaning of the death and resurrection of Jesus and of the event of justification.[162] God's Yes to us reaches to the highest heights and the deepest depths of our existence because through Jesus God has entered into everything that humans experience and suffer with this Yes. It is because of this that nothing can separate us any longer from God and the life that he has given us.

The Existential Dimension

What is it that sustains us when everything about our life is up for grabs? As Rom 8 shows, that is the question to which Paul is responding with the announcement of God's justifying action in Christ. Through Jesus Christ, God allies himself to humanity, in the face of any and all internal and external accusations and in the face of all the powers that desire to rob them of their lives.

This encounter with God's righteousness and love has consequences. People who allow their lives to be grasped and shaped by this cannot understand or see themselves and their lives as they did heretofore. The first consequence is a negative one: Through the justifying action of God in Jesus Christ any form of self-praise and hence also of self-justification is excluded. Following on from what he laid out in Rom 3:21-25, Paul continues, "Then what becomes of boasting? It is excluded. By what law? By that of works? No, but by the law of faith" (v. 27). Here, Paul once again picks up the analysis of the problem first set forth in 2:17-20. It is misguided, he says, to rely on one's being a part of the Jewish people and on having the law. It is misguided first of all because the law demands that it be fulfilled and not simply be used as a mark of identity and stamp of quality; and second, because in Christ God has shown us the way into communion with him. The question "Who belongs to God?" (or "Whose God is God?" See 3:29!) is therefore important in the context, but the basic existential questions of "On what do I depend in my life? What gives my life its quintessential worth?" are inextricably part of that same principal question.[163]

People can respond to this question by referring not only to their inherited status or their ethnic identity but also by referring to what they have achieved and attained for themselves. Not only contemporary experience of life but also a glance at Paul's personal witness of Phil 3:4b-9 demonstrates this. Paul's critique is directed at two goals: the self-certain trust in the privilege of being among the chosen people, and pride in what one has done, which one's sense of personal righteousness manifests. Only like this can the juxtaposition of works and faith be understood and only like this can the core of the Pauline doctrine of justification in Rom 3:28 be grasped: "For we hold that a person is justified by faith [alone] apart from works prescribed by the law."[164]

Faith is what is for Paul the distinguishing mark of the new existence before God that corresponds to God's justifying action. It does not matter whether Paul's theological opponents have more readily recognized in the "works of the law" external signs of the people of God or the possibility of achieving salvation through one's own works. For Paul, faith is what describes Christian identity, and it is an identity that thrives not by the erection of new boundary markers but completely from what God gives them in Jesus Christ.

This Paul describes in Rom 4 using the illustration of Abraham. Here, Abraham is, on the one hand, a salvation historical figure of unrepeatable significance. He is the father of all who believe, whether they are Jew or Gentile. But on the other hand, he is an example of faith by whose example the meaning of faith is clarified.

For after all, Abraham also would have had reason to boast if he had been justified on the basis of works (v. 2).[165] Here too, Paul refuses to engage in a simple leveling of the human situation—as long as it is a case of looking at things from the human perspective. In the presence of God what counts is what Gen 15:6 says: "And he believed the LORD; and the LORD reckoned it to him as righteousness." This sentence, which means so much to him, Paul analyzes in great detail. If "reckoning" were a matter of the relationship of work and achievement between God and Abraham, then Abraham would be compensated the appropriate rate for his proper behavior. But because it is faith that is being assessed, clearly it's a matter of a relationship that is determined by grace. And so the following proposition holds true: "To one who without works trusts him who justifies the ungodly, such faith is reckoned as righteousness" (v. 5).

Almost every word in this sentence is important:

1. The one who believes in God and entrusts his life to him is set in opposition to the one who works for pay. The profane meaning of *tōergazomenō*, "one who works" (v. 4), is transformed into the theological meaning of v. 5, "to the one who does works," as Luther translated it, i.e., "the one who relies on works." The classical Reformation understanding of works righteousness as a contrast to righteousness through faith has its clearest exegetical foothold right here.[166]

2. God as the object of Abraham's trusting faith is described by what he does: Abraham believed in the one who justifies the ungodly. Such characteristics of God seen through his creative and saving actions are not seldom found in Paul and early Christian literature.[167] In Rom 4 we find an example where God is named as the object of faith: Abraham believed in "the God...who gives life to the dead and calls into existence the things that do not exist" (v. 17) and this affirmation of Abraham's is true also of those "who believe in him who raised Jesus our Lord from the dead" (v. 24). Faith lives by God's creative being and actions. It is trust in the One who creates out of nothing and awakens life from death, it is trust in the One who welcomes precisely the ungodly into fellowship with himself.

3. The logic of the proof really should have demanded the conclusion that Abraham believed in the One who justifies the believer. It is not only for stylistic reasons that Paul avoids this formulation. Faith does not put itself into the equation but rather ascribes everything to God. Otherwise the theological declara-

tion would secretly become a purely anthropological one! The logic of the matter pushes Paul to the expression, "The one who justifies the ungodly." However, with this expression he marks a sharp break with tradition. The Greek word *asebes*, which Luther translates as "ungodly," in the Greek Old Testament is the equivalent of the Hebrew rš' (wicked). On the one hand the kind of person who is meant by this is the one who has to be declared guilty in a court of law because he has broken the peace of the law. It is part of the constants of the Old Testament tradition to warn insistently about "declaring the wicked to be righteous."[168] At the same time, especially in the Psalms, the "wicked" are the opponents of the righteous and therefore the enemies of God; they are those who deny that it is worth following God's will. So, to speak explicitly about the justification of the ungodly means formulating justification by faith in sharp contrast to the tradition of it as a paradox that brings healing, an act comparable only to creation ex nihilo and the resurrection of the dead.

The fact that Abraham is placed on the side of the ungodly sharpens this paradox almost to the point of blasphemy. For after all, Abraham is seen in the whole Jewish tradition, reaching right into the New Testament, as an example of faith and of someone who made something of himself, which is why his "faith" (= loyalty), which God reckons to him as righteousness, is so highly regarded.[169] Paul risks this break with tradition in order to make apparent the totally unconditional nature of justification by faith. The fact that faith is "reckoned to" a person does not mean that an achievement is entered into the merit account of a person but rather the recognition of a person who has nothing to offer and does only one thing, namely holds firm to God's promise.[170]

Paul summarizes his concern in a brief formulation: "For this reason it depends on faith, in order that the promise may rest on grace" (v. 16). In the first instance he understands this formula in terms of salvation history, because he sees embodied in the figure of Abraham God's promise for all peoples. The promise applies to the Jewish people, who consider themselves the progeny of Abraham and bear circumcision "as the seal of righteousness that comes from faith." But it applies also to the Gentiles to whom the blessing of Abraham applies and who are justified on the basis of their faith as was Abraham before he allowed himself to be circumcised.

But the promise that "it depends on faith, in order that the promise may rest on grace" is also true at a personal level for everyone who allows himself or herself to be infected by Abraham's faith. In Rom 4:17-22 Paul very persuasively depicts Abraham's faith as the reason why he became the father of many peoples: against all appearances he held fast to God's promise. It is because of this that he becomes an example to all who believe and to all who hold fast to the One who raised Jesus from the dead.

It is here that the dialectic of the Pauline understanding of faith becomes clear. Faith is always "faith in"; faith in the fact that God has raised Jesus from the dead (Rom 10:9) and thus "faith in Jesus Christ." Faith is acceptance of what God has done in Jesus Christ. The origin of faith is not the strength of my faith but the actions of God to which I hold myself in faith.

Yet at the same time faith describes the shape of the new way of being that is appropriate to the justifying action of God. So faith therefore stands in sharp contrast to the attempt to secure life by "works of the law" but also in contrast to the fruitless attempt to empower oneself in one's relationship to God through one's own wisdom (1 Cor 1:21) and to the desire to overcome the distance between oneself and God through enthusiastic visions (2 Cor 5:7). For Paul, faith is not simply an alternative rite of initiation to being accepted into the salvation community of the people of God. It determines a Christian's entire existence before God. Faith is both the step a person takes when letting himself be pulled over by God's hand to the safe ground of godly affirmation of one's life from a life that was far from God and dedicated to death, and the path that leads through temptation and resistance toward the goal of final communion with God.

Paul had already summarized his basic convictions very poignantly in Gal 5:5ff.: "For through the Spirit, by faith, we eagerly wait for the hope of righteousness. For in Christ Jesus neither circumcision nor uncircumcision counts for anything; the only thing that counts is faith working through love."

"What counts?" was the question that concerned the Galatian Christians with respect to their lives and with respect to their being Christians. Regardless of how Paul's opponents may have defined what counts—whether they referred to specific identifying marks that characterized their membership among the people of God or to the necessity of fulfilling the law—for Paul all that counts "in Christ" is faith alone, a faith that lives because of what God has done for everyone, a faith that shares this with others through love.

Besides this, according to Gal 5:5, what is also important to Paul with regards to "what counts" is another important aspect of Christian life. Christians await their future righteousness, their end-time salvation "through the Spirit" and "by faith." Faith and Spirit are two complementary dimensions that describe the fellowship with God enabled by the gospel from different perspectives.

- Faith comes by "proclamation" that passes on the word of Christ.[171] Christians receive the Spirit through the "message of faith," i.e., through the proclamation of the gospel, which preaches faith and calls it into being.[172]
- Faith is a person's response to the witness of the gospel; it is the opening up of one's life to what God has done in Jesus Christ. The Spirit is the presence of God in the life of the faithful, and it is this presence that fills a person with what God has done in Christ (Rom 5:5; 8:10).
- Faith is described as faith "in him who raised Jesus our Lord from the dead" (Rom 4:24). The Spirit who lives in the believer is the Spirit "of him who raised Jesus from the dead" (Rom 8:11). God's creative and renewing Spirit infuses divine life energy into the lives of Christians. The comforting words of righteousness are at one and the same time comforting words of life; being filled with God's spirit is a transfer of life into human existence that is nonetheless still marked by death.[173]

Just as faith takes into one's own life that which has happened in Christ, so the Spirit takes what God has done in Christ into an action of God in us. God's strength, God's wisdom, God's righteousness, and God's abundance of life do not simply become our strength, wisdom, righteousness, and life. But Christians claim as a reality for themselves what God has done for them in Christ, and in the Spirit that reality becomes effectively present in their lives. Through the Spirit, the *extra nos* of salvation happens in us.[174]

This has consequences in three arenas of Christian life:

1. *The Spirit imbues us with the confidence of being children of God.* Our relationship to God is that of children who are of age who live in communion with God full of trust.[175] *The Spirit is the breath of a living faith.*

2. *The Spirit is the dynamic power of hope.* Because through the Spirit some of the signs of God's kingdom—such as righteousness, peace, and joy—are actualized, the Spirit urges us on to an active hope in the fulfillment of that kingdom (Rom 14:17). The Spirit is the pledge or preliminary offering for the whole that will bring in God's all-encompassing reign. In this way the Spirit presents both the "already" and the "not yet" of salvation. And for that reason it is the Spirit that enables hope amidst a world still characterized by decay and destruction.[176]

3. *The Spirit gives the freedom to love.* Because through the Spirit the love of God becomes the center of our lives, the way out of captivity to one's own ego is opened up, and it becomes possible to understand others with their gifts and needs. Love is not only the basis for the helping deed but also for life together in a new community. Not in connection with the doctrine of justification but in another distinctive discussion, in 1 Cor 13 it is love that Paul presents "as the basis of all Spirit-inspired deeds." Because the Spirit makes present the love of Christ, 1 Cor 13 can also "not be understood as anything but a witness to the love of God in Christ, which wants to continue its effectiveness in and through believers.[...] Through the Spirit, the love of God revealed on the cross becomes the power that characterizes Christian life."[177] The new way of being that God gives believers becomes fruitful in this love for others and hence also for one's own life.

Faith, hope, and love, these are the aspects of the Christian way of life that take up in personal life what God promises in the Word of the gospel and gives us through his Spirit.[178] They are the elements that matter "in Christ" and make life valuable and fruitful.

"In Christ" is the most comprehensive basis for new life as Christians. The phrase describes what shapes their lives. What from the perspective of human understanding is described as a life of faith, from the perspective of God's salvation reality is life in Christ.[179] What God has done in the death and resurrection of Christ becomes the arena for the life of every congregation and every individual Christian. In Christ they are a "new creation"; what God has created anew in faith, hope, and love that can then also be an expression of a new kind of "boasting," a new self-confidence that is based upon what God has done and what God has given.

In Rom 5:1-5, Paul describes what this means for the everyday life of Christians. Anyone who is justified leaves in peace before God, at "peace with God" (Rom 5:1).[180] Because those who have been justified are secure in a state of grace, it is not only the hope of a future glory that is a reason for "boasting" but so is suffering, i.e., any kind of resistance in the world, because it leads to endurance and new hope. Being empowered and being disempowered, strength and weakness are not contradictions if they are understood by one trusting fully in God and in his life.[181] It is God who gives life a reason, a value.

The Ethical Implications

Paul himself had to struggle with the question of whether ethical behavior should be based on his doctrine of justification. In some of his conversation partners the conviction that only the law could induce and sustain people to do God's will was too deeply rooted. Some felt that the power of grace was too overwhelmingly praised, that there could still be room besides grace for humans' personal responsibility (cf. Rom 6:1). And even Paul found himself driven to warn the Galatian Christians not to make the freedom to which they were called through Christ into a starting point for approving the desires of the flesh (Gal 5:13).[182]

We have previously touched several times on the first of the lines of argument with which Paul responds to these questions. God's spirit fills the hearts of the believers with the love of God that enables them to love God and their neighbors. The will of God, as witnessed to by the law, is fulfilled by the twofold love commandment (Gal 5:13-15; cf. Rom 13:8-10). Believers still experience the battle between "Spirit and flesh" (Gal 5:16ff.) in their lives. But this battle has essentially been decided, and so anyone who allows himself or herself to be led by the power of the Spirit can avoid the "works of the flesh" and will yield the "fruit of the Spirit."[183] The law will not raise any objections to people who act this way (Gal 5:18-23). Believers are thus not only in principle but also de facto exempt from such a judgment according to the law. And yet this phrase also suggests that even for Christians the law still has a deterrent function, namely when they are at risk of falling out of the sphere of Christ's rule and of his spirit.

The second line of argumentation also already begins in the Letter to the Galatians and proceeds from the question of what circle of power Christians live in. The power of sin has no hold any longer over anyone who has died with Christ. Paul expresses it this way here: "Those who belong to Christ Jesus have crucified the flesh with its passions and desires" (Gal 5:24). Whatever agonizing worry about themselves or whatever insatiable greed to grab as much life as possible for themselves has ruled them up until this point has all died with Christ.

In Rom 6:1-11 Paul offers far more expansive reasons for these thoughts in order to avoid the false conclusion that as a result of Paul's teaching on grace one might suggest, "Should we continue in sin in order that grace may abound?" What Paul sets in opposition to this is the switch in power that occurred at baptism: "We have been buried with him [Christ] by baptism into death, so that, just as Christ was raised from the dead by the glory of the Father, so we too might walk in newness of life" (v. 4). To this Paul adds an explanation that shows that death makes people free from any liability for their debts or from any claim of whatever power. If Christians have died with Christ in baptism, they should consider themselves as persons who are "dead to sin and alive to God in Christ Jesus" (v. 11).

This idea that baptism is the foundation for a new way of life is one we have encountered before in connection with statements on justification. In 1 Cor 6:9ff. the former way of life of the Corinthian Christians is characterized by a catalogue of vices. Anyone who lives in this manner is excluded from God's kingdom. As a counterpoint to this, Paul says, "But you were washed, you were sanctified, you were justified in the name of the Lord Jesus Christ and in the Spirit of our God" (v. 11). Baptism has changed the lives of the Christians; it has not only purified ("washed") their incriminating pasts but has also taken them up into fellowship with God ("sanctified") and placed them in the sphere of influence of his righteousness ("justified"). Baptism gives them not only "freedom from the *guilt* of sin, but also from the *power* of sin."[184] This enables a new way of being together in the congregation and a life of righteousness (cf. 6:1-8).

These two texts lead us to an important observation about the connection of baptism and justification in Paul. At each point where Paul expressly links baptism and justification with each other, he does so with reference to what has occurred to the person through baptism.[185] He presents the new way of being into which the person is placed and makes it clear how this also must lead to a new kind of behavior and new kinds of actions. This is the place where the indicative of salvation and the imperative of ethics are linked together.

But where he describes how a person becomes a Christian and enters into the saving fellowship with God, Paul speaks about faith. And he does it precisely when circumcision is demanded. Paul does not set one initiation rite against another. He speaks of faith because, for him, it's a matter of a totally new relationship with God, a relationship that encompasses the whole of existence, and when he speaks this way he reminds us of baptism in order to show what God has made happen to Christians personally.[186]

In this connection, the baptism event makes clear that for Christians, power relations have changed. There is no longer any reason to place one's body and members at the disposal of sin; "but present yourselves to God as those who have been brought from death to life, and present your members to God as instruments of righteousness" (Rom 6:13).

What is important about this sentence and the argument that builds on it in Rom 6:12-23 is the following: In place of law and sin, the old powers, which reigned over people and led them into wickedness, come the new powers of grace, righteousness, and God himself, and these lead a person to salvation. Humanity's true freedom is not some fictional total independence, but obedience to the power that leads to life.[187] Whereas the rule of sin leads to death, obedience to God leads to righteousness, sanctity, and eternal life. "Righteousness" in this context is therefore both the life power of God that takes us into service and leads us to right behavior, as well as the reward of fellowship with God, whose last and greatest gift of grace is eternal life, whereas the appropriate wages that sin deals out is death (6:23).[188] Just as in the Old Testament, righteousness is life lived out of God and in thanks to God, lived as a life concretely shaped according to God's will, and it is life that is ultimately given to one.

Although in this section Paul nowhere speaks of practical consequences, it is nonetheless important to him that he communicate that this is not only about having a good inner feeling but also about concrete actions. It is for this reason that he repeatedly speaks of "members" who should be put at the disposal of God and of righteousness. He's speaking of physical obedience to the utmost degree.

It is this that is also the aim of Rom 12:1ff., where Paul encourages the Roman Christians "to present your bodies as a living sacrifice, holy and acceptable to God" and to "be transformed by the renewing of your minds, so that you may discern what is the will of God" (v. 2). God's mercy allows persons the freedom to give themselves and enables persons to recognize the will of God out of a renewed sense of thinking and desiring.

What this all means Paul then explains quite practically in what follows. It's about a way of being in the congregation that is oriented toward common responsibility and the mutual interplay of gifts and tasks. It's about how one behaves in the everyday, a behavior that is oriented by the love command (12:9-21). It's about responsibly integrating oneself in civil society (13:1-7), and it's about a way of living together as Christians in which different forms of insight are accepted and are not misused for spiritual oppression (14:1–15:7). But that's touching on the subject of the next section.

The basic tenor of the way this ethic is grounded in the doctrine of justification is: Whoever has been freed from sin is free to serve righteousness. Freedom from sin is tantamount to freedom from the worry of having to justify one's own life and, hence at the same time, freedom from the greed of having to make one's own life rich and fulfilled, and freedom from the worry about coming up short and being robbed of opportunities and space by others. All such matters have "died with Christ" and have been overcome by his sacrificial giving of his life. The way is clear to live life as a gift that can be given to others and that can be received anew over and over again. The power of sin is fundamentally over and space for life in the spirit of righteousness has been created both for the community and for the individual.[189] Therefore, the phrase "righteous and a sinner at the same time" (*simul iustus et peccator*) does not match Paul's conception of how to describe the life of a Christian.[190]

The Social Consequences

This section ought really to be entitled "Ecclesiological Consequences." But I did not want to so much as suggest the possible misunderstanding that what is of concern here is primarily church structures or organization. Neither, of course, am I intending to speak of what nowadays is called "social work." What this section is really about is simply the "social form of the gospel," and how this is shaped in the teaching on justification by the Christ event itself and its exegesis.[191]

We have already noted that how teaching on the doctrine of justification was shaped in Galatians originally had far less to do with comforting tormented consciences and far more to do with the question of "Who belongs to the people of God?" But we have also already established that for Paul what was at issue was not just the entrance qualifications into the salvation community or the identification marks needed for membership but a new way of being before God. And this new way of being not only has a personal dimension but a social one too. The line of argumentation in Gal 3:25-28 moves seamlessly from the salvation meaning of justification by faith over into the description of the new reality in Christ. All who, in Christ through faith, have become children of God and therefore number among the descendants of Abraham have grown together into a unity in Christ in which all divisive religious and social differences are done away with: "There is no longer Jew or Greek, there is no longer slave or free, there is no longer male and female" (3:28). This unconditional acceptance through God that is received "by faith" finds its social realization in what happens "in Christ."

The conflict concerning the continuing integration of Gentile Christians into the Antioch church shows that for Paul this matter is not merely a set phrase. The very being of the congregation is its inclusivity; it is a social counterpoint to the universality of the gospel. But this inclusivity takes concrete form and is expressed just as much in eating with one another as it is in the conviction that all participate in God's salvation in equal measure.

Paul fights on very different fronts for the form and life of the congregation to correspond to the essence of the gospel. In *Corinth* there is the danger that the striving for esoteric wisdom and pride about pneumatic experiences will lead to discrimination against other Christians. To confront this, Paul holds up "the word of the cross" by which all wisdom in one's own strength, all derivative power, and all self-confident boasting both inside and outside the congregation are exposed for what they are. This then gives space for the calling of the least of these, for the uneducated and those who are nothing and count for nothing. Just as in Rom 4:17 Paul connects the *creatio ex nihilo* with the event of the justification of the ungodly, so in 1 Cor 1:28 he connects this with the election of those who are nothing and count for nothing in this world. The fact that Christ became righteousness for us not only has significance for salvation but also forms the basis for the inalienable inclusivity of the Christian congregation.

This is also what determines the conflict about the celebration of the Lord's Supper in Corinth. Because the meal entitles a person to participation "in the sacrificial death of Jesus Christ and in the salvation connected with this death," the deplorable circumstances at the communal meal of the Corinthians, where some starve and others feast, deeply contradict the essence of the Lord's Supper. "Inconsiderateness, indifference, and lovelessness toward the 'brothers, for whom Christ died' are therefore nothing less than the denial of the [*hyper hymōn* = for you]."[192]

In the final analysis, this same principle also guides Paul's argument about the meaning of the gifts of grace. The gifts are not evidence of an individual's having the Spirit, but are gifts for the building up of the congregation. The multiplicity and diversity of the gifts enable mutual help. The image of the congregation as an organism [or body] makes this clear. But the persuasive power of this comparison is only a part of the argument; it is when they were baptized into the one body and were given to drink of the one Spirit that Christians have experienced that God is the one who has brought the body together, regardless of whether they were "Jews or Greeks, slaves or free" (1 Cor 12:12ff.).[193]

Basing the church soteriologically in the Christ event has social consequences: Just as it erases the discrimination between slaves and masters, so also it prevents people from deriving ideas of people being differently qualified before God because of the diversity of the gifts. Such an understanding is far more an organic development of their basic unity in the body of Christ. Because Paul wants to highlight this diversity as God-given and God-willed, in 1 Cor 12:28 he inserts the service of the apostles next to that of the prophets and teachers in the list of charisms. Yet this list is by no means intended to serve as an "ordering for charismatic churches" or even a democratic basic structure for congregations, although "democratic" elements are not to be denied in this design.[194] But what must become clear is that no matter what task God has entrusted to an individual, everyone is dependent on God's actions, and because God does not do everything through one person and, thanks to the participation of everyone, the whole body is effective, therefore all are dependent on one another. Therefore it is true that "Paul's teaching on charisms is nothing but the projection of the doctrine of justification into ecclesiology."[195]

For this reason it makes sense that in Rom 12:3-8, where Paul develops the social consequences of the doctrine of justification, he once again takes up the image of the body of Christ and of the organic working together of the gifts of the spirit. Here he no longer speaks of the broad spectrum of activities and gifts that he included in 1 Cor 12. Paul names those gifts that particularly serve the community. What Paul describes have not yet become "congregational offices," but nevertheless they are relatively firmly set functions that are important for the life of the congregation. The possibility of their being practiced with faithfulness and modesty depends on those to whom they have been assigned recognizing in "the grace given to us" the concrete forms of the grace in which all together participate equally.

This is also how Paul understands his *apostolic authority*, which, on the one hand, he differentiates from the charisms and yet also repeatedly includes in their number (Rom 12:3). This authority quite fundamentally is in service to the gospel. This becomes particularly clear in the confrontation with his opponents in Galatia; it is their connection with the gospel that leads to a thoroughly dialectic relationship to authority in the church. For it is noteworthy that Paul, on the one hand, submits to adjudication the matter of his apostolic authority to the point of declaring a hypothetical anathema on anyone who proclaims a different gospel yet, on the other hand, rigorously and provocatively refuses any formal safeguarding of the truth of the gospel—whether in the form of an angel or of the apostle himself. For the identity and truth of the gospel is not guaranteed by either the person or the office of the one proclaiming it, but alone by its content (Gal 1:6-9).

This same dialectic pervades the discussion in 2 Corinthians on the apostolic office, where the concern is the question of the authority of this position and its derivation. Paul impressively connects basic tenets of the message of justification not only with comments on his personal existence before God but also more pointedly with the form of his task.

The point of departure for the whole letter is the question, "Who is competent and empowered as an apostle to proclaim the gospel, to carry forth the message that decides about life and death?" (2:16). The basic response Paul gives to this is, this competence comes not from ourselves but from God (3:5). It is for this reason that an apostle cannot commend and praise himself.[196] Paradoxically, "an apostle's legitimacy" is based in his weakness.[197] The reason for this is how his "office" or rather "service" [*diakonia*] is linked to his message.

Paul is in service of the "new covenant" and thus in service to the Spirit and to righteousness—in contrast to being in service to the death and judgment linked with the law of Moses (3:4-18). It is for this reason that the gospel is described as being the content of a ministry that is far more determinative of one's being and far more empowering. And so the differentiation between law and gospel becomes the criterion for apostolic authority.[198] So the message of justification also has direct consequences for ecclesiological questions; in this connection also it is a "message of freedom" (3:17), an expression of life-giving proclamation and missionary authority.[199]

What all this means, Paul explains in 5:11-21. He closely links particular elements of his service with fundamental sayings about the salvation event and Christian life. That apostolic ministry is not self-satisfied exhibitionism of enthusiastic circumstances but rather a way of living for the sake of the community, is for Paul based in the *proexistence* of Christ and in what transpires from that for every Christian. The love of Christ "is the controlling principle, the decisive measure and driving force of apostolic activity all in one."[200] The new way of being that is given to everyone who belongs to Christ also determines the nature of apostolic ministry.[201]

As one who has been reconciled with God, Paul is entrusted with the task of reconciliation. This means that he carries forth the message of reconciliation that God has set up in Jesus Christ's deed of reconciliation as "an ambassador for Christ" through whom God then carries into the world his call to reconciliation. Real reconciliation is not dictated but granted to the enemy. Not that there is still something to negotiate about this, or that conditions still had to be negotiated, but that God's peace for a person can only become a reality of life when that person puts his or her hand into the hand of God that has been stretched forth as an offer of reconciliation. This reconciling hand of God encounters people through the apostolic proclamation. In this context Paul even dares to speak of a pleading for Christ's sake in order to underscore the urgency and sincerity of God's offer of peace.[202]

The apostolic task is therefore an integral component of God's reconciling action; it is part of God's movement toward humanity. But even though here they are closely connected, nonetheless God's actions remain distinct from the service of the apostle. The "word of reconciliation" and the "ministry of reconciliation" are not identical. The ministry is borne up, fulfilled, and authorized by the Word. The gospel defines what is apostolic and not the reverse.[203]

This differentiation between God's actions and apostolic ministry is emphasized by the catalogue of sufferings that Paul links with the presentation of his task. The leitmotif is 2 Cor 4:7: "We have this treasure in clay jars, so that it may be made clear that this extraordinary power belongs to God and does not come from us."

Paul isn't so much concerned with a completely clear-cut division: here the overwhelming power of God and there the human suffering of the apostle. For, after all, even in this suffering something of Jesus' suffering becomes visible, the proexistence of Christ continues to have an effect in the apostle's experience of suffering, and allows the life-giving power of his giving of himself in a world of death to become effective for people. Thus in his suffering itself and in his intervention for others the apostle proves himself to be a "servant of God" (2 Cor 6:3-10). Paul shows this again in 11:23–12:10: here he describes an inner process at the conclusion of which is the affirmation of Christ that "my grace is sufficient for you, for power is made perfect in weakness" (12:9). But for Paul this provides the basis for a final authority that he hopes the Corinthians will also recognize (13:1-4).[204]

Who is empowered to apostolic ministry? Paul's response to this question in 2 Corinthians is hard to generalize because it is so strongly determined by the particular relationship between the apostle and the churches founded. But it is not difficult to recognize an underlying stance: The authority of ministry fundamentally derives from the authority of the gospel itself; while there are formal avenues for such ministry, there are no formal guarantees, whether institutional or with reference to particular spiritual experiences or gifts. The ministry of proclamation and the work of "building up congregations" is at one and the same time the legitimate form of humans' "participation" in God's salvific actions (cf. 1 Cor 3:9; 2 Cor 6:1).

One last observation in this connection: Through his message of justification, Paul is obviously driven to advocate for groups that are in danger of being discriminated against and pushed to the edges in churches. Sometimes this coincides with his basic theological orientation, for example when he advocates for Gentile Christians in Antioch from whose fellowship Peter and the other Jewish Christians draw back. In the conflict in Rom 14:1–15:12 about the so-called weak and the strong, it is surprising that Paul advocates for a minority whose conscience is endangered, the views of whom appear to be contrary to the very consequences that Paul himself draws from the teaching on justification. The theological truth that is not concerned about its effect on others cannot itself become a reason for egotistical self-satisfaction (Rom 15:1). The fact that

Christ has accepted everyone unconditionally (15:7) cannot be of no consequence to life together in community. The truth of the gospel is also concrete.

Romans 11:17-24 shows just to what extent the truth of the doctrine of justification evidences itself in its implementation and therefore should not be reduced simply into an external sign of identity. In this text, Paul warns the Gentile Christians against boasting about their status as opposed to Israel, which has not yet come to faith. After all that Paul himself has said theologically in Rom 9 and 10, this is a surprising text whose importance cannot be overestimated. Even faith should never become either a possession or something done through one's own effort on account of which one boasts about oneself in contrast to others. (This would be a kind of "tax-collector self-righteousness" in contrast to the parables in Luke 18:9-14.) Faith lives solely out of God's goodness; if it does not, it becomes lack of faith and is subject to judgment. What is exciting about this thought is that here the theology of grace underlying the doctrine of justification is also applied critically to the stance of Gentile Christians. This is the most impressive proof that, for Paul, the scope of the doctrine of justification is not limited to the discussion about the lawless Gentile mission but rather is the criterion for all interpretation of the gospel. But it is based not on what is appropriate human behavior but on the sovereignty of God in his salvific actions.[205]

The Eschatological Perspective

Justification is an eschatological event. It is true that in Paul we only find occasional references to the fact that the actual occasion of the decision regarding justification will be the Last Judgment. Because God in Christ has already now revealed his salvific righteousness and has judged sin in Christ's death, in the proclamation of the gospel, justification occurs wherever a person accepts the gracious judgment of God.

And yet this way the eschatological perspective remains intact. Occasionally justification itself is still described as being in the future.[206] Paul often differentiates between present justification and future salvation.[207] But it is precisely in the most fundamental sayings of Rom 1:16ff. that the salvation that God gives appears as present in the gospel. And in an especially eschatological section like Rom 8:18-30, in which unredeemed earthly existence is portrayed very vividly, Paul at the end presents as already realized the entire path of salvation right up to glorification (v. 30).

Apparently Paul is not following some fixed plan but rather can at one and the same time emphasize the presence of justification as well as the fact that Christians are still on the way to their goal in God. Everything has been given, but no one has finished the course yet. For justification means being accepted into fellowship with God; it is the current reality in which we live, yet it is neither a right nor a property that has any validity independent of this relationship. And all are included in God's wrestling for the whole world, which one day will as an entirety be placed under the reign of his mercy (cf. 1 Cor 15:28; Rom 11:33-36). It is not just about the salvation of individuals but about the redemption of the whole of creation—as is emphatically presented in Rom 8:18-30. The entire creation is to be freed from the bondage to decay for the "freedom of the glory of the children of God" (v. 21). What already in the Old Testament was mentioned as the goal of the revelation of God's righteousness finds its fulfillment in the perfection of the revelation of Christ.

On the other hand, with Paul the judgment of the world, particularly the judging of the unbelievers, has at best a secondary place. Whenever the judgment is spoken of, it is in the context of Christians and their actions (Rom 14:10; 1 Cor 3:13–15; 2 Cor 5:10). This has often been perceived as being in contradiction to the doctrine of justification. But Paul in fact does not situate this teaching in connection with the event of justification. For him, there is no "double" justification, one by faith at the beginning of a person's Christian walk, the other based on a person's works at the end-time judgment. The connection between justification by faith and judgment according to works for the Christian depends precisely on this differentiation between works and person in justification. As a responsible being, a person does take seriously the judgment about works and the praise or shame about what one has done with one's life, and yet at the same time a person does not irrevocably tie his or her worth and fate to his or her works. "The Pauline presentation of the divine, or Christological, end-times judgment is the obvious conclusion of his theology of justification to the extent that the judgment of God is understood as the final manifestation of his righteousness: The eschatological saving of a person is independent of their character and deeds (1 Cor 3:14-15; 5:5)."[208] And yet the fate of the individual is only a part of the eschatological events in which God will reveal his righteousness in the gospel through the proof of his mercy on everyone (Rom 11:33-36).

Paul also outlines this perspective in Rom 5:12-21. The contrast between Adam and Christ demonstrates the universal meaning of the salvation event. God's actions intend a new humanity. What happened in Christ is God's act of justification that is valid for all persons. Just as all became sinners through Adam's disobedience, so all are intended to become righteous through Christ's obedience.[209] Even though the promise of participation in God's glory is promised to those who receive the gift of righteousness (v. 17),[210] nonetheless God's aim is for it to be universal. God's justifying action is not a restricted offer of amnesty. It finds fulfillment in that "grace might also exercise dominion through justification leading to eternal life through Jesus Christ our Lord" (v. 21).

What Paul presents in this section is true for his entire theology: the Christ event is the justification event and the justification event is the Christ event. They both describe the same thing, namely the fulfillment of the one, unbreakable, saving, and life-giving Yes of God to those who hold fast to him, until the destructive No of sin and death is overcome.

5. PAUL'S LEGACY

With the Pauline correspondence that has been preserved for us, the doctrine of justification has seen strange advancement. The Letter to the Ephesians as well as the Pastoral Letters take up the motifs of the doctrine of justification and apparently attempt to reformulate it for their era.[211] How well they succeeded in doing so is debated by scholars.[212]

Justification among Paul's Disciples

In Eph 2 the author shows through two parallel trains of thought how those addressed by the letter have come to participate in salvation. The text of 2:1-10 speaks of the personal, existential aspect of the event. Life before the encounter with Christ is characterized as an existence under the lordship of the spirit of disobedience and desires of the flesh and hence as life that has fallen prey to death. This is contrasted with the following: "But God, who is rich in mercy, out of the great love with which he loved us even when we were dead through our trespasses, made us alive together with Christ" (2:4ff.). And before the writer concludes this sentence ("and raised us up with him and seated us with him in the heavenly places"), he interrupts himself, as it were, and qualifies himself with a kind of reminder: "by grace you have been saved." Apparently this whole phrase alludes to an idea from the Letter to the Romans. The image of dying and being raised with Christ comes—with a typical change—from Rom 6:1-11.[213] The interruption, "by grace you have been saved," reminds one of Rom 3:24; and yet instead of saying "being justified" the text says they "are now saved," which Rom 5:9 only depicts as being the end-time fulfillment of justification. For the Ephesians, salvation in Christ is already present. It is apparently precisely for this reason that it is so important to emphasize that what validly happened in Christ for us once and for all time remains a gift of grace from God. This is spoken of in Eph 2:8-10 with obvious connection to the terminology of the doctrine of justification: "For by grace you have been saved through faith, and this is not your own doing; it is the gift of God—not the result of works, so that no one may boast."

Three motifs of the Pauline doctrine of justification are picked up here: (1) It is "through faith" that Christians participate in salvation; as in Rom 4:16, the *sola fide* anchors the *sola gratia*.[214] (2) Salvation does not occur "because of you," i.e., not on account of personal qualifications and one's own efforts, i.e.,—to pick up on Paul's wording—"not by works." Here, the sharper antithesis of "not by works of the law" is missing; apparently the argument about the conditions for the Gentile Christians to be accepted into the salvation community of the people of God has long since been resolved. The question of "works," of the necessary "prerequisites," is thus generalized (and therefore it is not by accident that the question concerning "good works" surfaces in v. 10). (3) And this leads to the rationale that repeatedly shows itself to be the leading indicator for the basic affirmations of the doctrine of justification, even where other terminology is used—namely, why boasting before God is not allowed.[215]

But then Ephesians takes an additional sly step. Basing himself on the Pauline declaration that justification is not only a matter of being vindicated of a past determined by sin but also signifies a new creation for a future with God (cf. 2 Cor 5:17; Gal 6:15), Paul comes to the far-reaching conviction: "For we are what [God] has made us, created in Christ Jesus for good works, which God prepared beforehand to be our way of life." A responsible life as a Christian is the fulfillment of what God has already done for him or her. This is a quite original attempt to solve the problem of ethics on the basis of the doctrine of justification. Even those good works that need to be done in the life of a Christian are already, in fact, God's work. "God's salvific activity reaches into the actions of the redeemed."[216]

From a salvation historical-ecclesiological perspective, Eph 2:11-21 then describes the salvation event in a related parallel section. In Ephesians it is no longer the task to fight against Jewish Christian criticisms of the justification of the unconditional acceptance of Gentile Christians into the people of God. Instead, as in Rom 11, it seems to be far more necessary to make it clear to the Gentile Christians what a miracle of God's grace it is that they have been accepted into the covenant of God with his people. It is for this reason that the salvation event is in the first instance described as the acceptance of the Gentiles into the citizenship of Israel and into the covenants of promise "in the blood of Christ." It is through this key phrase that the cross takes center stage in the depiction of the salvation event. Through his death Christ has set aside the hostility between Jews and Gentiles, has reconciled them with each other, and has created "a new humanity" through his act of peace. Verse 17 strongly emphasizes that both Jew and Gentile are now equally dependent on God's action in Christ. Through his coming, Christ "proclaimed peace to you who were far off and peace to those who were near."[217] Perhaps this is the point at which the writer of Ephesians most profoundly understood the message of the justification of the ungodly and translated it into his ecclesiology.[218] The Letter to the Ephesians, too, contains no word of ecclesiological transmittal of salvation, though there is an ecclesiological dimension and expression.[219]

This is confirmed in Eph 3:6 through the Ephesian form of a summary of the Pauline gospel: "the Gentiles have become fellow heirs, members of the same body, and sharers in the promise in Christ Jesus through the gospel"; in other words it is the inclusivity and universality of the gospel of Jesus Christ that become predominant in the church.

The author of the Letter to the Ephesians did not only go to great trouble to keep a few Pauline expressions in the letter, he tried to interpret the Pauline theology of grace afresh for the theological demands of his time and in so doing apparently viewed the Pauline doctrine of justification as the decisive criterion. He did not perpetuate the old discussions about the "works of the law." Instead, in a new situation in which he was concerned to bring together the rootedness of the salvation event in the promise to Israel, he held fast to the absolute predominance of the gracious action of God in Jesus Christ.

The resulting presentation in the Pastoral Epistles is comparable to the Letter to the Ephesians and yet, nonetheless, is quite distinct from it. It is comparable because certain typical formulations of the teaching on jus-tification also occur with typical variations in the Pastoral Epistles (2 Tim 1:9; Titus 3:5-7). It is distinct from Ephesians because the Pastoral Epistles are not about new interpretations of the salvation event but about preserving the Pauline gospel and about the church proving itself against the threat of false teaching. The typical formulations of the teaching on justification are pressed into service for both these tasks.

Second Timothy 1:8-16 is about preserving the gospel. It is a passage that, to a certain extent, presents the message of the Pastoral Epistles *in nuce* and makes its testamentary nature particularly clear.

The reminder to Timothy to rekindle the gift of God that was given to him through the laying on of hands make two things clear: being com-missioned and being empowered to ministry is no longer the free gift of God's grace for every Christian, but is now founded on the institutional-ized action of ordination.[220]

Yet, the official power is not totally formalized by this. It has the effect of rekindling the gift of grace over and over again.[221] De facto this hap-pens through the following reminder of the task of proclaiming the gospel, a reminder that is clearly dependent and styled after Rom 1:16ff.

Regarding content, the gospel is now characterized by a newly formu-lated summary of the Pauline message of justification.[222] As in Eph 2:8, the term "justification" is replaced with being "saved"; the clearest dependence of this passage on the Pauline doctrine of justification is, as in Eph 2, the expression "not the result of works." Now it is no longer a matter of works of the law but rather of one's own deeds and efforts that cannot be the basis of one's relationships with God. This gospel is the content of the teaching with which Timothy was familiar. It is the "gift entrusted to him"[223] that he is to nurture. Here the reference to the doc-trine of justification does indeed seem to serve the function of being an "identity marker" for the Pauline tradition.

The various formulas in the Pastoral Epistles, like soteriology itself, are in service of the *paraenesis* and its origins. This is shown in Titus 2:1-15 as well as 3:1-7 where the command to obey those in authority is justified by the fact that the appearance "of God's goodness and love toward humanity in the form of our savior" that has saved Christians out of "all iniquity" of the world and "through their behavior toward the surrounding non-Christian world is meant to reflect the goodness and friendliness of God toward humanity."[224]

God's goodness and mercy are then described in 3:5-7 using motifs from the Pauline teaching on justification and the early Christian baptismal tradition.[225] The traditional expression, "not because of any works of righteousness," again underscores salvation's "exclusive character of grace" that happened "without any human effort";[226] the warning in verse 8 does, in fact, very expressly not preclude that Christian faith should manifest itself in good works.[227]

This theological basis finds agreement with Paul: "Salvation is given to the unholy one through the grace that has been revealed in Jesus Christ. This affirmation of salvation is the basis of ethical demands."[228] Even the decisive reason for Paul's linking the indicative and the imperative, the renewal and being gifted by the Holy Spirit, is named here. And yet the linking of the two seems stronger here than by Paul himself (cf., for example, Gal 5:13-26) and hence immediately points to a problem with which the proclamation of the message of justification repeatedly has to engage. The "fruits of the Spirit" and the necessary "good work" often do not so automatically grow out of the salvation experience that such probing questions about them would arise.

Surveying the further history of the Pauline tradition, we notice that in a writing like the Acts of the Apostles, which seems to be indebted to the work and legacy of Paul like no other, the doctrine of justification plays virtually no part. In the first of Paul's speeches, it appears as almost only a reference or citation meant to mark his missionary proclamation (13:38ff.) and plays as small a part in the presentation of his theology as it does in the discussion about a Gentile mission free of the law.[229] Luke comes closest to Paul's intention when he describes the effects of the gospel. For although the individual episodes of Acts seem to depict the acceptance of the Godfearing rather than the justification of the ungodly,[230] its presentation of the history of the church as a history of mission does witness rather impressively to the power of the gospel to cross boundaries. It is, above all, the working of the Holy Spirit that keeps helping the church to advance into new regions that it does not itself at first recognize as possibilities.

The Obligating Legacy

The impression conveyed by this earliest history of interpretation of the Pauline doctrine of justification is two-sided. On the one hand, what becomes clear is that the message of justification really does present a kind of "identity marker" of Pauline theology, something one could not and would not want to overlook. Yet at the same time what becomes clear as well is that the teaching on justification is not simply something one can pass along like any other piece of information. The critical function it has established for itself in the whole of Pauline theology opposes this. A simple assumption of its most important elements would carry with it the danger of it being used simply as a kind of decorative element, an add-on, or give it a kind of alibi function as the seal of approval for establishing what is correct Pauline theology.[231] Conversely, any attempt to transpose the theological content into a new situation and reformulate it for that next context is subject to the accusation that important points of doctrine may be given up.[232] Do we not, in fact, already see within the New Testament that the effectiveness of the doctrine of justification thrives on its context and that, though it can spring up to new life (for example, in the Reformation discussion of the late scholastic theology of grace), it is by no means always assumed nor can it or should it be reintroduced over and over?

Paul himself was convinced that the doctrine of justification was more than a polemical accentuation of the message of Christ for a particular situation of political importance to salvation history or Christian mission. If the Letter to the Romans constitutes anything like a legacy—and the Letter to the Ephesians and the Pastoral Epistles obviously saw it this way—then it is clear that for Romans the doctrine of justification was fundamentally the most basic and unequivocal interpretation of the Christ event. Said even more clearly: *Justification is the self-interpretation of God who acted for the salvation of the entire world on the cross of Jesus Christ.*

Such an interpretation determines the missionary perspective for the proclamation of the gospel and for the life of the church. It leads people into an encounter with God in which God reveals himself as being beyond people's imaginings and projections. It leads one to an encounter with oneself in which one's own lostness is put on hold because knowledge of that lostness is surrounded by the affirmation that one is accepted by God; it leads into an encounter in which people take off the masks of their egos and can find themselves in Christ. Such knowledge then forms the basis for a life of love and begins to form a community in which people formed by different influences and with different origins encounter one another as beloved children of God, and thus accept one another and are present for one another. This, in turn, opens up a vision of God's rule and righteousness and peace and encourages people now to live and act from out of this vision.

All of this is the content and consequence of the gospel's message of freedom and justification of the ungodly and the reconciliation of enemies in Jesus Christ. This is Paul's enduring legacy for the Christian church.

6. CONTRASTING MODELS FROM THE NEW TESTAMENT

The fact that the doctrine of justification is not uncontested as the center of the theology found in Paul's letters almost necessarily leads on to the question of how things stand in this regard in the rest of the New Testament. Understandably, it was often the Roman Catholics who pointed to the fact that even within the New Testament there are quite different responses to the question of how people experience salvation through Jesus Christ than simply that of the Pauline doctrine of justification. Conversely, Reformation scholars already saw in this question the attempt to muddy the clarity of the message of justification and domesticate its power. With reference to such discussions Luther came out with the bold saying that "therefore, if the adversaries press the Scripture against Christ, we urge Christ against the Scriptures."[233]

Yet Protestant exegesis and theology would not be well advised to toughen themselves against such critical barbs in this way. In an earlier phase of his ecumenical work, Hans Küng has pointed out that there must be an injunction of *tota scriptura* to correspond to that of *sola scriptura*.[234] And when the Vatican's original response to the common declaration on the doctrine of justification warned that "said deepening [of the study of the biblical foundations of the doctrine of justification] should be applied to the whole New Testament and not only to the Pauline writings," then doubtless this occurred because of a conviction that there would yet be other important arguments in favor of their own position to be found in the other writings of the New Testament with reference to some unresolved questions about which they were still in conflict, such as what part a person plays in his or her own salvation.

In the context of this particular book we can only suggest three tentative responses to these questions. Are there different soteriological models in the New Testament to that of Paul's doctrine of justification, models that we ought to pay attention to when addressing questions of whether the doctrine of justification must and can offer the decisive criteria for contemporary proclamation of salvation?

In considering this, the term "contrasting models" need not necessarily be limited to offering opposing options, but should, however, make clear that it is conceivable to consider routes for what God in Christ has done for the salvation of humanity other than what Paul has shown with his doctrine of justification. For the purposes of these tentative alternative responses I am choosing to focus, on the one hand, on James, because a discussion about the Pauline doctrine of justification can be assumed from the get-go with James, and, on the other hand, on Matthew and John, since both these gospel writers undoubtedly had their own particular influence on the theological development of Christian teaching.[235]

James

Things are quite clear in the Letter of James. What he's concerned about is a faith that manifests itself in deeds. This is shown not only in the discussion about the Pauline doctrine of faith in 2:14-26.[236] It even determines his criticism of behavior toward the poor and the rich in the congregation (2:1-13). After all, if, as all early Christendom does, one speaks of the preference for of the poor,[237] then the behavior of the congregation must correspond to that. However, if, on account of thoughtlessness the commandment regarding the love of neighbor is not fulfilled with regard to the poor, then one is falling short of the entire law.

When James speaks of the law—and especially of the Decalogue—he speaks quite exceptionally of the "law of liberty" (cf. also 1:25). This law sets the standards for mercy, particularly regarding the Final Judgment, but hence also regarding what we do now. For precisely this reason it frees us to live in a way that finds fulfillment in doing the will of God. This is how we are to teach, but this is also how we are to act (2:12).[238]

It is on the basis of this conviction that James takes to task the statement that it is faith alone that saves. He considers a faith without works as totally misguided. Because otherwise it would be possible that someone could pass by a neighbor in need completely unmoved, without this having any consequences for his or her relationship to God. This cannot be. A faith without works does not evidence signs of a life lived with God. A faith that does not prove itself by deeds is, seen by itself, dead.

For James this is shown by the verse in Gen 15:6 where God reckons Abraham's faith to him as righteousness. Together with the entire Jewish tradition of interpretation, James considers this verse to allude to Gen 22: Through his willingness to sacrifice his only son, Abraham proved his faithfulness and trust in God, and this was reckoned to him as righteousness. So his faith worked together with his deeds in a sign of practical obedience, and it is through these deeds that faith was first made complete.

And yet we can also see by way of this text that James assumes a completely different understanding of faith than Paul (and basically also than the Jewish tradition on which he depends). The faith of which he speaks is Israel's confession, "God is one," and particularly as an intellectual recognition of this truth that even the demons share—albeit without being able to participate in the saving power of faith as a result of it (2:19).

But this is not Paul's understanding of faith. Paul's response to James's question is found in Gal 5:6: "In Christ . . . the only thing that counts is faith working through love." This verse pulls the foundation of James's entire argument away from under it. Faith that ignores the needs of the neighbor does not need to be fulfilled through works; what it needs is far rather to be totally newly based in the love of Christ.

We do not know if there were proponents of Pauline theology around when James wrote his letter, people who lived and taught this idea of "through faith alone" in as distorted a way as James describes. Perhaps he was simply reacting with a simplistic caricature to a particular theology whose consequences seemed dangerous to him or whose basis he could not understand.

Three things are clear:

1. Paul's teaching on justification is not affected by James's argument.

2. James's concern is nonetheless justified. A faith from which no loving action springs forth is indeed questionable. So James's questioning becomes an important warning against a "solafideism" in which "through faith alone" withers to a dead formula that either does not have an effect in a person's life or leads a person astray into a trust in a "cheap grace."

3. The path that James suggests is not one Paul can advocate and one with which his theology could not agree. The cumulative understanding of faith and works, i.e., the way they work together for salvation, would throw humanity back on itself and

its own desires and actions, instead of grounding human lives and actions in God's salvific deed in Christ. Regarding this question, one therefore has to decide between Paul and James.

Matthew

The Gospel of Matthew does not offer a similarly univocal alternative model to Pauline theology. In terms of its effect, one might well imagine that the influence of the First Gospel primarily contributed in the early church and in the Middle Ages to these basic questions about the Pauline messages of justification being relegated to the peripheries of spiritual and theological efforts. The call to a more exceptional righteousness (Matt 5:20) and the invitation to perfection as the path to eternal life (19:21) primarily shaped the thoughts and actions of those who struggled for a credible basis for being a Christian.

What is noteworthy here is that the Gospel of Matthew is the only non-Pauline writing in which the key word "righteousness" attains a programmatic significance. Everywhere it occurs it is influenced by Matthew's redaction, and therefore has particularly important significance regarding the theological intentions of its author.[239]

This intention seems to be quite explicit. In Matt 5:20, Jesus warns the disciples, "Unless your righteousness exceeds that of the scribes and Pharisees, you will never enter the kingdom of heaven." Likewise Matt 6:1, where the NRSV tellingly translates the word as "piety" is apparently about the will of God that people are expected to fulfill, i.e., it is about appropriate behavior and uprightness before God. It is on the basis of this explicit foundation that a whole raft of exegetes interpret all other examples of the key word "righteousness" in Matthew.[240]

Corresponding to this is the importance of the Final Judgment in Matthew, a judgment that serves to "separate the evil from the righteous" (13:49; cf. 13:41-43; 25:31-46). According to 25:33-46 what determines this separation is one's behavior toward the suffering "least of these who are members of [Jesus'] family." However, those who are characterized as the "righteous" are not conscious that by their actions they are doing something toward their righteousness and their acceptance at the Final Judgment. This is meant to warn people to be careful and not jump to the conclusion that Matthew represents "righteousness through works."

So where does Matthew describe the path to salvation to be?

Undoubtedly it is the way of imitation, the way of discipleship. It is not only the total thrust of the gospel, in which, for example, the Sermon on the Mount as the first exposition of the gospel of the kingdom is tightly connected with the calling of the first disciples. It is particularly shown by the ending of the gospel, and the resurrected One's commission to his disciples: "Make disciples of all nations, baptizing them in the name of the Father and of the Son and of the Holy Spirit, and teaching them to obey everything that I have commanded you" (28:19). Baptism and being instructed in the teaching of Jesus, those are the decisive steps into discipleship and into the church. Baptism in the name of the triune God, i.e., becoming a part of God's saving revelation, comes before handing on the commandments.[241]

The main reason for Jesus' way and for his call to repentance and discipleship is the coming of the kingdom of God, which Matthew in his Jewish translation of the God-concept often calls "the kingdom of heaven." What the consequences of the nearness of God's kingdom are, what the promise of a salvific presence of God is, and what demands arise from this to turn completely to God as a result Matthew shows particularly through the Sermon on the Mount. In an exemplary way the gospel of the kingdom is presented in this sermon, and for Matthew this is essentially what constitutes Jesus' message.[242]

The Sermon on the Mount begins with Beatitudes that describe who will benefit from the blessings of the coming kingdom. Matthew takes up Jesus' Beatitudes that were transmitted through the tradition and expands upon them through clarifying additions and further Beatitudes from his own tradition.

Among these new interpretations, what is particularly exciting is how the first Beatitude is expanded: Matthew has the "poor in spirit" praised rather than the "poor." By doing this, the blessing given to the suffering and needy is internalized and spiritualized. This does not necessarily constitute a falsification of what Jesus said. For already in the Old Testament the promise of help for the poor included a spiritual dimension. Early Judaic piety toward the poor takes this up; the witness of the writings of Qumran shows that this piety resulted in similar formulations as Matthew includes.[243] Yet this begs the question of who is meant by "the poor in spirit." Are they the "lowly before God," meaning basically the truly pious,[244] or are those meant who truly stand before God with empty hands knowing that in every respect they are beggars? Is the kingdom of

God promised to those who have the correct attitude toward God or to those who survive only by God's good gifts?

The observation that Matthew has grouped the Beatitudes in two batches makes this decision easier. The first four Beatitudes concern those persons who are completely thrown on others' help, whereas the second group of Beatitudes praises those whose behavior is appropriate to the coming kingdom.[245] Thus the second Beatitude refers to those who mourn and the fourth to those who hunger and thirst for *righteousness*. The picture we get from this makes it unmistakably clear that what is being sought is not a striving for a way of being that is pleasing to God but a hungering and thirsting for what will really bring some fulfillment to what is lacking in life, namely the gift of the saving presence of God and his righteousness.[246] The second group of Beatitudes then makes clear that the gift of righteousness also shapes the lives of those who are open to the coming of the kingdom. It is this last of eight Matthean Beatitudes that, by its promise that "theirs is the kingdom of heaven," once again reminds us of the first Beatitude, which shows us the interconnection between God's gift and the role of duty it plays in the term "righteousness." For after all, righteousness, for which reason the disciples are being persecuted, encompasses both God's desire for salvation and justice, to whom they open their lives and for which they are engaged, and their own behavior, which they allow to be shaped by God's righteousness.

This interconnection between God's working and the openness with which people allow the activity of God space in their lives is also shown in 6:33, a first summary of the message of the Sermon on the Mount. "Strive first for the kingdom of God and his righteousness, and all these things will be given to you as well." Instead of daily anxiety concerning food and clothing, Jesus establishes the first and decisive goal as being to orient one's life totally to God's kingdom and his righteousness. Once again, we hear the Old Testament parallel with God's reign and the revelation of his righteousness. Once again, the objective here is the saving will of God who so touches the life of each individual that the anxiety about matters of their daily needs is taken from them. "To seek" the kingdom and God's righteousness, and to make it to the goal of one's own life, however, also means allowing them to become the life-determining power and norm for one's own life. It means "striving to allow God's righteousness to be effective in one's life. Said even more clearly: to strive for God to transfer his righteousness to oneself,"[247] thus making righteousness the predominant factor in one's life, one that will shape one's own behavior.

This is also the basis on which the other side of Matthew's proclamation of salvation is to be understood. God's salvific action is deeply obligating. It is for this reason that the disciples' righteousness has to far exceed that of the scribes and Pharisees if they truly want to enter into the kingdom of God. This is a teaching not lacking in danger if what is being spoken of here is "your" righteousness as if it could also mean one's own, and if a comparison is deliberately intended as Jesus so critically illuminates in Luke 18:9-14. Yet in light of the radicality with which this is developed in the following antitheses, any attempt to boast of one's "own" righteousness or to hint at the success or failure of others must be nipped in the bud. For in this text we are presented not with "additional requirements" for entry into the kingdom of God but what is described is the lifelong task of fulfilling God's will and by one's life showing others mercy and love. Undivided devotion is the sign of belonging to God. This is the sense of Matthew's call to perfection, whether it be found in Matt 5:48 with reference to the all-encompassing mercy of God or in 19:21 where the text is about liberating a person from the thralldom of his possessions.

This also seems to be the basis of the obviously deeply anti-enthusiastic saying of 7:21: "Not everyone who says to me, 'Lord, Lord,' will enter the kingdom of heaven, but only the one who does the will of my Father in heaven." Whoever does the will of God shows whose he is and what shapes and determines his life. This also clarifies the earlier comparison with a tree that one recognizes by its fruits. The question about "good works" is not the question about what one has managed to do by one's own strength but the question about the why and how of our lives. We also find such an imperative that is totally driven by the indicative of Jesus' promise in 5:13-16. "You are the salt of the earth. . . . You are the light of the world," is what the disciples are told as a background to the Beatitudes. But then there is the serious question of what will happen if the salt loses its saltiness (which is actually an impossible possibility!). The disciples' "good deeds" are no more than the inevitable working out and radiance of the "lightness" of their being disciples. The fact that the "good works" are seen does not put the disciples into the spotlight but rather God's work, which people will then praise and glorify.

Even at those places where Matthew calls blessed those who try to order their lives according to the will of God, for him this is "a full and pure bestowal of grace." "The Christian who makes an effort, who is supported by God…is precisely not the one who wishes to be righteous by his or her own works."[248]

This same point is shown very clearly by the section of Matthew's Gospel that one might variously consider to be the center of the gospel: Matt 11:25-30. The revelation to the simple corresponds to the Beatitude about the poor, the invitation to the children to enter the kingdom of God, as well as the election of the foolish and powerless about which Paul speaks in 1 Cor 1:26ff. It is likewise true of the invitation to all those who threaten to collapse under the burden of their lives. The "peace" promised to them and in which their lives are hidden and taken care of will not take the weight of their lives from them. Rather, it is an invitation to a task and an assignment that will not demand too much of them but instead will lead their lives into the responsibility for which they were created. The christological center of this text makes it clear that this passage is not about a "better way of life" that Jesus conveys but rather that his person and the revelation of God through him (v. 27!) stand in the center of the gospel. For Matthew too, the question, "Who is God?" and the response, "In Jesus God is with us" constitute the central message of the gospel (cf. 1:23; 28:20).

Such a scheme is hard to grasp and judge using Pauline interpretive categories. Undoubtedly Matthew would have had little understanding for a "justification by faith alone" or even a "justification of the ungodly."[249] But neither would the Matthean solution have been adequately portrayed by phrases such as "faith and works" or even "works alone." In Jesus, Matthew sees the way of Jesus and the teaching of God's acts of salvation that touch persons who neither have nor need any prerequisites for it but which nonetheless put them fully at God's service and reshape their lives. So it's not a matter of humans "working with" God to add something toward their own salvation; rather, it's a matter of a person being taken into the activity of God for the salvation of all, with all that that person is and can do.

This then leads to a paradoxical thesis regarding the relationship between the message of justification and the gospel "according to Matthew": Anyone who tries to interpret Matthew's gospel solely through the lens of the doctrine of justification will fundamentally misunderstand it—as the examples gathered by U. Luz from the history of interpretation of the Reformation period show. Anyone who tries to understand the Gospel of Matthew without the context of the doctrine of justification places the gospel in danger of becoming *nova lex*.

John

Whereas the Gospel according to Matthew is very practically oriented and one might almost begin to fear that "works" really are once again pivotal to a person's salvation, the Gospel according to John seems rather to tend in the opposite direction. Much of what it reports seems to be strangely unreal, and life seems to be totally reduced to the relationship between God and human.[250]

The epitome of the salvation of which John speaks is eternal life. The central phrase of his message of salvation goes, "For God so loved the world that he gave his only Son, so that everyone who believes in him may not perish but may have eternal life" (3:16). He then adds the reason for this: "Indeed, God did not send the Son into the world to condemn the world, but in order that the world might be saved through him" (v. 17). The framework of a judgment isn't totally given up, even though John emphasizes that the Son does not have the function of a judge. Instead, the judgment is fulfilled in the here and now when a person accepts or rejects the Son: "Those who believe in him are not condemned; but those who do not believe are condemned already, because they have not believed in the name of the only Son of God" (v. 18). This reason for this statement is given yet again: "And this is the judgment, that the light has come into the world, and people loved darkness rather than light" (v. 19). The positive parallel to this is given in a saying of Jesus in John 5:24: "Very truly, I tell you, anyone who hears my word and believes him who sent me has eternal life, and does not come under judgment, but has passed from death to life."

Whereas Paul speaks of a justification that leads to a final salvation and to eternal life, John (like Ephesians) proclaims salvation through faith in Christ that in itself brings one into the presence of and fellowship with God and in so doing gives a person life.

In John, the revelation of the saving presence of God is not described as a revelation of his righteousness but as the appearing of the glory of God in the works of Jesus and as the encounter with the truth of God in the person of Jesus.

What is of central importance is the saying in the prologue to the Gospel: "And the Word became flesh and lived among us, and we have seen his glory" (1:14*a*), a saying that is explicitly taken up again in 2:11 and 11:40 of the Gospel. What "glory" means in John can only be understood with the background of the Greek Old Testament.[251] Independent of usual Greek word usage, *doxa* (glory), like its Hebrew equivalent *kabôd*, means the powerful and holy presence of God among God's people or in God's temple. This glory appeared in the works of the "only begotten Son" (cf. the parallelism of the glory of God's Son and the glory of God in 2:11 and 11:40). Thus, the Pre-Johannine Logos hymn already determines the glory of God's Son as a glory "full of grace and truth" and then takes up the Old Testament predicate about God, *hesed we'emet,* which characterizes God in his eternal goodness and graciousness and everlasting truth (cf. Exod 34:6ff.).[252] John 2:11 and 11:40 initially connect the "appearance of glory" to the miracles of Jesus.[253] But it is not limited to this. Just as the signs are just a part of the work of Jesus, so too the glorification of God through him occurs in a far more comprehensive sense than only in the appearing of the glory of God in the miracles. Glory is evident in the unbreakable faithfulness of the Son to his task (cf. 17:4) and in the fact that he does not seek his own honor (*glory*) (5:44; 8:54) but rather does the will of the one who sent him, and that he comes in God's name and not in his own name. In this way his speech and actions become transparent for the working of God. Through his total dependence on the Father he makes present God's care for the world.

With reference to the life of the earthly Jesus, the Fourth Gospel here gathers together the same content that derives in 2 Cor 4:6 from a post-Easter perspective: "For it is the God who said, 'Let light shine out of darkness,' who has shone in our hearts to give the light of the knowledge of the glory of God in the face of Jesus Christ."[254] For Paul, the fact that people encounter the glory of God in Jesus Christ is based in the revelation of the *righteousness* of God and in the saving faithfulness of God that creates spirit and life (cf. 2 Cor 3:4ff.).[255] In John, the appearing of the glory of God in the life and death of Jesus is described as the revelation of the divine "truth," or *alētheia.* Its Old Testament equivalent, *'emet,* which could be the parallel term to *tsedaqah* (righteousness or right; cf. Isa 48:1; 59:14), characterizes the faithfulness and loyalty of the God of Israel.[256] It is where this Old Testament understanding, that was taken further in Judaism and particularly in the writings of Qumran, and encounters the Hellenistic Greek history of the term "truth," that the Fourth Gospel connects with it.[257]

From the Johannine perspective, *"truth"* is the *"reality of God"* shown in the person of Jesus, which frees people from the life lie through which they have become entangled in sin and which places them in a living relationship with God (8:30ff.; cf. 3:21; 18:37). This truth occurs and reveals itself in the "unity of being and love" of the Father and Son,[258] which is shown in Jesus' actions and in his way to the cross, as the love of God directed to saving humanity. Therefore Jesus is not only a witness to the truth but is himself "the way, and the truth, and the life" (14:6). We cannot overlook the close resonance between this and the Pauline expression that "he . . . became for us . . . righteousness," in whose death on the cross God's righteousness was demonstrated and revealed (1 Cor 1:30; Rom 3:21ff.).

Among the strangest sayings of John's gospel is the one that says that Jesus was glorified through his death on the cross. A glance at the idiom of Second Isaiah in the Septuagint helps us understand this text. Not only in 52:13 but also in 49:3-5, God's Yes to his servant is characterized as a glorification, exaltation, or honoring, as likewise is Israel's reacceptance—where being glorified is paralleled with being justified![259] Seen against this background of language usage, Jesus' glorification is his justification, analogous to the Christ hymn in 1 Tim 3:16. This hymn apparently has the resurrection of Jesus in mind, whereas John refers to the lifting up of the Son of Man on the cross. From this springs the conviction that where the Son of God himself has gone into the realm of death, death can no longer remain death but rather becomes a gate into eternal life and a path into the undisguised reality of God—his glory.

Thanks to this, a door to everlasting life is opened for all. The path into fellowship with the Father, and hence to life, occurs through coming to Jesus and believing in him. Whoever believes has eternal life. The core meaning of "faith" in the Fourth Gospel is to accept the divine presence in Jesus, in other words to accept him as Messiah and the Son of God (3:18; 4:39; 6:69; 11:27; 20:31).[260] Such faith can arise as a result of his signs or miraculous knowledge (cf. 1:50; 2:11, 23; 4:53, etc.). But such faith is only fully realized if a person, as a result of this faith, draws radical consequences for his own life. This is demonstrated in chapter 3 by Nicodemus and in 8:30ff. by those Jews who come to faith. Anyone who gives up everything his life has meant and allows his life to be formed anew by the free, wonderful, and irrestrictable action of God, anyone who is loyal to the One whom God has sent from heaven, and anyone who in faith puts himself under the sign of the Son of Man who has been raised up and in him recognizes God's love, that person has eternal life and has been taken up into the saving and protective fellowship of God. Anyone who recognizes the reality about his own life through his encounter with the truth of God, and who sees the insistence on religious security and the search for personal honor exposed as a kind of self-aggrandizement in opposition to God, that person can truly become free (8:31ff.).

Yet this is about more than just understanding oneself differently in the sight of God. God creates new life in a world that has fallen into death. "The hour is coming, and is now here, when the dead will hear the voice of the Son of God, and those who hear will live" (5:25). It is the dead who will live, the blind who will see (while the seeing will become blind) (9:39). This is the Johannine message of justification. Even if the terminology of a carefully thought through doctrine of justification is lacking in this Gospel, there are nonetheless even in John basic elements if it described through the salvation event: in place of the total depravity of those who have become distant and enemies of God despite higher religious demands, the presence of saving divine love steps in through Jesus. Whoever hears his word and opens himself to the claim and promise of divine truth in him, whoever turns his back on "all seeming security and every pretense"[261] and, like that Samaritan woman, allows himself to be led to faith (ch. 4), that person is saved, which means he is included in that fellowship with God that welcomes him into a new way of living in the unity of the Son with the Father (15:9). In this way, the lost are saved and pulled away from the brink of judgment (3:16ff.), those who have been enslaved to sin are freed (8:32, 36), those trapped in the vicious cycle of corporal existence discover, through the creative working of the Spirit, the wonder of new birth (3:3ff.), and those who have destined to die will receive eternal life (5:24ff.).

When the Johannine Christ says that "no one has greater love than this, to lay down one's life for one's friends" (John 15:13), admittedly this seems to be in sharp contrast to the Pauline declaration that Christ died for us "while we were enemies" (Rom 5:10). Do we not see here the tendency of the Johannine community of becoming a faith community that is closed off and turns away all outsiders? But it doesn't say Christ died (only) for those who were his friends. For even John knew full well that the disciples weren't always friends, but, in fact, up until now, were servants (15:15). But in his text he describes what has come to be, what God's love has effected. And therefore, as in every systematic theology of grace, the way of those who are saved has to be described through predestination: "You did not choose me but I chose you..." (15:16). Enemies have become friends, and in Jesus' perspective believers cannot be those who have come to him but rather only those whom the father has given him!

Conversely, the decision of those who do not believe remains their own decision, whatever the consequences. The decision is not punished but simply seriously owned for what it is: A No to God, a No to life, a Yes to darkness. A judgment is no longer necessary. And yet at the same time the entire gospel is one long invitation to believe that "Jesus is the Messiah, the Son of God" and that those who believe will have life in his name (20:31).

7. The Heart of the Scriptures

It ought to be uncontested that the Pauline teaching on justification represents a theological highpoint of the biblical message. Its function as part of the range of biblical theology remains open to discussion. Is it one of many versions of the ancient Christian message—perhaps one of the most significant, yet also potentially one of the most one-sided and most situation-specific? Or is it the objective center of the Scripture, a kind of canon within the canon and hence the decisive criterion for the interpretation of the biblical message as a whole?[262]

As we saw, even as regards Pauline theology itself, this matter is debated. Ever since William Wrede and Albert Schweitzer, biblical interpreters have emphasized that Paul's devotion to Christ, or rather of his interpretation of the Christ event, forms the center of Pauline theology, whereas the teaching on justification represents a "militant anti-Judaic teaching," a "secondary thought" of the Pauline teaching on salvation, or a situation-specific further development of his theology that refers to a particular presentation of a problem to do with the history of salvation. This assumption is not always linked to a critical attitude toward the doctrine of justification; sometimes all that is behind it is the effort to adequately categorize historically and systematically the various strands of Pauline theology.[263]

Before we pursue this topic further, we need to clarify what we mean by "the heart of the Scripture" and similar descriptions. The heart or center of a literary work or a collection of religious documents, after all, cannot be mathematically or geometrically established for certain as the middle of a row of numbers can be. Is the "heart" or "center" of a writing the theme out of which all the other themes can be derived in all their variations, interpretations, or sometimes even counterpoint? Or is what is meant the measure by which the theology of the individual biblical writings is considered as regards its appropriateness?

This is not the place to work through this question in detail. All that is important for us is whether one of these positions can be an adequate expression of the importance of the teaching on justification. What should be clear here is that the teaching on justification cannot assume to be the thematic center of the Scriptures in a historically descriptive sense. Such an insistence would not do right by the multiplicity of theological themes and formulations within the biblical message. But if by the term "heart of the Scripture" we mean the "predominant perspective"[264] that is intended to help us to understand God's revelation from its center, then there are good reasons to denote the teaching on justification as such a center. Seen in this way, the teaching on justification is not one thematic variation on the biblical proclamation of salvation among many but rather the "hermeneutical principle," the pivotal key to understanding that biblical message as a whole.[265]

Basically, by starting with this definition we have already determined in advance that from this particular perspective the question cannot be answered from a neutral standpoint. So the answer instead arises in an ever-changing shape from the circle of understanding between the insight gained through the message of justification into the nature of God's revelation and the openness to quite varying shapings of this revelation in the witness of the biblical writings.

This should also clear up another one of the questions with which we started. If by "the heart of the scripture" we mean the dominant way it is exegeted, we will not end up with an alternative "Christ event" or "doctrine of justification."[266] Without a doubt, God's salvific action in Christ forms the center of the New Testament message. And yet at the same time, the Pauline message of justification, with its inner connection to the theology of the cross, is the most authentic and unequivocal interpretation of the good news of God's action in Jesus Christ, which time and again determines this center to be the heart of the Scriptures.

The shape, history, and message of Jesus Christ can, after all, be proclaimed and interpreted very differently. Jesus can be seen as the new Moses and the new lawgiver. Jesus can also be understood as a gnostic savior. Whether or not one of the New Testament writings portrays such an understanding is debated. But at the very least the Gospel according to Matthew or the Gospel according to John were open to such interpretations for some of their readers. Even the proclamation of Jesus' death on the cross can be interpreted in different ways. Between an understanding of his death as an exemplary martyrdom of a suffering righteous man and the interpretation of his death as a cosmic redemption drama lies a plethora of different possible interpretation, some of which are far from what Paul understood as the "word from the cross."[267]

In contrast to this, the teaching on justification emphatically holds fast to how God revealed himself to humanity in Jesus Christ and what kinds of consequences this has. This teaching points to God, who, in Jesus Christ, has enfleshed and strengthened his Yes to his creation and to us humans. At the same time, the teaching on justification reveals the deepest reason for our human failure: alienation from God, which has the effect that both the successes and failures of our self-empowered actions lead us under the sway of the life-denying power of sin. Through this teaching we are made clear how, through the death and resurrection of Jesus, God has conquered this No that ruled over our lives and thus opened to us the possibility and reality of new life in fellowship with him. This life is one that will survive even the ultimate questioning of our existence because it is life created and given by God. It is a kind of life that we live when, trusting in Christ, we invite God's Yes into our lives. It is a kind of life in which God's love and righteousness determine our desires and actions, while God's holy presence forms us and at the same time puts us in communion with others with whom we live as a result of God's grace. Last but not least, the message of justification points to the path of righteousness on which we attempt, step by step, to fulfill God's Yes to God's creation through our "doing of righteousness," through actions that further and protect life, a path on which we both struggle and suffer with the opposition that other forces muster against that righteousness, until God finally establishes his righteousness and his kingdom.

This interpretation of the gospel's message of liberation finds its deepest resonance in the proclamation of Jesus about the inbreaking reign of God and the liberating acts through which he was empowered. In blessing the poor, in promising the children the kingdom of God, and in welcoming the sinner, Jesus lived the justification of the ungodly. And for that reason he intervened by giving his life "for many."

Based on this dominant perspective we can then interpret and understand a writing such as the Gospel according to Matthew. It is a perspective that will prevent us from seeing the intertwining of the indicative and imperative that is so characteristic of his message as a new law. It makes clear how a powerful encounter with Jesus' teaching can be experienced as empowerment to a life lived in the strength of the righteousness of God.

From this perspective, the encounter with Jesus as the revealer of divine glory and truth in John's gospel becomes an experience of the saving presence of God in the final existential lostness of humanity in an (apparently) godless world. Yet salvation and redemption do not mean bringing home those children of God who have lost themselves in the world; rather, they mean new birth for those who have fallen into death and liberation for those who have become enslaved by the power of sin. Salvation and redemption do not lead a person out of the world but rather enable people to live a missionary existence that is independent of the world's power structures.

From this perspective even James's critical concerns can be understood and taken up without his theological intentions necessarily becoming an equally valid alternative.

Such an interpretation of the "heart of the Scripture" is sufficient to prevent us from forcing the individual biblical writings into a straitjacket or even censoring them. This interpretation centers its message on the core of the Scripture, yet also allows it to speak for itself and thus manages to place the message of justification in a wider perspective. As important as the central perspective is for a consistent and clear picture of the gospel of Jesus Christ, the picture as a whole is richer and more diverse than this one single line of interpretation.

This is particularly true of its relationship to the Old Testament. For a Christian understanding of this part of the Scripture, both are equally important: to be able to see the clear thread that connects his message with the testimony of God's revelation in Jesus Christ and to be open to allowing the Old Testament to have its own say. There are few New Testament themes claiming that they are already testified to by the law and the prophets that are as well grounded as the teaching on justification.[268] Here a dimension of the encounter between God and humanity is touched upon that is fundamental to and typical of the entire biblical revelation.

An ambiguous interpretation is the result. Without its Old Testament grounding, the New Testament teaching on justification is hard to understand. It is only with the Old Testament background that it becomes clear how pervasively the legal-sounding terminology addresses the social dimensions of human existence and to what extent justification encompasses the processing of guilt, the overcoming of the past, and, with regard to the future, being openly integrated into the community. It is only understandable from the perspective of the Old Testament that God's righteousness is as responsible for the dependable order of creation as it founds and anticipates life-giving interaction in human society. It is significant that it is where God's righteousness is made valid as the basis of God's salvific actions toward Israel that the universal aspect of God's claim on this world and his promise of his gracious law for all persons is expressed. And even if it is only minimally testified to, the christological dimension of the teaching on justification also has its roots in the Old Testament, namely both the identification of the messianic king as a representative of righteousness and also the linking of the substitutionary suffering of the servant of God with the justification of the sinner. It is only on the basis of this linking of justification and atonement as the "coming to God by passing through the sentence of death"[269] that the justification of the ungodly and of the sinner who has succumbed to death becomes understandable in the New Testament.

If the New Testament message of justification becomes comprehensible in light of its Old Testament precedents, so too does the reverse happen and the doctrine of justification becomes a principle hermeneutic for the Christian interpretation of the Old Testament, which then understands what might otherwise be a message open to a variety of other interpretations as most centrally to do with justification. The self-revelation of God, "I am Yahweh, your God," thus appears in light of the revelation of his creative and saving righteousness. The story of creation is an expression of God's Yes to the world and to humanity. It places humanity in a particular relationship to God with the mandate to be God's "image," God's responsible partner, and "governor" in creation. Seen this way, it becomes apparent that creation and salvation "have the same face."[270] At the same time, the Primeval Narrative shows how God wrestles with humanity's No to God's Yes and with humanity's questioning of and denial of fellowship with God. Human life has only had permanence from the beginning because God continually saves despite the judgment of death, as can be seen in very differing ways by the examples of Cain (Gen 4:14ff.) and Noah and his family (Gen 6:5–8:22).

The story of Abraham and his descendants is a model for God's unconditional call, a call that contains the seed of universal effectiveness (Gen
12:3). It is the story of obedience and failure and thus always a story of
faith. Healing and saving community with God is experienced wherever
a person totally trusts in God's promise. In this sense, Gen 15:6 is the
authentic summary of the story of Abraham.

Thus the basic grounding experience of Israel—the exodus from Egypt
of the people of Israel—is in the most profound sense also an "experience
of justification." Granted, the enslavement of Israel in Egypt is not
described as being a consequence of the people's guilt. But it is a situation
of profound alienation from God and from their own calling, and so exodus is a liberation for God and for themselves: "I am the LORD; I sanctify
you, I who brought you out of the land of Egypt to be your God: I am the
LORD" (Lev 22:32-33). This is the interpretation that gives the Holiness
Code its basic introduction of God for Israel (Exod 20:2).[271] Using cultic
terminology that God "declares holy" his people by the act of liberating
them describes the same thing as the legal or social terminology of God
"justifying" (cf. 1 Cor 6:11). By doing away with everything that stands
in the way of fellowship, God brings persons into saving fellowship with
him. For the Old Testament people of God this was linked with the par-
adigmatic action of being freed from slavery in Egypt; for the New
Testament people of God, with God's actions on the cross and the resurrection of Jesus. The Old Testament story of liberation encompasses the
Passover event, the sparing of the people in face of the death sentence,
and their passage through the floodwaters of the sea. The New Testament
salvation event is most profoundly expressed in the saying that God did
not spare his only Son; rather, he went through the floodwaters of the
death sentence for the sake of all. Whereas in the Old Testament God
was called the One who "led the Israelites out of Egypt," now his "new
name" is "the one who raised Jesus from the dead."[272]

But what does all this mean with regard to the theme that, at first
glance, seems most strongly to contradict an interpretation of both testaments from the perspective of the doctrine of justification, namely the
theme of the law? Doesn't the Old Testament speak repeatedly of the joy
of following God's commandment that shows the path to life, whereas
Paul is convinced that the promise of the law will lead people astray (Gal
3:10-12) and that the "letter [of the law] kills" (2 Cor 3:6)?

It is this last passage that shows that even for Paul the law and the
gospel are not fundamentally opposed and separate parts of the Bible. As

"Scripture" (i.e., as the Word of God transmitted in written form), what the law does is precisely to witness to righteousness through faith and to be fulfilled by love. Gese poignantly says, "It is not gospel and law that are contrasts to each other, but gospel and the human attempt to become ourselves the law."[273] In that the doctrine of justification helps to identify this distinction, it "uphold[s] the law" (Rom 3:31). It is by this that the teaching on justification proves itself as the hermeneutical key to the interpretation of the whole Scripture.

EVERYTHING IS GRACE: DIVERGENT POSITIONS IN THE TRADITION

T he doctrine of justification has had a very diverse history. To describe its course in the requisite detail would demand an extensive and comprehensive volume.[1] And yet we cannot simply ignore this history and ask about the contemporary significance of the message of justification by simply appealing directly to the biblical witness. For every contemporary understanding of justification is consciously or unconsciously formed by some traditional preunderstanding. Only when we are conscious of that can the question of the underlying biblical formulations become a critical conversation partner. And so in this section at least a few of the highlights in the history of the doctrine of justification must be named. We will subsequently see that clear and obvious lines of development lead to contemporary ecumenical discussion of justification from the foundational decisions made here. The diverse emphases of the various Christian traditions necessitate this present need for clarification.

1. NEW HISTORICAL EMPHASES

What we must first establish in the task we've set ourselves is that for long periods in the history of Christian theology the doctrine of justification was hardly noticed or at most comprised a part of the traditional teaching on grace. This development already began in later Pauline epistles, where the doctrine of justification was, we acknowledge, still mentioned in shorthand but was no longer developed, and it ended in the early church's eloquent silence on the whole topic.[2] The question about salvation is focused on the question of the incarnation. Redemption "happens by the Logos of God becoming human and in himself making completely visible the image of the human as the image of God, and then through his spirit establishing humanity once again to match this image."[3] It was Irenaeus who stated, "For to this end, the Word of God was made man, and He Who is the Son of God, Son of Man, that man blended with God's Word, and receiving the adoption, might become the Son of God. Since we could not otherwise receive incorruption and immortality, but by being united to Incorruption and Immortality."[4] Athanasius encapsulated this conviction by saying, "He, indeed, assumed humanity that we might become God."[5] This is how the term "divinization" (*theōsis*) became the central theme of the Eastern church's doctrine of salvation. We must not misunderstand this to mean that a saved person had pretensions of becoming divine: " 'Divinization' of the human means that a person only becomes completely *human* by once again becoming completely in the image of God."[6] But this happens through participation in God's being through the incarnation, and above all means participation in immortality. This becomes the epitome of salvation in the Orthodox tradition.

This is the reason why the doctrine of justification never became central in orthodoxy but rather remained foreign to it.[7] In his *Dogmatics*, D. Staniloae says, differentiating himself from the Protestant and Roman Catholic understanding of salvation:

> So salvation should not be understood as justification that is promised to the believer in some legal way, nor is it to be understood as a gift that is to be shared out by the church as if it were a treasure that had been created and earned as grace by Christ. Rather, it is a new life that overflows from the sanctified and resurrected body of Christ in to the members of his mystical body, which is the church, thus showing the result of the believers' personal fellowship with Christ. Thus, it is not an external, legal, and static condition, but rather a new quality of humans which is constantly transforming itself.[8]

This does not mean that Pauline statements about justification have no meaning for Orthodox theology. But they are considered from their own particular perspective. Staniloae therefore characterizes the Orthodox understanding in the following way: "In brief: Christ became our righteousness. And in fact he became not only an outer but an inner righteousness, for we live in him (1 Cor 1:30). He gives us the strength to be righteous and to live righteously according to his image in which we were created."[9] So here the message of justification and soteriology oriented to the incarnation merge into each other.

That the development of the doctrine occurred differently in the Western church can be primarily traced to *Augustine*. It is through him that the concepts of sin and grace step into the center of the Christian teaching of salvation. In so doing, grace is understood as the helping mercy of God that frees persons from the vicious cycle of desire and the power of sin occasioned through it. It is not participation in the divine nature that is the essence of salvation but being freed for fellowship with God. Salvation means the healing of one's relationship to God and it is because of this that love becomes a central dimension of Christian life. Yet this love is simply and only a gift of God's grace, for "God's love has been poured into our hearts through the Holy Spirit that has been given to us" (Rom 5:5). Since Augustine, this saying of Paul's has been one of the most basic expressions of Catholic teaching on grace.[10]

Yet Augustine's teaching on grace was only taken up again and developed further in the late Middle Ages by the eminent scholastic theologians. It is as a part of this teaching on grace that the justification of the ungodly becomes an important subject—no more and no less than that.[11] Despite significant differences between the particular schools and systems of thought, we can recognize two basic thrusts: For their salvation, humans are entirely indebted to free grace, that which cannot be earned by any human effort whatsoever. Yet this grace so pervades a person that he or she is enabled to turn away from sin and do the good God demands as the fruit of grace and return of a life filled by grace, something that can certainly be termed their "just merits."

This has to do with the basic characterization of grace, Thomas Aquinas's understanding of which O. H. Pesch characterizes as follows:

> Grace is the creative arrival of the eternal love of God in the I-center of a person. Through it, a person is yanked up out of the limits of his nature and into fellowship with God. Simultaneously he is equipped with abilities that make it not only possible but even easy and taken for

granted: From grace "flow" faith, hope, and love. Yet all of this is the work of a God who shows his power precisely in ruling over the ways his creatures find their way to him "suaviter"—gently—through the irresistible lure of his love.[12]

At the center of this understanding is the creating equivalence between grace and love, to the background of Rom 5:5.

The "infused grace" (*gratia infusa*) upholds the process of justification. As "prevenient grace" (*gratia praeveniens*) it moves the free will of human beings to turn to God through the faith which justifies. As "grace which makes agreeable" (*gratia gratum faciens*) it causes the justification of human beings, in fact through the forgiveness of sins as well as through the inward transformation that moves a person from the state of sin to the state of righteousness.

If, therefore, the justification of the ungodly is based in "effective grace" (*gratia operans*), then it occurs in the course of life through the effect of "cooperative grace" (*gratia cooperans*), which aims for the "merit of the acceptability of a life for eternal blessedness."[13] Through this, Thomas Aquinas hopes to make clear that the effect of grace is a personal event that pulls the person and his desires and actions into its orbit of action and recognizes and rewards its cooperation. Aquinas determinedly wants to hold fast to the fact that the reason for all meritorious works is justifying grace, which is totally undeserved.[14]

Balancing out this paradox of course necessitates a very complex system, a system in which the "through grace alone" (*sola gratia*) remains but the "through faith alone" (*sola fide*) doesn't come into play as a critical counterpoint, or at least only in the form of a faith formed and made effective by love.[15] Yet it is to be doubted whether "justification by love" really corresponds to "justification by faith."[16]

Luther did not explicitly engage Thomas Aquinas's teaching on grace. The representatives of scholastic theology that he encountered in his studies were William of Ockham and Gabriel Biel, whose doctrine of God, being strongly influenced by philosophy, strangely distorted the teaching of grace and justification.[17] In the end, the question of whether familiarity with Thomas Aquinas and his subtle discourses on the effect of grace would have significantly helped Luther as he wrestled with the question of justification is hypothetical. De facto, Luther arrived at his teaching on justification through intensive exegesis of the Bible and particularly of Paul's letters and in so doing arrived at solutions that had different emphases.

Justification becomes the center of his theology. "For in the doctrine of justification what surfaces is who God is and who humanity is—in light of this God."[18] God manifests his righteousness in making righteous the sinner who entrusts himself to God through faith in Jesus Christ.

In his celebrated retrospective on his life's work, Luther designated his new understanding of God's righteousness in Rom 1:17 as the turning point of his Reformation understanding. God's righteousness lies not in his making decisions that arbitrate the justness of the punishments he metes out to sinners; God's righteousness lies rather in the gift through which he grants righteousness to a sinner and through which the one made righteous through faith then lives.[19]

But none of this persuaded Luther to separate the gift from the giver. The righteousness given to a person for Christ's sake always remains God's, or Christ's righteousness, meaning that in this sense it remains an "alien" righteousness that, while it is owned through faith, yet never becomes one's "own" righteousness. Since God's righteousness is both the gift of an alien righteousness and signifies the participation in its transforming power, God's justifying action includes "both the ascription of righteousness and how a person becomes increasingly righteous."[20] "Justification and making righteous belong closely together. They act in the same way as means and purpose do. One and the same will of God encompasses the wholeness of what he does to a person."[21] Even if the process can only be completed in the hereafter, for Luther what is clear is that "a person truly is made righteous in the sight of God. So righteous, that he can even stand at the Judgment."[22]

And yet we cannot speak of Luther advocating for a double justification, as if the sinner were justified by faith in the initial justification, yet in the Final Judgment only the one who had actually become righteous. The basis of justification always remains God's judgment, which, as God's creative word, always effects what it promises to effect.[23] It is for this reason that a person can only depend on whatever God promises him. If he were to rely on himself, he would be led into temptation or doubt or boasting.

This is the reason why for Luther the recognition that humans are always at one and the same time righteous and sinners (*simul iustus et peccator*) was so important. If a person looks only to herself, she remains a sinner; if instead she looks to what God promises, she is righteous. This remains fundamentally true, right until God perfects a person in death. And yet this is no static determination. Luther also knows of a way in which there can be some advance in the life of a Christian, for he knows that through the working of God's righteousness the rule of sin is broken and a life of righteousness becomes possible. It is because of this that Luther understands humans as partly sinful and partly righteous.[24] It is noteworthy that the first time the phrase *simul iustus et peccator* occurs in Luther's lecture on the Letter to the Romans it does so by way of comparison with a sick person, someone who, in the eyes of the doctor, is at one and the same time sick and well: "He is sick in fact, but he is well because of the sure promise of the doctor, whom he trusts and who has reckoned him as already cured, because he is sure that he will cure him; for he has already begun to cure him and no longer reckons to him a sickness unto death." The person who "Christ, our Samaritan" has taken into his care at the inn is in a similar position. He "is at the same time both a sinner and a righteous man; a sinner in fact, but a righteous man by the sure imputation and promise of God that God will continue to deliver him from sin until God has completely cured him. And thus he is entirely healthy in hope, but in fact he is still a sinner; but he has the beginning of righteousness, so that he continues more and more always to seek it, yet he realizes that he is always unrighteous."[25] Thus Luther wants both to take seriously the saving power of the gospel and also warn persons against putting their hope of salvation in anything but the promise of Christ, such as, for example, some improvement they notice in themselves.[26]

Luther's doctrine of justification has a comprehensive scope. He summarizes many different aspects of the biblical message of justification that his followers, who tried to develop a system, had difficulty in holding together. After all, Luther by no means only developed his teaching on justification from the perspective of a fearful sinner. The pivotal reference point for Luther remains the sovereignty of God's actions in the revelation of his righteousness in the gospel of Jesus Christ. It is for that reason that Luther also cannot separate the pronouncement of being righteous from being made righteous.

For Luther, a sinner's being declared righteous was not a judgment that occurred "as if" that person were righteous, yet "allows the person to remain who he is, quite unchanged. Instead, he saw in the judgment of declaration of righteousness the word of power of the creator and redeemer who will realize what he has promised.[...] This event begins even now, as certainly as Christ becomes *effectively* present to the faithful through his Spirit. For sure, there is still sin in him, and it will only finally be taken from him completely through death. But its power over him is broken, for the Spirit counters it in pursuit of the beginning of a new life. And so faith certainly does not remain passive with regard to the needs of the neighbor in the world, though for its own part it can be only pure receptiveness. Because faith means to enter into the life-giving power of Christ, works of love proceed from it spontaneously. Indeed Luther would say that true faith cannot even exist without such works."[27]

It was no easy task to systematize Luther's teaching on justification. The task fell to *Melanchthon*, and his efforts to undertake the task provoked a series of difficult arguments between Protestants. He gives a summarizing definition of justification in his *Loci* of 1535: "Justification means the forgiveness of sin and the reconciliation or acceptance of a person to everlasting life."[28]

Although for Melanchthon, too, in the process of justification being accepted by God and renewal through the Spirit objectively belong together, for the sake of terminological clarity he nonetheless prefers to separate justification and sanctification. But by doing so he exacerbates the problem of their precise relationship. Does sanctification then become the imperative that follows the indicative of justification, or does sanctification remain the obvious fruit of the Spirit that is received through justification?[29]

Calvin attempts to reconnect these two threads. Justification is based solely in faith, but faith and justification are not "devoid of good works." We are justified by faith "because by faith we grasp Christ's righteousness by which alone we are reconciled to God. Yet you could not grasp this without at the same time grasping sanctification also. For he 'is given unto us for righteousness, wisdom, sanctification, and redemption.'...Therefore Christ justifies no one whom he does not at the same time sanctify."[30]

The Roman Catholic Church's response to the challenge presented by the Reformation teaching on justification was the justification decree of the *Council of Trent*. Without drawing attention to the fact, in this decree important Reformation positions are taken up, for example, through a newly revised edition of the classical scholastic teaching on grace, particularly that of Thomas Aquinas, and are taken up with particular attention to the language of the Catholic teaching on grace. On the other hand, central concerns of Reformation theology are discarded by the doctrinal decisions of this decree.

This two-sided aspect of the decree on justification is the reason why the Protestant judgment on Trent is both divided and fluctuating.

Whereas some have suggested that no Reformation would have been needed if Trent had already existed at the beginning of the sixteenth century, others see this decree as nothing less that the classical summary of everything that the Reformers had opposed.[31]

What is characteristic of Trent's teaching on justification is the close linking of God's gracious action and the human cooperation enabled by it to work for salvation.

This cooperation already commences at the beginning of the way of salvation, when the "prevenient grace" in the sinner awakes the "faith in the truth of the proclamation of salvation . . . along with the first awakenings of hope and love toward God" and through this at the same time enables the sinner to cooperate freely with God's grace. This is set in outright contrast to the Reformation *sola fide*.[32]

And so justification by faith is also only the beginning of the justification event. Faith is the "basis and root of all justification," out of which the actual transformation of becoming righteous happens thanks to a lifelong process of a working together of faith and works that arise from the gift of righteousness. Trent understands the complementarity of the three characteristics of Christian life—faith, hope, and love—as being sequential. Love and hope have to be added to faith. That is why for Trent there is no justification *sola fide*, because faith is part of the preparation, and a person is justified by the love poured into him by God.[33] So we are left with the emphatic conclusion that while the Council's text works very intensively with Pauline terminology and concepts, it runs the risk of completely discarding Paul himself by dismissing *sola fide*.

In the Protestant arena, we find one of the most independent developments of Reformation theology in *John Wesley*. Some aspects of his teaching on justification seem to approach Trent quite closely.[34] For Wesley, the justification event is embedded in God's way of salvation with humans, a way that begins with the work of "prevenient grace," which has the effect of awakening in a person the first questions about God's existence and the sense of being separated from God.[35] God's salvation is then continued thanks to the "convincing grace" that leads a person to confession and repentance. This is followed by the "proper Christian salvation, whereby 'through grace' we 'are saved by faith.'" This grace is composed of "those two grand branches, justification and sanctification. By justification we are saved from the guilt of sin, and restored to the favour of God; by sanctification we are saved from the power and root of sin, and restored to the image of God."[36]

Through God's justifying and sanctifying actions a person's inner transformation commences, whose goal is perfection, in which "the heart is cleansed from all sin, and filled with pure love to God and man."

Thus, for Wesley the active nature and the creative work of grace are central to his understanding. Grace is real action of God in the hearts of human beings;[37] "it is the actual effect of God's love on human existence." For Wesley Rom 5:5 is the central description of God's saving action in human beings.[38] Yet at the same time Wesley is adamant that all of this is solely the work of God. Justification "implies what God does for us through his Son," sanctification "what he works in us by his Spirit."[39] It is for this reason that Wesley holds resolutely to the position that we are not only justified *sola fide* but also are sanctified through faith alone, for only faith receives the love that God gives us.[40]

And yet even at the beginning of Wesley's ministry there were strong caveats from theologians of a reform disposition against Wesley's linking of "ascribed" and "inherent" righteousness. Calvinists and the Moravians feared that people might be led astray into thinking they could rely on justification as coming from their own righteousness if they believed this righteousness indeed to already live in their hearts.[41]

In his sermon, "The Lord, Our Righteousness," Wesley attempts to make clear that it is not the righteousness abiding in our hearts that is the reason for our being accepted by God, but its fruit.

> I believe God implants righteousness in every one to whom he has imputed it. I believe "Jesus Christ is made of God unto us sanctification," as well as "righteousness;" or, that God sanctifies, as well as justifies, all them that believe in him. They to whom the righteousness of Christ is imputed, are made righteous by the Spirit of Christ; are renewed in the image of God, "after the likeness wherein they were created, in righteousness and true holiness."[42]

It is because of this that the righteousness of Christ is "the entire and only reason for all our hope"; not even faith can take its place. "Through faith, the Holy Spirit enables us to build upon this ground. God gives us faith, and it is because of faith that we are accepted by God—not because of this faith, but rather because of what Christ has done and has suffered for us."[43]

This is an impressive attempt to unite Catholic soteriology (in the broad sense) with biblical Reformation knowledge. Using the category of *solus Christus*, the creative power of his righteousness is emphasized.

It is not possible to present in detailed fashion the rest of the history of the doctrine of justification up until the present. However, particular twentieth-century emphases were:

- the discovery at the beginning of the twentieth century of Luther's teaching on justification through the discovery and research on his early lectures;[44]
- the integration of the doctrine of justification into Karl Barth's doctrine of reconciliation through which he both released the "anthropological constriction" of Neo-Protestantism, but at the same time moved the justification out of the center;[45]
- the hermeneutical function of the doctrine of justification in Paul Tillich and Ruldolf Bultmann's theology, which takes it out of the context of classical soteriology and reframes then in the arena of epistemology, thus making it a basic principle of Protestant theology;[46]
- the new interpretation of the doctrine of justification through liberation theology, which identifies aspects of Old Testament terminology on justification in Paul's soteriological sayings and interprets them within their social contexts and refers them to contemporary situations of oppression and marginalization.[47]

2. THE ECUMENICAL NEED FOR CLARITY

If one surveys the inter- and intrachurch debates about the doctrine of justification, what becomes clear is that there is unanimity that Christian theology must always be a theology of grace. There is a consensus that the basis and content of all Christian proclamation is the message that in Jesus Christ, God came near to humanity and quite aside from all their efforts "to will and to work" has acted for the sake of their salvation. The open question is in what measure human cooperation is included in this event. It is on this point that very different emphases are owned, and this not so much between Lutheran and Roman Catholic theology as one might have imagined, but also in the discussion among different Protestants or with respect to the teaching of Orthodox churches.

Yet these differences don't so much stem from the fact that some people find it hard to be gifted by others. The tensions can already been seen in the New Testament:

- When Paul, on the basis of Gen 15:6, describes faith as the stance of receiving God's justifying action, then it is unavoidable that the question of whether an individual's decision for faith becomes the condition of justification.
- Because in Paul Christ's death signifies not only an "exclusive" substitution (Christ bore our punishment) but is also understood "inclusively" ("We die with Christ"), then the question arises of how people are actually included in the Christ event.
- Because our being ascribed righteousness for Christ's sake is not intended to be imagined as an accounting procedure with respect to a heavenly account, but rather transposes us into the arena of the effectiveness and power of God's righteousness, the question as to the meaning of God's righteousness in the life of a person remains open.
- If Christians have to be warned not to let the freedom of the gospel become "an opportunity for self-indulgence" (Gal 5:13), then one also must ask what the significance is of their efforts to battle sin and their pains to give the Spirit of love space in their lives.
- Because justification occurs directly between God and the individual, and yet also not independent of the connection to the people of God and the body of Christ, the relationship between individual experiences of salvation and ecclesial mediation must be variously determined.

A serious discussion of the different traditional standpoints is only possible if its origins in particular biblical questions are recognized. It is also only in that way that common response can be found that can give contemporary understanding energy to continue the discussions.[48]

With this in mind, I want to attempt to sketch out some response for at least a few preliminary questions.

The Path to Faith

Among the most hotly debated questions of the Reformation and Post-Reformation age is the one about how persons contribute to their faith. Though just one of many, in his writing, "On the Bondage of the Will" (*De servo arbitrio*), Luther said, referring to John 1:12, that humans participate in an exclusively passive way in their becoming Christian.[49] In saying this, Luther gave us an important key term for the Reformation understanding of grace.[50] Because God's grace is unconditional, it cannot be dependent on any human activity.

The Council of Trent saw this quite differently and rejected this understanding: "If anyone says that man's free will moved and aroused by God, by assenting to God's call and action, in no way cooperates toward disposing and preparing itself to obtain the grace of justification, that it cannot refuse its assent if it wishes, but that, as something inanimate, it does nothing whatever and is merely passive, let him be anathema."[51]

The Council's more detailed explanations are, of course, much more differentiated than this. But here the Council Fathers attempt to show that it is on account of "prevenient grace" that persons who are "disposed through His quickening and helping grace" can "convert themselves to their own justification by freely assenting to and freely cooperating with that grace." Therefore, a person "neither does absolutely nothing . . . nor yet is he able by his own free will and without the grace of God to move himself to justice in His sight."[52]

The Formula of Concord posits a quite different position in response to this attempt to draw a mediating line: "But before man is illuminated, converted, reborn, renewed, and drawn by the Holy Spirit, he can do nothing in spiritual things of himself and by his own powers. In his own conversion or regeneration he can as little begin, effect, or cooperate in anything as a stone, a block, or a lump of clay could."[53]

Now it is true that the Formula admits that a person cannot simply be considered a lump of wood or a stone. But with regard to God this only heightens the situation, for a person can oppose the working of God, which a stone could not do.[54]

This position has not endured in such an intransigent way in Protestantism either. So, for example, Methodist theology also speaks of a "prevenient grace" that awakens in persons "the first wish to please God, the first dawn of light concerning his will, and the first slight transient conviction of having sinned against him," without, however, there being any mention in this context of humans working with God.[55] In the "call to decision" of the evangelism and revival movements, people are appealed to about the need and possibility to "convert." Some would say in response to this that we have no need to call people to decision but rather have only to tell people that a decision has already been made about them.[56]

The biblical testimony seems to bear out both sides on this point. To support its middle-of-the-road position, the Council of Trent had already previously called upon biblical passages that both say "Return to me, says the LORD of hosts, and I will return to you" (Zech 1:3), as well as "Restore us to yourself, O LORD, that we may be restored" (Lam 5:21).

This twofold theme can likewise be traced through the New Testament. People are called to change their ways and come to faith. To his question of "What must I do to be saved?" the jailer in Philippi receives the simple response, "Believe on the Lord Jesus, and you will be saved, you and your household" (Acts 16:31), not at all the theologically correct information that he couldn't possibly do anything to be saved, for that is God's work alone.

At the same time, all this "coming to faith" is described as the work of God. Only a few verses earlier, in Acts 16:14, it is said about Lydia, a dealer in purple cloth, "The Lord opened her heart to listen eagerly to what was said by Paul." And the Gospel of John repeatedly emphasizes, "You did not choose me but I chose you" (15:16), or "No one can come to me unless drawn by the Father who sent me" (6:44).

One cannot simply ascribe these two strands of interpretation to diverse layers of the biblical witness. Apparently they address a dialectic: People are asked about their Yes to God's Yes. If someone responds to this Yes, the only explanation he or she has for this is that God has spoken God's Yes to him or her. It is the same dialectic expressed by Paul when he speaks of us knowing God because God knows us (Gal 4:9; 1 Cor 13:12).

There is thoroughgoing agreement about this nowadays between Protestant and Roman Catholic theologians. The only differences that remain are in regard to the nuances of the description of the way and means in which people come to this point. Thus, in the text entitled *The Condemnations of the Reformation Era*, it says, "The response of faith is itself brought about through the uncoercible word of promise which comes to human beings from outside themselves. There can be 'cooperation' *only* in the sense that in faith the heart is involved, when the Word touches it and creates faith." But it is admitted that the word *cooperation* is subject to misunderstandings.[57] So too the *Joint Declaration on the Doctrine of Justification* says: "When Catholics say that persons 'cooperate' in preparing for and accepting justification by consenting to God's justifying action, they see such personal consent as itself an effect of grace, not as an action rising from innate human abilities."[58] E. Jüngel basically describes faith quite similarly, as "the heartfelt human Yes to God's

Word," yet in so doing he excludes the possibility of "any of their own effort or collaboration."[59] So, correspondingly, the Lutheran side of the *Joint Declaration* writes that the Lutheran teaching of the "mere passive" justification negates "any possibility of contributing to one's own justification, but do not deny that believers are fully involved personally in their faith, which is effected by God's Word."[60]

H. Weder aptly characterized this paradox: "Faith is [...] not a subjective human possibility, not a spiritual activity to which I could rouse myself. Faith occurs where the salvific appears. Faith is something that is awakened in me, just as a laugh is awakened by a joke, or a dance by music."[61] It is this comparison of Weder's that also points to the real problem of proclaiming faith today. For, in the face of the prevalent lack of faith, the question cannot only be how much or how little "cooperation" we can assume on the part of an individual in the process of coming to faith, but rather we should be asking how faith comes to be at all. Are we grasping the crux of the gospel when we preach it, so that people have no choice but to believe? Could this crux perhaps be precisely an engaged passing along of the message of justification? Do we have the courage (the *parrēsia*) to proclaim this message with the goal and intention that it awaken faith?

By Faith and Therefore by Grace

The most explicit step toward unity on the doctrine of justification is the common witness to *sola fide*. If it was not yet totally clear in the *Joint Declaration* on the doctrine of justification whether both partners really meant the same,[62] then the "Official Common Statement" says unequivocally, "Justification takes place 'by grace alone'...by faith alone; the person is justified 'apart from works.'"[63] This is truly a breakthrough, for even the Council of Trent still condemned this statement.[64] This establishes once and for all that the love a person lives is not what justifies them, but faith alone: "Justification is a pure gift, and is always grace."

The fact that mistrust continues to be raised about this *Joint Declaration* possibly has less to do with interdenominational unclarities than with the intra-Protestant dilemma that means for some theologians even faith cannot take a sufficiently invisible place for the sake of the "invisibility of justification."[65] Here there is a very real risk that faith will now only be defined as "doing nothing" and "achieving nothing." Because *sola fide* is to prevent any and all works of righteousness, there is the concern that faith might itself be made into a work,[66] and this, in turn, can lead to suggestions such as that a person is "neither an active nor a passive" participant in the faith event,[67] and this can lead to the impression that if one pursues the notion of *sola fide* to its logical conclusion, it, in fact, aims for the notion of *sine fide* (without faith).[68] But this would dishonor the personal aspect of the justification event, which, in the New Testament is held onto precisely by the notion of the necessity of faith. So *sola fide* carries a dual possibility for liberation in it: It liberates us from the oppressive notion that our relationship with God depends on our moral or ecclesial achievements. And at the same time it liberates us for a personal relationship of trust, a relationship in which our strengths and possibilities are both recognized and mobilized. Paul describes this aspect of the justification even in Rom 5:5: "God's love has been poured into our hearts through the Holy Spirit." It is not a case of love having to be added to faith in order that the justification of the ungodly occur.[69] When the love of God takes ownership of the center of our being (cf. also Gal 2:20ff.), justification through faith occurs and at "peace with God"(Rom 5:1) becomes the reality of our lives.

Participation in Salvation

The fact that faith is active in love is not called into question but rather emphasized by *sola fide*. This should be a matter of ecumenical consensus by now. "The working of God's grace does not exclude human action...."[70] In fact the opposite is true; it calls it into being and liberates it for positive possibilities.

Luther never tired of speaking of faith being such "a lively, busy, active, mighty thing...[that] it is impossible for it not to be doing good works incessantly."[71] It is in this connection that he also talks about how God imparts the Holy Spirit "through the Word, so as to have us as cooperators with him."[72] The formula suggested in the Concordia also holds true, "that as soon as the Holy Spirit has initiated his work of regeneration and renewal in us through the Word and the holy sacraments, it is certain that we can and must cooperate by the power of the Holy Spirit, even though we still do so in great weakness."[73] This takes up what Paul says in his oft overlooked paradoxical word of Phil 2:12ff.: "Work out your own salvation with fear and trembling; for it is God who is at work in you, enabling you both to will and to work for his good pleasure." Although this text speaks of working out one's own salvation, it is not meant in an oppositional way to complement God's actions with human work. In contrast, what is meant is that "because God effects everything, therefore you ought to do all things, and it is because of it that you can do all these things."[74]

Does this enable us to create a bridge to the Christian traditions for whom a person's "participation" or "cooperation" in his salvation is a central concern? After all, this is not only the tradition of the Roman Catholic Church but also much more intensively so of Orthodox theology. "Synergy," the term applied to the cooperative working of God and humans, is "a central term of the Eastern Orthodox and patristic soteriology."[75] To understand it correctly it is important to clarify "that Eastern Orthodox theological thinking as a whole is less oriented to the beginnings of the way of salvation, to conversion and to the justification of the sinner than to the perfection, sanctification, and divinization of persons. 'Synergeia' is thus not so much participation in one's justification but participation in the whole process that includes redemption, justification, sanctification, and divinization, and which, looking back with praise, insists that all of Orthodox theology derives from God's grace alone."[76]

From the perspective of the New Testament, this participation in salvation can by no means be understood as a cooperation between the actions of God and the efforts of persons. Rather, Christians are taken into the work of God for the salvation of persons. What is important here, but seldom attended to is whenever Paul speaks of himself or others being "co-workers with God" he does so in the context of God's grace being brought closer to others through apostolic ministry (1 Cor 3:9; 2 Cor 6:1). So participation in salvation is precisely not individualistically focused on the questions of personal salvation, but rather occurs within the context of our ministry in God's work of salvation for all.

This close connection of the missionary task and of our existence is nowhere expressed more clearly than in 1 Cor 9:22b-23: "I have become all things to all people, that I might by all means save some. I do it all for the sake of the gospel, so that I may share its blessings." The apostle has been swept up in the movement of the gospel toward people. It is only in this way that he is and remains a "participant" in the gospel, also with respect to his own life. It is in the fulfillment of this task that being protected and provided for by grace occurs. This happens without relying on "meritorious" behavior; it is simply part of the nature of the gospel.

It would be good if ecumenical theology of the future could let go of the mutually offensive terminology of the past and could instead unequivocally develop this ministerial and missionary dynamic of the gospel of justification.

The Triumph over Sin

This, in turn, leads to the question of the enduring significance of the "counter reality," namely sin, in the life of the Christian. As a logical addition to the contention that our righteousness always remains the righteousness of Christ, in short, "alien" to us and not our own, Luther very early on shaped the expression of Christians being *simul iustus et peccator* (at one and the same time both righteous and sinners).[77] This designation forms the heart of the Lutheran interpretation of the justification event. For through it the *extra nos* of the reality of justification is preserved and held on to, namely that we could never in our lives establish something like our own righteousness. This is also the reason for the reticence about ascribing to good works any saving status as "fruits of faith" for the keeping or deepening of one's own righteousness over and above what they do for others.

On the other hand, Catholic teaching and also, for example, Methodist theology, wants to hold fast to the idea that Christians have not received God's grace in vain, i.e., not without effect (cf. 2 Cor 6:1). So liberation from sin can also be existentially experienced, and the believers' actions made possible by grace contributes to the growth and deepening of faith and to fellowship with God.

If one looks from this controversy back into the New Testament, a strange observation transpires. Almost no one has portrayed the dangerous reality of sin, as seen by the New Testament, quite as clearly as Luther. In contrast to Luther's portrayal, the Catholic and the Wesleyan are pretty much harmless.[78] And almost no one has explored the Pauline message of the liberating reality of Jesus' victory over sin quite so powerfully as has Luther. And yet it is just here that a profound difference arises. Paul does not call those who have been made righteous sinners. Neither does he call them "righteous" because the fact that they will be made righteous is an eschatological reality (Rom 5:19).[79] But the believers have been "justified" and therefore have peace with God and live with God's protection and hope until the time that God finishes his work with them (Rom 5:1-11). Their sinfulness is fundamentally now in the past (Rom 5:8–6:15). Even Rom 7 doesn't describe the life of a Christian but the life of a person under the law, albeit from the perspective of one who has been freed from the power of the law through Christ. Paul presents this circumstance in such a way as to also depict something in it that threatens Christians. It is thought provoking that it is this description with which many serious Christians identify themselves.[80] Paul Althaus was even of the opinion that we should prefer Luther's interpretation over Paul's here because his "insight into the soul is more piercing" and his "reflection is sharper."[81]

Looking at the Bible as a whole then, we could point to the dialectic of 1 John (cf. 1:8–2:2 with 3:4-8). But because with John, as with Paul, the encounter with Christ signifies "at one and the same time the disempowerment by God of the sin that holds persons captive,"[82] the "theological imbalance" between the reality of grace and the reality of sin must be brought to expression in the Christian message.[83]

Whether this can be accomplished through the traditional formulas seems doubtful to me on the basis of the discussion about the joint declaration on the doctrine of justification. For those who are not at home in the particular linguistic traditions, these formulas are far too laden with potential misunderstanding.[84] We must try together to listen to the witness of the Scripture regarding the overcoming of the power of sin through God's justifying actions, and yet must also at the same time take seriously the reminder of the continuing threat of this power. It is a power whose reality encroaches into the life of the Christian and always wants to direct that person's life when it is not being shaped by Christ.

In this connection it will be important to consider this question not only individualistically from the perspective of the interaction of these powers in the individual's life but also to try to proclaim the reality of liberation from sin in light of social reality in which, after all, these destructive powers of sin manifest themselves more than elsewhere.

The Ecclesial Transmittal

Not long after the Second Vatican Council a Lutheran observer of the same summarized his impressions this way: "If we look carefully we can see that after the most recent Council of the Roman church the decision is demanded of us even more clearly than before: Church or justification, unity or truth."[85]

Even back in 1969 this was no doubt already a simplification, and it points to a problem we have still not solved.[86] So although twenty-five years later, in 1994, the study "Church and Justification" was able to initiate a general rapprochement, nonetheless continuing differences in the relationship between salvation and the church remained.[87] This, in turn, led to the critical question of whether one really could be of one mind on the doctrine of justification as long as such an agreement did not also include church and table fellowship.

Before this argument is too self-righteously pursued by the Protestants, we should remind ourselves that cordial church relations between Lutherans and Reformed were only reached in 1974 through the Leuenberg Concord, and this although, as far as the doctrine of justification goes, there never were any differences about doctrinal accusations that split the church. The fact that the doctrine of justification was seen as "Master and Prince, Lord, Leader, and Judge over all kinds of doctrine,"[88] apparently could not prevent the churches remaining divided for more than 450 years on account of differences in eucharistic doctrine.

The peculiar blurring of distinctions between official doctrine and church practice belongs in this context too. People had long pointed to the "compensatory division of function between theology and praxis" regarding this question: "The Protestants proclaim justification through faith and are untiringly oriented against works righteousness; the Catholics represent justification by works and live out their faith."[89]

Undoubtedly, the blurring of distinctions between theory and praxis had to do with ecclesiological transmission of salvation. Through institutional and sacramental representations of grace, the Catholic Church, which had huge problems with the Lutheran teaching on assurance of faith, made its members more sure of their salvation than did the Protestant church, for whom this teaching represents a very important sticking point for the truth of the doctrine of justification, yet one that it leaves deliberately abstract out of a concern that the certainty of salvation would otherwise become determined and measured by particular "experiences."

But exactly because a person can't grant himself salvation, salvation cannot be experienced without the participation of other people who pass along the message of the gospel. Of course it is up for discussion whether this also assumes a certain institutional form of this "ecclesial transmission" and if so, what status this takes on in the salvation event. On this point, contemporary Catholic theology establishes that "the priority of divine action in the transmittal of grace must be preserved and remain the critical measure of ecclesiology. On the other hand, the social-ecclesial transmittal of the action of God (as 'mediated immediacy' of God to every person) should be critically enforced against all attempts to 'shortcut' this immediacy individualistically."[90]

We can find the critical function that the doctrine of justification realizes in these questions at those places in the New Testament where, in order to safeguard one's own ecclesial identity, others are excluded (Gal 2:11-14), where particular identity markers are insisted upon as necessary for salvation (Gal 3–5),[91] and where spiritual authority is supposedly given legitimacy by formal conditions or personal spiritual experiences (1 and 2 Corinthians).

Yet the significance of the doctrine of justification for ecclesiology is not exhausted with this critical function. It also has a creative power. Perhaps this has been remarked upon too little in Protestant circles, possibly because people truly thought they had to decide between church and justification.

- For church order the authority of the gospel is foundational. The apostles' authority is linked to it; apostolic tradition and succession were oriented by the transmission and guarding of the gospel. Yet this is intended to be not only a way of setting limits against a too formally conceived and preserved authority; it is also a challenge to so establish church order that it really gives the gospel opportunity to exercise its authority.
- Church and community are social outworkings of the gospel. The reality of reconciliation and acceptance by God also shapes interaction between people in communities and the ways in which they interact with those outside of the church. The constructive mutual aid of the different ministries and gifts is a consequence of justification by faith.
- Church is a community of the faithful. The personal aspects of the salvation event must influence the shape and life of the church just as much as the fact that faith always remains a gift. This is why the discussion about the doctrine of justification also has significance for the conversation between mainline churches and Free churches.

Social Duty

The controversial debate on the question concerning one's "participation" in the gospel raises a pressing question. Isn't the fact that these fights are always about basics and nuances indicative of the fact that the theology of the Western church has misunderstood the doctrine of justification too much as an "introspective conscience of the West"?[92] Isn't there a danger in this question about an inherent self-preoccupation, even where one decisively negates every possibility of participation and yet, even in negating things, turns it into the central theme?

On no account should the social demands that arise from the doctrine of justification be neglected. This is what the ecumenical theology of the young churches demands of us today. The Pauline focus of the texts on justification on the relationship between God and persons by no means excludes embracing in the proclamation and ministry of the church all that the Old Testament theology of justification says concerning the social effects of the revelation of God's righteousness.[93] When Paul calls upon the justified in Rom 6:12ff. to present their members as instruments of righteousness, he makes them "instrumental" in embodying and realizing God's social righteousness through their lives.

In light of a society in which more and more people are excluded from the possibility of living their lives with dignity, there is a particular challenge to inclusivity, an inclusivity grounded in the message of justification. Newer works of liberation theology rightly take this up.[94]

The most important question posed by the ecumenical preoccupation with the message of justification is this: Does this newly won common (or alternatively the tightly held own) doctrine of justification help us to find our way out of the permanent ecclesial or ecumenical self-preoccupation and instead to live out God's righteousness in this world and to pass along to others the revelation of this righteousness in Jesus Christ?

The Missionary Challenge

We once again find ourselves at the point that has attained decisive meaning for the Pauline teaching on justification. The fact that God's righteousness is revealed in the gospel of Jesus Christ gives this teaching the power to cross boundaries and touch everyone. It is no accident that this way of considering the matter had already helped the presence of God in the people of Israel attain salvific meaning for the peoples of the world.

This is why, if there is any agreement about the doctrine of justification, it is not only the question about inner concerns that are posed. What does this mean for the relationships between churches, particularly for their fellowship at the communion table? But what about those outside the church? What does this mean for joint proclamation of the gospel to the people of our society? Does it, in fact, become clear through this that the churches have become unified on this one point; that they live because of God's grace, and do they then consider this likewise to be the basis for all people's lives, a basis that should pervade and mark everything that happens in the church and through them?[95]

WHAT IS JUSTIFICATION? SUMMARIZING THESES

I will attempt in a few sentences to respond to the question of "What is justification?"

Justification is being set free to live. It is the gift of a new life, a life that finds its place and its goal in fellowship with God, a fellowship that becomes possible through God's word of judgment that deems us righteous.

Justification is being set free from death, being set free from the accusation of a failed life, and being set free from a deathly lack of relationship.

Justification is being set free from the delusion and anxiety that we have to justify or are even capable of justifying our own lives and accounting for their value and sense.

Justification is being set free to determine our own lives; it is being set free to live God's righteousness as God's mature sons and daughters.

Justification happens for Christ's sake: In his death God has borne away and overcome the burden and sorrow of our alienation from him.

Justification happens on account of faith: It happens wherever God opens people's hearts so that they embrace their lives and, full of trust, consider those lives to be good.

Justification opens us to the working of the Spirit and enables us to act in response to God's love, forgetting self and yet conscious of it, knowing that we have God to thank for everything.

Justification is an aspect of God's salvific action toward the whole world. God's gracious Yes, which believers hear in the word of the gospel, is also God's Yes to his whole world, a world that we proclaim as the basis of the biblical message, live out as the task of our lives in the world, and hope for as eschatological fulfillment.

To pass along this message, whether in a sermon, in conversation, or in the classroom, is the task of our proclamation of justification. It is our common theological responsibility to keep on giving the necessary clear shape to this message through carefully formulated and reflective teaching on justification. In conclusion then, ten theses regarding this task:[1]

1. The message of justification proclaims God, who in his saving faithfulness turns to all persons and speaks the Yes of his love to them.

The proclamation of justification by faith alone is the outworking of the self-revelation of God in Jesus Christ. It is not tied to a particular form of human questioning. We are bound to offer the gospel of God's justifying and saving actions in Jesus Christ to all, regardless of whether or not they ask for it. The question about a "gracious God" is not limited to the doubting of a fearful conscience in face of the threatening judgment of the Last Judgment. Correctly understood, it is the very question about God himself, at least insofar as it is not only the question about the ultimate creative and ordering power of the universe, but rather the question about a God who enters into a healing relationship with us.[2] But even if people no longer ask this question, we pass along to them the word that, in the person and history of Jesus of Nazareth, God has spoken the Yes of his love to them. The proclamation of justification is at one and the same time the proclamation of God and of salvation.

2. The message of justification calls people back to their real vocation of living in fellowship with God and relating responsibly to God.

The event of justification considers seriously how dignity and work arise in human life. It is responsible living. It is about responsibility in response to a gracious God who does not overburden anyone and yet asks each person to fulfill his or her potential. The significance of legal language with regard to the doctrine of justification lies not least in the fact that it holds fast to this aspect. Even if a secularized person no longer knows nor wants to know about responsibility toward God, nevertheless he is conscious of the particular responsibility people have for one another and for life on this planet, a responsibility that arises from the peculiar human capacity to both create and destroy. The law is written on the hearts even of contemporary people (Rom 2:15)!

The biblical message describes this fundamental characterization of human beings through people's destiny to be made in the image of God. God's justifying action points people back to this destiny.[3] For, after all, it is not only the being acquitted of sins committed that follows on the judgment of justification; what also follows is the taking up again of the relationship with God that had foundered and the recapturing of the dignity that God gave but people themselves squandered. The justification event not only does away with a disastrous past it also establishes a new forward-looking reality: the reality of a new creation in Christ and of being justified through him.[4] As a work of God's grace on and in a person, justification and sanctification cross over. Justification is a kind of rehabilitation, not in the sense that an innocent condemned person is rehabilitated, but rather that those who find themselves at the end of their capacities are enabled to serve God and in this way to live their own lives. God's justifying action provides the foundation of the true dignity of human existence and directs us anew toward our goal.

3. The message of justification uncovers the sources of humanity's failure: its incurable alienation from God and from themselves, through which sin becomes the determinative power in their lives. The message of justification at one and the same time proclaims the overcoming of this alienation through God's actions in Jesus Christ, who took upon himself the destructive power of sin and the consequences of humanity's enmity toward God and thus heals the relationship between humanity and God.

The connection between the theology of the cross and the message of reconciliation makes visible the totality of human lostness and at the same time witnesses to the radicality of the saving love of God. It is in this that the seriousness but also the wonderful depth of the justification event is grounded. After all, the message of reconciliation doesn't simply say to a person: "You're O.K." It says to him: "God accepts you, as you are, because in Christ he has taken upon himself everything in you that is unacceptable." It is only when they know that their lives are safe in the love of God that people can even recognize and grasp what is really going on in their lives. The transformative power of the justification event also lies in this liberating effect. It is the Pauline theology of the cross that above all emphatically underscores that through Christ's death we are not only liberated from the guilt of sin but also from its power (cf. Rom 3:23-26; 4:25; 5:12-21; 6:1-23; 8:3ff.). Because Christ, and therefore God's love, has become the center of their lives, people discover that they do not have to sin. They know, at one and the same time that they continue to be firmly entrenched in the paradoxical nature of human life that makes their lives open to the power of sin. But they also know that they no longer have to let themselves be torn asunder by this battle for power, but can be assured of forgiveness and can continually allow themselves to be led wherever God's love leads them.[5] In the face of a social reality in which destructive powers of sin exercise their death-dealing power, Christians are transformed into messengers and carriers of life that God gives them with his love.

4. In the justification event, people experience God accepting them unconditionally; they experience that he puts aside all that separates them from him and that God shapes their lives anew through his love. The fact that people are enabled to open themselves to these events and to accept God's actions in them is a miracle that God's Spirit causes through the word of proclamation (Gal 3:2-5; Rom 10:17). This miracle takes place through faith in Jesus Christ.

This reference to faith describes both the manner and the way in which people both accept and hold firm to salvation, particularly the fact that this happens completely without a person's "achievement."

Among the important and big steps on the way to regaining church unity is the fact that, in the meantime, a consensus really has been reached—with reference to *sola fide*—between the Lutheran and Roman Catholic churches.[6] In light of this, all the more do we owe people an explanation of what we understand by "faith." What needs to become clear as we explain it is that it's not a case of substituting some religious achievement in place of nonexistent good works, nor is it about a *sacrificium intellectus*, nor about making some big effort at obedience to the church's teaching. But it has to be equally obvious that faith is not simply an abstract circumscription for people's "doing nothing," where the person is, if possible, not at all involved, so as to preclude any notion of "participation." Faith is the trusting acceptance of what the gospel promises. Faith is about opening one's life to God's salvific promise. Faith is "creative receptivity and passivity"[7] and also therefore at the same time "actively lived grace."[8]

This is why the call to faith belongs inseparably to the message of justification and the persistent plea of "Be reconciled to God" to the transmission of the gospel.

5. The message of justification liberates people not only from the destructive pressure of justifying their lives through success, achievement, or material property but also from the deadly despair of thinking that without such self-justification one's life is useless, worthless, and senseless. Justification gives one a sense of identity, an identity that is grounded in God's acceptance.

In our society the question about justification by works seems to have died down. And yet our society is permeated with the conviction that the worth and meaning of human life is determined by what one does or achieves or has. This basic orientation of contemporary existence outwardly manifests itself in quite a secular fashion, but existentially it is a deeply religious phenomenon, a "last-ditch" questioning about the justification, the meaning, and the value of life. Many in our society experience quite painfully how decisions about life are made on the basis of achievement and success, and they suffer tremendously as a result of being written off by this society.

If it's true that such self-justification without and, in fact, against God is a consequence of sin as a result of which not only those who can't keep up go to their doom but also those who think they can justify their own lives, if this is true then our age needs no message quite so urgently as the sermon about justification by faith alone. It is vital that we explain step by step to the successful and to the unsuccessful, to the contented and to those who doubt and despair that it means to accept life in God; it means being set free to enjoy a life that is not the "product" of one's doing or that founders on unfulfilled achievements but one that is grounded by God's love toward us. "This way, one's own life story becomes a place in which justification comes into its own and simultaneously frees persons from self-justification and self-realization."[9]

The message of justification at the same time contains a plaidoyer for the worth of each human life before God, no matter whether a person has already realized this in faith or not. To God there is no life that is "unworthy of life."

6. The proclamation of justification occurs in service of the border-crossing power of the gospel; it can be reformulated over and over again as we tell people that God's faithfulness and love apply to them, no matter the ecclesiological, religious, social, ethnic, or cultural borders we have to cross.

Remembering Paul's saying that God is not only a God of the Jews but also of the Gentiles (Rom 3:29), these days we need to reflect together what it means that God is not only a God of the Christians but also wants to be God of Buddhists, Muslims, and atheists. Paul did not come up with his statement as a result of some pluralistic theory of religions that sees the truth of God represented in all religions. He held firm to the singularity of God's revelation in Jesus Christ, yet tried at the same time to overcome the linkage of God's salvific deeds to human prescriptions and to break through all the current human ascriptions of what constituted clean or unclean areas. The effect of the gospel is also not limited to the sociocultural conditions of traditional Christianity. Among the most important ecumenical challenges for the doctrine of justification is to continually discover anew and to trust in its border-crossing power.

7. The gospel of God's righteous actions in Jesus Christ has a social form. It was responsible for convening a community of persons who were led to one another because they live by God's

Word and by the presence of Christ in his supper. They welcome one other despite their differences because God in Christ welcomed them (Rom 15:7). They keep their promises to one another even though they must also say No to particular ways in which they each behave.[10]

The justification even is the basis of a social structure whose most important feature is its inclusivity (Gal 3:28). Its external feature is its table fellowship. Anyone who abstains offends against the truth of the gospel (Gal 2:11-14). So there cannot be any real consensus regarding the questions about the doctrine of justification unless one side includes the other in eucharistic fellowship or at least offers them hospitality. To insist on this is not only a question of the inner logic of the gospel but rather also a matter of the credibility of our common proclamation to those beyond our fellowship circle. We share an ecumenical responsibility for the gospel; this responsibility must also be proved by the teaching on justification always wanting to show itself as a critical force opposing all efforts to tie the existence of the church of Jesus Christ to particular constitutional structures. For the church to be the church of Jesus Christ, it must remain tied to the gospel, and this tie creates life in the church that is made up of a community of different people who have become one through the call of Christ and through being graced by God's Spirit.

From this follows that:

- the church is a community of those who believe and are called. This call, that places the entire being of a person in personal fellowship with God, also strives for a person's committed and engaged membership in a particular congregation. But because faith is a gift, an unforced response to God's call, the church is always also a community of believers and seekers.
- the church is a church of the poor, the despised, and those who have been pushed to the edges. But it is also precisely because of this that the church offers space for all, without regard to their origin or income.
- seen from the outside, the church is an "earthen vessel," characterized by persecution, troubles, fears, weakness, and despair, but precisely because of these things, also ever anew an

159

instrument of grace. Through the church, people experience the beauty of God and the warmth of brotherly and sisterly love.

• the church is a mission, a living expression of how the gospel continually crosses borders to others and shares with them life and the gospel (1 Thess 2:8).

8. The message of justification places the justified in a life in which the anxiety about one's own worth has been taken away and one is freed for lovingly caring for others. The commandment about love of neighbor becomes a possibility that is realized with gratitude, a chance to live out this newly created existence that has been given by God in fellowship with one another, a chance to experience the life-giving power with which God has permeated this new existence.

There is no additional attribute of human behavior that describes how faith becomes effective through love (Gal 5:6), only the way in which faith allows itself to become a part of God's action. For this reason, "participating" in salvation can never be understood as something extra or added on to God's action, but rather as an active embrace into the work of God.[11]

"Co-workers with God," those who help with what God does, are those Christians who, by preaching, building up community, or by offering deeds of kindness, work to bring salvation to others (cf. 1 Cor 3:9-14). Justification does not preclude such "assistance" toward salvation but, in fact, assumes it. For there is no more believable form of accepting or treasuring another person than to say to her that she is needed. It is for this reason that for Paul's being taken into service for the sake of the gospel, and being gifted and called despite having been a persecutor, is the most profound expression of the justification of the ungodly (1 Cor 15:9ff.; Gal 1:15ff.; Rom 12:3-8). Here, in the discussion of ministry, one can also speak of recognition, reward, or praise from God as an expression of the enduring responsibility before God (1 Cor 3:13; 4:5); and yet in this context there is no "payment" to which we have a right or for which we enforce God's recognition and valuation of our lives. After all, what is so liberating and fortunate about this kind of "participation" in salvation is precisely that those who have been justified no longer have to worry about their own salvation. It is because of this that they can be so happy and grateful about what God is doing in their lives.[12] The fact that the almighty God needs co-workers, whom he does not select on the basis of human capacities of ability and endurance, might indeed be an important refinement of the message of justification for our time.

9. The message of justification draws into service of the life-affirming righteousness of God the fact that God has created and sustains everything that serves such life. This includes basic critique of all systems and ways of relating that show disrespect toward life.

The doctrine of justification cannot be translated into direct political instructions for use. But because the doctrine does nothing but make God's righteousness applicable to all, it will have social repercussions in those instances when rights of life and space for God's creatures must be protected and newly won.[13] In cases of conflict, this can have very significant political consequences.

Seen from the perspective of the whole Bible, the depravity of human existence in all its various dimensions is the arena for God's justifying action and the revelation of his righteousness. And so the matter of justification opens up not only with regard to humanity's guilt but also more generally with regard to the suffering of the world, "hurting life, hurting society, and hurting nature."[14] The Old Testament legacy of teaching on justification, its concern about the integrity of society that depends on a legal system imbued with social responsibilities, has a continuing critical and constructive function. Where it is not misused as a path to salvation, God's commandment can regain its original meaning as a sign to living rightly.

The justification event straightaway puts the justified into the process of God's justification, whose righteousness is put in question. The fact that God examines the justified in light of all the depravity in Jesus Christ through his sympathy with and in this world also determines the path of those who live as a result of his righteousness. "The doctrine of justification does not attribute all the guilt for the evil and suffering of the world to people. Rather, the doctrine challenges people to face up to God's brotherly judgment and—without fear of judgment and punishment—to own up to their own part in humanity's history of depravity."[15]

10. The message of justification gives us certainty that the path that God in Jesus Christ has taken ahead of us into life, suffering, and death fills our emptiness of God, thereby conquers death, and will lead us through him into a final, perfect communion with God.

God's Yes to us is the underlying reason for our existence. This is true even beyond death. Justification is life. And therefore justification leads to hope, a hope that is not restricted to our own lives but, at the same time, includes hope for the redemption of the entire creation (Rom 8:18ff.). The justification of the ungodly is an expression of the creative energy of God, an energy that creates from nothing and thus at the same is the basis of our hope in the One who gives life to the dead (Rom 4:17).

NOTES

Chapter 1: The Contemporary Question

1. In E. Wilkens, ed., *Helsinki 1963* (Berlin und Hamburg: Lutherisches Verlagshaus, 1964), 456.

2. Lutheran World Federation and the Roman Catholic Church, *Joint Declaration on the Doctrine of Justification*, English language edition (Grand Rapids: Eerdmans, 2000), 25.

3. Ibid., 42.

4. Compare J. Reumann, *Righteousness*; E. P. Sanders, *Paul, the Law*; K. W. Niebuhr, M. Seifrid, *Justification*, 6-76; ibid., *Christ, Our Righteousness*; K. W. Niebuhr, "Rechtfertigungslehre"; D. A. Carson, P. T. O'Brien, M. A. Seifrid, *Justification and Variegated Nomism*; S. J. Gathercole, *Where Is Boasting?*; S. Westerholm, *Perspectives Old and New*; J. D. G. Dunn, *New Perspective*.

Chapter 2: Righteousness Is Life: The Old Testament

1. J. Scharbert, "Gerechtigkeit I," *TRE* 12, 1984, 405; F. Horst, "Gerechtigkeit Gottes II," *RGG* 3 II, 1958, 1403.

2. Hebrew: bsædæq; cf. also Isa 11:4; Pss 9:8; 72:2; 96:13; 98:9. Two words in Hebrew that are related and close in meaning and yet different correspond to the English words *justice* and *righteousness*: sædæq (m.) is an abstraction and first and foremost describes the quality and principle of an action and is used in contexts "that are about correctness and order" (also "to judge in sædæq"); sdaqa (f.), on the other hand, describes an action itself, the doing of it and the "the actions in which righteousness is manifested" (cf. B. Johnson, "sadaq," *ThWAT* 6, 1989, 912; F. Crüsemann, "Jahwes Gerechtigkeit," 431ff.). K. Koch wants to ascribe even more divine action to sädäq and to see in sdaqa the consequences of human behavior (K. Koch, *Sädäq und Ma'at*, 59).

3. Compare also Isa 5:23; 29:21; Ps 82:2-4.

4. H. Cremer, *Biblico-theological Lexicon*, 191-93.

5. Compare K. H Fahlgren, sedaka; K. Koch, sdq; G. v. Rad, *Old Testament Theology I*, 383-98.

6. This is the accurate translation; cf. with H. J. Boecker, *Redeformen*, 127.

7. K. Koch, "Wesen und Ursprung," 110.

8. Compare Jer 22:3; Prov 31:8. On the king's function in matters of justice, compare H. J. Boecker, *Law and the Administration of Justice*; H. Niehr, *Rechtsprechung*, 66-83.

9. Compare with Wildberger, *Isaiah 1–12*, 189-90.

10. On this, cf. with G. Liedke, spt, *THAT II*, 1005. On the topic of the frequent com-

bination of justice and righteousness (mispat and saedaeq/s'daqa) that occurs more than eighty times in the Old Testament, see B. Johnson, *ThWAT* 6, 907f.; E. Otto, "Recht," *TRE* 28, 204. Moreover, it is striking how often matters of payment of wages and pledge appear in this connection; cf. Deut 24:10-18; Job 22:6; Ezek 18:7.

11. On the formation of the text compare H. W. Wolff, *Amos*, 271. Compare also Amos 6:12 and Isa 5:7: "[H]e [Jahweh] expected justice, but saw bloodshed; righteousness, but heard a cry!" On the general topic compare K. Koch, "Die Enstehung der sozialen Kritik."

12. Compare Isa 1:17; Mic 6:8; H. J. Stoebe, *tob*, *THAT I*, 659-61; Koch, op. cit., 163: The "justice" (mispat) of the people "is, according to this, something like the behavior based on community faithfulness and appropriateness...that is, the basis of the community which is to be appreciated day by day, basically its cultic, political, and economic existence itself."

13. Compare with Prov 11:30; 12:28; and 14:34 among others.

14. Compare with Prov 21:3: "To do righteousness and justice is more acceptable to the LORD than sacrifice."

15. Compare Isa 9:6-7; Jer 23:5-6.

16. Compare Wildberger, *Isaiah 28–39*, 264; see also, Ps 85:9-13.

17. Compare also Ps 33:5; 99:4.

18. Compare Mic 6:5d, "that you may know the saving acts of the LORD," and 1 Sam 12:7, "and I will declare to you all the saving deeds of the LORD" [in both instances the plural of righteousness is used!], and also in Deut 33:21b, "he executed the justice of the LORD, and his ordinances for Israel."

19. Righteousness and justice as the foundation of God's throne and majesty can also be found in Pss 89:14 and 103:17-19. (Concerning kings and righteousness see Prov 16:12 and 25:5.)

20. Thus H. H. Schmid. *Gerechtigkeit als Weltordnung*, 166. For a discussion of Schmid's thesis, cf. Crüsemann, "Jahwes Gerechtigkeit," 428ff., and J. Assmann, *Ma'at*, 31-5, who suggests replacing the formula "righteousness as world order" with "world order as righteousness" (34) following Egyptian presuppositions and who identifies Ma'at emphatically as "connective righteousness," as "considerateness (...) that binds people together by bringing about responsibility and trust" (91; cf. also 163).

21. On conjectures that the (demythologized) conception of a Canaanite deity saedaeq could be at the root of this idiom, cf. Schmid, op. cit., 75, and particularly K. Koch, "Die hebräische Sprache," 44-50.

22. Compare 65:5; 71:2; 143:1, 11; see further 69:14, 17.

23. Compare Ps 71:14ff., 19, 24, but also Pss 22, 33; see also, Crüsemann, 440-43, on the whole tradition complex, and Schmid, 144ff.

24. Compare Ps 31:15, 18; Ps 35:1, 11; and Ps 71:9, a psalm that shows how the weakness of old age also leads one to be socially and legally without assistance.

25. Pss 40:12; 51:3-16; 143:1ff. (cf. also Ps 103).

26. Crüsemann, "Jahwes Gerechtigkeit," 442.

27. Crüsemann, 443.

28. Crüsemann (op. cit.) clashes with H. Graf Reventlow's *Rechtfertigung* in wanting to avoid the term "justification" precisely because it "is confusing rather than clarifying." However, I think there is some urgency about using the term because it highlights the actual process, and the term thus gains biblical breadth.

29. Compare Ps 69:13, "But as for me, my prayer is to you, O LORD. At an acceptable time, O God, in the abundance of your steadfast love, answer me." Ps 40:10ff.: "I have not hidden your saving help [literally: righteousness] within my heart, I have spoken of your faithfulness and your salvation; I have not concealed your steadfast love and your faithfulness from the great congregation. Do not, O LORD, withhold your mercy from me; let your steadfast love and your faithfulness keep me safe forever." See further Pss 51:1; 103:6-8; and especially Dan 9:16-18!

30. Compare Pss 4:1; 18:1-24; for a different emphasis, see Job 27:5ff., 35:1. On Ps 7, compare B. Janowski, "JHWH der Richter."

31. H. Graf Reventlow, *Rechtfertigung*, 92. Compare G. Barbiero's survey in *Psalmbuch*; the one praying cannot fulfill the conditions of Ps 24; he therefore confesses in Ps 25: "He can only be righteous if JHWH forgives him his sin. His righteousness, one could affirm with Paul, comes from his faith, i.e., from his trust in God's mercy" (Ps 25:21). It is in this context that the declaration of integrity in Ps 26:1 should be considered: "It is a case of someone who has become justified through the forgiveness of his sins" (360).

32. H. J. Kraus, *Psalms 1–59*, 173. Reventlow, op. cit., 91; "What the righteousness of the righteous" is about is "in no way about a quality that emanates from a person of his own doing, but rather about a gift that he receives only as a member of the congregation through the care of God, as a beneficiary of God's righteousness" (re Ps 5:8, 12); also cf. Ps 89:16ff.

33. K. Koch, "Hebräische Sprache," 50.

34. W. H. Schmidt, "Werk Gottes," 27

35. The so-called Jahweh-King Psalms: 47, 93, 96–99.

36. Compare Pss 82:8; 96:13; see further, G. Liedke, art. "sapat," ThWAT 8, 425.

37. Isaiah 43:14-21; 48:20ff.; 49:8-12; 51:9-11; 52:1-6.

38. H. J. Hermisson, *Deuterojesaja*, 7.

39. Compare Isa 51:1-8 (esp. 4-6); 42:4-6.

40. H.-J. Kraus, *Jesaja 40-66*, 131.

41. I understand Isa 56–66 to be a discrete composition.

42. Crüsemann, "Jahwehs Gerechtigkeit," 447; further, he says, "In tradition-historical terms, two heretofore distinct ways of speaking about sdaqa become amalgamated here: the demand for human sdaqa so familiar from Wisdom and the Prophets is combined with what the individual experiences in worship and becomes, as Deutero-Issaiah says, the universal and eschatological sdaqa of Yahweh's salvation."

43. Compare Isa 61:10ff.; 62:1ff., and the parallel tradition of Hos 2:18-20.

44. Compare L. Köhler, *Hebrew Man*, 127-50; H. J. Boecker, *Redeformen*; ibid., *Law and the Administration of Justice*; H. Niehr, *Rechsprechung*.

45. Compare Ruth 4:1-12; there was no basic difference between a civil and a criminal case. Compare Jer 26:10-19.

46. Compare Boecker, *Redeformen*, 122ff., and the oft-cited saying by Köhler, "To judge means here [for the Hebrew legal community] to settle" (op. cit., 133).

47. H. J. Boecker, *Redeformen*, 124.

48. The NRSV translates even in Proverbs 24:24: "You are innocent," describing how we would say it, but not how the Hebrews spoke.

49. H. J. Boecker, *Redeformen*, 132.

50. K. Koch, "Wesen und Ursprung," 113.

51. Koch, *op cit*.

52. Compare Neh 9:33: "You have been just in all that has come upon us, for you have dealt faithfully and we have acted wickedly." See similarly Dan 9:14b.

53. It is, perhaps, hinted at in Dan 12:1-2.

54. Compare G. v. Rad, "Gerechtigkeit" und "Leben," 225-47; K. Koch, "Tempeleinlassliturgien," 169-83. H. Spieckermann in *Heilsgegenwart*, 201ff., A.13, is skeptical about this classification of genre.

55. Compare Ps 24:3-5; Deut 26:12-15; Isa 33:15ff.; and Ezek 18:2-9. All the texts quite impressively witness to the fact that there is no fundamental rift between cultic purity and social uprightness.

56. Spieckermann, op. cit., 204, here translates sdaqa as "justification."

57. Thus Koch, op cit., 182.

58. Compare the former principle in Exod 20:5ff.; 32:7.

59. Compare W. Zimmerli, "Leben" und "Tod," 186. See similarly H. Ringgren, "hajah," *ThWAT2*, 885: "einvollwertiges, reiches und glückliches Leben führen" (trans.: to live a fulfilled, rich, and happy life).

60. Compare K. Koch, "Vergeltungsdogma" and, summarizing the critique, B. Janowski, "Die Tat kehrt zum Täter zurück" (on which also see again Koch, *Sadaq-Ma-at*, 57f.).

61. J. Ebach, "Hiob," *TRE* 15, 367.

62. G. v. Rad, *Old Testament Theology* 1, 379. J. Schreiner ("Deklaratorische Formel," [esp. 285]) is critical of accepting a declaration formula.

63. On this understanding of the Hebrew term hæsæd, cf. H.-J. Stoebe, "hæsæd," *THAT* I, 600-621; H.-J. Zobel. *ThWAT* 3, 48-71 (esp. 56ff.).

64. Compare Hos 10:12; Ps 24:5; Prov 21:21.

65. Compare G. v. Rad, "Anrechnung"; W. Schottroff, "hsb," *THAT* I, 645.

66. H. H. Schmid, "Gerechtigkeit und Glaube," 408.

67. Ibid., similarly, D. Michel, "Ansehen des Glaubens," 113; yet M. Oeming ("Genesis 15:6," 182-97) proposes a completely different interpretation; R. Mosis, "'Glauben' und 'Gerechtigkeit,'" 225-57; H. D. Preuss, *Old Testament Theology* II, 160-65.

68. In contrast to H. Gross, "Rechtfertigung," 20.

69. Compare R. Stahl, "Die glaubenden Gerechten," 250: In faith "is seen the reason for righteousness. Israel wins its identity as a 'people' thanks to justification which accrues to Israel through God in correlation to Israel's close linking of its livelihood to God."

70. Schmid, op. cit., 408.

71. Compare also Pss 79:10; 115:2; Joel 2:17—as a question of the heathens.

72. Compare Ps 79:10-12 (and Rev 6:10!); also, on this, see Reventlow, *Rechtfertigung*, 101f.

73. Ch. Levin, "Altes Testament und Rechtfertigung," 168ff.

74. Regarding this, see L. Perlitt, "Anklage und Freispruch Gottes;" and Ch. Levin, op. cit., who writes: "One can understand late Old Testament theology with a grain of salt as teaching on justification—with the difference that in the New Testament the justification of *persons* is in the foreground, whereas in the Old Testament it is the justification of God" (169).

75. On the differing judgments on these expressions, compare H.-J. Hermisson, "Diskussionsworte."

76. Literally, "The way of the Lord is not just" (Ezek 33:17; 18:25).

77. Jeremiah 31:29; Ezek 18:2; cf. Lam 5:7: "Our ancestors sinned; they are no more, and we bear their iniquities."

78. Isaiah 40:27. Here "way" means the fate of the people (cf. 48:17).

79. Compare v. 25. Crüsemann, "Jahwes Gerechtigkeit," 445f.

80. Understood in this sense, v. 23 is taken up again in Rom 14:11 and Phil 2:10ff.

81. Compare Niehr, *ThWAT* 8, 417, and Boecker's observation in *Redeformen*, 135, that there is no "speech to the guilty that corresponds to the positive judgment" ("You are guilty") handed down in the Old Testament.

82. This point is among the most disputed questions of our theme. Although von Rad (*Old Testament Theology* I, 377) and K. Koch (*THAT* II, 518) explain that a "punitive righteousness" would be a contradiction in terms, others prefer not to totally exclude this option (Reventlow, *Rechtfertigung*, 36; J. Scharbert, *TRE*, 409). That having been said, there are only three or four places where sdq could possibly be construed as being an expression for a punishing righteousness: Isa 5:16; 10:22; (28:17); Zeph 3:22. What is far more commonly used to describe condemnatory judging is sft, cf. H. Niehr, *ThWAT* 8, 426f.; Liedke, *THAT* II, 1002, 1006.

83. In this sense, God's anger is "something downright necessary" (C. Westermann, "Boten des Zorns," 153), and to a certain extent the negative counterpart to God's righteousness (Ps 103:6, 9). God's anger can be an expression of God's "judgment," but not of his righteousness. Compare Dan 9:16: "O Lord, in view of all your righteous acts, let your anger and wrath, we pray, turn away."

84. On this assumption, cf. H. Gese, "Atonement."

85. "Double [punishment]!" means Yahweh repays the full term, i.e., double for all her sins, namely first for the sin itself and second, the legally appropriate replacement for damage done. Yahweh has allowed Israel to repay her debts "fully according to the law and justice" (Elliger, *Dtjes*, 16).

86. Thus also K. Seybold, "Gericht Gottes, I," *TRE* 12, 1984, 462ff.

87. On this connection between v. 25 and v. 28, cf. Elliger.

88. On this, see B. Janowski, "Auslösung des verwirkten Lebens."

89. The term, "offering for sin," is confusing: the word asam refers not to a cultic sacrifice but to an "obligation of debt"; cf. R. Knierium, "asam," *THAT* I, 251-57; B. Janowski, "Er trug unsere Sünden."

90. B. Janowksi, op. cit., 19f., describes the process in this way: Yahweh "allows an alien process of deed—effect—consequence to be so expressed in the servant of God that the actual guilty party—meaning Israel—takes on the position of the one saved—while the innocent party breaks apart in the process."

91. On this, see Janowski, op. cit., 20. On the theological level, this interaction between distance from and acceptance of one's own guilt has something to do with the scapegoat motif, with which Isa 53 traditio-historically had no connection.

92. The term "the many" seems to be consciously multivalent. One has to see it as having a double meaning: "Because Israel returns to Yahweh through the servant, therefore Yahweh's plan will succeed, and thus the peoples also come to salvation" (H.-J. Hermission, "Der Lohn des Knechts," 287). Surprisingly, hardly any interpretations of Isa 53 attempt to explain the exact meaning of the quite singular connection between standing in for someone and justification (but cf. J. Blank, "Gottesknecht," 72-74; B. Johnson, *ThWAT* 6, 921f.).

93. Daniel 12:3, "those who lead many to righteousness" is not of parallel content to Isa 53:11b. Compare W. Zimmerli, "Alttestamentliche Prophetie," 590.

94. The original version of a "judgment doxology" (German: "Gerichtsdoxologie") in

a legal process is found in Josh 7:19 where Joshua says to Achan: "My son, give glory to the LORD God of Israel and make confession to him. Tell me now what you have done." On this cf. G. v. Rad, *Old Testament Theology* I, 358.

95. Compare W. Zimmerli, "Altestamentliche Prophetie," 585ff.; R. Stahl, "Die glaubenden Gerechten," 247f.

96. G. Braulik has explored this development into a doctrine of justification in "Gesetz als Evangelium"; and "Development of the Doctrine of Justification."

97. However, 9:4-6 is one place that Braulik, along with N. Lohfink, characterizes as "the closest terminological and topical parallels to the Pauline justification texts" in the Old Testament ("Gesetz," 147), particularly the negative of "Not on account of our righteousness." There is a lack of any positive indication of God's righteousness; it can be found in Deut 7:7ff.: "It was not because you were more numerous than any other people that the LORD set his heart on you and chose you....It was because the LORD loved you."

98. Compare Ps 130:3: "If you, O LORD, should mark iniquities, Lord, who could stand?"

99. Compare Reventlow, *Rechtfertigung*, 100f.

100. Verse 5: "Indeed, I was born guilty, a sinner when my mother conceived me," is no confirmation of a kind of "original sin," but probably for a "total depravity which is determinative for humans from the beginning" (Kraus, *Psalms 1–59*, 503).

101. Kraus, op. cit., 504. It is noteworthy that the word br' is used here as well for creating, when it is usually only used of God's creative actions.

102. H. J. Kraus, *Theology of the Psalms*, 157: "The justification of the ungoldly [sic] is made known." Compare Rom 4:5.

103. Psalm 32 gives an example of such a confession. Now compare this with Barbiero's *Psalmbuch*, 435.

104. In contrast, cf. J. Becker, *Heil Gottes*; O. Betz, "Rechtfertigung in Qumran."

105. Compare also 1QH 19:17ff.: "And I know [that] righteousness is Thine"; 1QH 20 (Vermes, 288): "For Thou art just and none can oppose Thee" (Vermes, 292). Translation of Qumran texts follows G. Vermes, *Complete Dead Sea Scrolls*.

106. On the translation of mispat (justice), cf. J. Becker, op. cit., 122ff., who prefers to say "salvation help" or "salvation status" rather than "justification."

107. Compare J. Becker, 277ff.

108. O. Hofius, "Das vierte Gottesknechtslied," 421; H. Gross, "'Rechtfertigung,'" 27.

109. J. Wellhausen, *Israelitische und jüdische Geschichte*, 204; similarly, see Ch. Levin, "Altes Testament und Rechtfertigung," 172ff.; in a more differentiated voice, see Perlitt, "Anklage und Freispruch Gottes," 300.

110. Compare Isa 40:27, the people's complaint: "My way is hidden from the LORD, and my right is disregarded by my God."

111. Job 34:12; cf. 8:3, and the depiction of the sinners' fate (15:20ff.; 18:5ff.; 20:4ff.). Even Job thinks in this way, only he comes to the opposite conclusion.

112. Compare 4:17; 15:14; 25:4 (and see Ps 143:2). Job partly adopts this argument as his own—albeit with an ironic undertone! A human cannot be just before God, for "one could not answer [God] once in a thousand" (9:2ff.).

113. On this, see J. Ebach, *Streiten mit Gott*, XIII: "For it's not just a matter of *what* is said but rather of *who* says it, *from what position* he says it, *to whom*, in what position he says it, and *when* he says it. When Job and his friends say the same thing, it doesn't necessarily mean the same thing, and when the friends say and predict the *right* thing,

nonetheless it's not necessarily true for the person suffering in this position." Or ibid., "Hiob/ Hiobbuch." *TRE* 15, 1986, 368: What the friends say "remain *truths* told by whose *not affected* and hence only *correct words.*"

114. Compare H. Gese, "Lebenssinn," 168-72; G. v. Rad, *Old Testament Theology* I, 414.

115. Compare Job 9:14-20, 31-35; 13:14-19; 16:18-22; 23:3-9.

116. Compare 7:21; 9:2; 14:4.

117. Compare the depiction of his uprightness in chs. 29 and 31, which is summarized in the expression: "I put on righteousness, and it clothed me; my justice was like a robe and a turban" (29:14; cf. Isa 11:5; 59:7; 61:10; Ps 132:9).

118. In Job 2:3 God praises Job to Satan for continuing to hold fast to his "integrity," meaning his integrity before God, is one of the few literary brackets between the narrative framing and the Job poem (cf. 2:9). Most translators don't show this connection, a connection that hints that Job's sentence is not simply a fitting self-justification but represents his holding fast to the judgment of God!

119. J. Ebach, *Streiten mit Gott*, 142.

120. Compare R. Kessler, "I know that my redeemer lives."

121. Compare 9:14 (following Ebach): "How then can I answer him, choosing my words with him? Though I am innocent, I cannot answer him; I must appeal for mercy to my accuser."

122. Ebach, *TRE* 15, 370.

123. G. Fohrer, *Hiob*, 536.

124. Gese, "Lebenssinn," 168ff.; cf. also W. Zimmerli, *Old Testament Theology in Outline*, 164, on 19:25: "Thus Job stands here as a dead man, but he knows there is one who will take up his cause even after death and demand his rights."

125. Ebach, *TRE* 15, 364, countering Gese's (op. cit.) altogether too strident emphasis on the transcendence of God's fellowship.

126. In this connection, R. Kessler points to the social implications of the institution of redeemer. Whoever claims a redeemer "thereby admits that he himself is at his wit's end." In naming God his "redeemer," Job "admits to God and to himself that he is standing there with empty hands" (op. cit., 151).

127. Compare Job 1:9; on this see Ebach, *Streiten*, 13; Kessler, op. cit., 146ff.

128. R. Stahl, "Die glaubenden Gerechten," 246.

129. Op. cit., 246f.

130. I use the term "Hebrew Bible" not because the term "Old Testament" seems problematic but because much of what I will be saying in this section is true first and foremost of the original Hebrew text of the Old Testament, but not of its Greek translation, the Septuagint.

131. In contrast, compare the Egyptian conception of the death trial. Here, justification means both being exonerated and being transformed into a "living god" and being taken up into an other-worldly realm "without fight and turmoil" (J. Assmann, *Ma'at*, 130, 135ff.; cf. also the similarities between the declarations of innocence in the Book of the Dead and Ezek 18, esp. the liturgies surrounding the entrance into the temple; op. cit., 146ff.).

132. In suggesting this I am trying to conflate the perspectives of K. Koch (for example, in *THAT* II, 516 ff.) and J. Scharbert (*TRE* 12, 404-11).

133. Compare Isa 56:1 as a way of connecting the message of Second and Third Isaiah.

134. To compare what Ps 24–26 and 32ff. say about forgiveness and the gift of righteousness, see Barbiero, *Psalmbuch*, 360, 435ff.

135. K. Koch, "Rechtfertigung I," *EKL III*, 1959, 472; cf. ibid., *THAT II*, 520: "A sdaqa gifting of a rasa, in other words, a 'justification of the ungodly' is not only unthinkable in the Psalms but in the entire Old Testament."

136. Compare Braulik, "Gesetz," 151; O. Hofius, "Rechtfertigung," 132.

137. Compare Exod 23:7; Prov 17:15; 24:24; Isa 5:23. In contrast, Hofius (op. cit., 56) argues that these texts deal only with " human law."

138. H. Graf Reventlow, *Rechtfertigung*, 100f. Compare Ps 25:8: "Good and upright is the LORD; therefore he instructs sinners in the way."

139. See W. H. Schmidt, "Rechtfertigung," 157; O. Hofius, op. cit., 132; Reventlow, *Rechtfertigung*. Also cf. Preuss, *Old Testament Theology* II, 184, and F. L. Hossfeld's survey in "Gedanken."

140. Hofius, op. cit., 136.

141. Compare Reventlow, *Rechtfertigung*, 60f.

142. Reventlow, op. cit., 62.

143. This is hinted at in Isa 45:22-24a and 51:4-6.

144. On this, cf. Ps 73:26 and H. Gese, "Death in the Old Testament," 41-59.

145. On "justification" in the judgment of the dead, cf. J. Assmann, Ma'at, 130ff.

146. Compare P. Stuhlmacher, *Gerechtigkeit Gottes*, 145-84; K. Kertelge, *Rechtfertigung*, 15-32.

147. 1 Enoch 91:12 (following S. Uhlig, *JSHRZ* V, 6, 713); cf. 51:2: "He will choose from among them the righteous and the holy, for the day on which they will be saved has come"; further, see 61ff. and 100ff.

148. Wintermute, "Jubilees," 102. The text of 5:13-18 describes the judgment in greater detail.

149. 1 Enoch 93:4ff.; 99:2 (on this, see Ziesler, *Meaning of Righteousness*, 95ff.). The theology of the Qumran group manifests a similar overall relationship between election and obedience to the Law; cf. Becker, *Heil*, 125.

150. Compare Klaiber, *Rechtfertigung und Gemeinde*, 258-64.

151. The English translation of these texts follows the NRSV, whereas the German edition follows J. Schreiner, *JSHRZ*, V, 4.

152. Stuhlmacher (*Gerechtigkeit Gottes*, 173) compares this saying with that of Jas 2. Sanders (*Palestinian Judaism*, 409) is of the opinion that in 2 Esd the Jewish faith was made into "religion of individual self-righteousness" and "legalistic perfection."

153. This is established by the fact that he has "found favor" and "been accounted righteous" (12:7) but also by the fact that he has "a treasure of works stored up with the Most High" (7:77).

154. Compare also the rabbinic understanding of Torah obedience, as the Way to Life, in which present and end-time salvation are seen as one (F. Avemarie, *Tora und Leben*, 578-83).

155. Compare C. H. Dodd, *Bible* 42-59; D. Hill, *Greek Words*, 98-109; J.A. Ziesler, *Righteousness*, 52-69. Following Hill's lead, the Septuagint translates 462 of a possible 476 cases of words that have the word stem sdq with words having the word stem dikai- (Ziesler sees the proportion as being 449 to 481).

156. Compare, for example, "to judge with justice" (Lev 19:15) with "to judge with righteousness" (Ps 96:13; Isa 11:4). See J. Fitzmyer, "Romans," 257ff.

157. Compare A. Dihle, "Gerechtigkeit," *RAC* 10, 1978, 257f.

158. Thus Dodd, op. cit., 42.

159. R. Baumann, *Gottes Gerechtigkeit*, 55f.; E. Jüngel, *Justification*, 57-62.

160. Compare Dihle, op. cit., 240ff., Luke 1:75; and Eph 4:23.

161. *Eleos* and *eleēmosyne*; cf. Pss 24:5; 33:5; 103:6.

162. Compare Gen 19:19; 20:13, etc.; Hill, op. cit., 106.

163. Compare C. H. Dodd, *Bible*, 48-50.

164. The uncertainty about how to translate Sir 42:2 hints at this difficulty. Is what is meant: "of rendering judgment to acquit the ungodly" (as translated by the NRSV, following the underlying Hebrew text) or "to punish the guilty one, or in any case not to acquit him" (thus Sauer, *JSHRZ*, following the meaning of the Greek text).

165. On this, see Ziesler, *Righteousness*, 67-69.

Chapter 3: Justification Is Freedom: The New Testament

1. Thus H. Wolff, *Neuer Wein*, 84.

2. All examples of the use of the term "righteousness (of God)" are found in Matthew. When compared with the other Synoptic Gospels, these instances are found to be typical of his theological interpretation (cf. 3:15; 5:6, 10, 20; 6:33).

3. In this, the summaries of his proclamation in Matt 4:17 and Mark 1:14ff. are certainly in the right, even if they are redactionally formulated (compare to the original wording in Matt 10:7; Luke 10:9, 11). On the whole topic, cf. E. Zenger/A. Lindemann, "Herrschaft/Reich Gottes" II, IV, *TRE 15*, 1986, 176-89; 196-218; H. Merklein, *Jesu Bostschaft*; J. Becker, *Jesus*; R. Baumann, *Gottes Gerechtigkeit*, 205-24; E. Jüngel, *Paulus und Jesus*.

4. O. Camponovo, *Königtum*, esp. 443-46.

5. On this, cf. J. Becker, *Johannes der Täufer*; ibid., *Jesus*, 33-83.

6. In contrast to Matt 5:3, Luke 6:20 has preserved the original form of the Beatitude. This is also true of the form of the formulation in the second person (thus J. Becker, *Jesus*, 157-58).

7. Compare Stuhlmacher, *Biblische Theologie*, 72. In the final analysis this is also true of the Old Testament spirituality of poverty itself. By "the poor and the suffering" are meant those people "whose external circumstances force them to expect everything from God, and whose inner disposition is such that they really do expect everything from God alone" (J. Schniewind, *Matthäus*, 41).

8. Compare H. Weder (*Rede*, 48-50), who is almost the only commentator who goes to great lengths to understand what is meant by the unusual formulation "yours is the kingdom of God."

9. H. Weder, op. cit., 48.

10. H. Weder (op. cit., 47) speaks of the "act of speech" that must be effective.

11. Compare Isa 26:19; 29:18ff.; 35:5ff.; 42:18; 61:1. The text fragment from 4Q521, 2, II, shows that the expectation was that God would fulfill these promises in the days of the Messiah; cf. G. Vermes, 391-92.

12. This is true although the term "good news" is not a theme in Jesus' proclamation. Mt 11:5 should really be translated: "The poor have salvation announced to them" (G. Strecker, "euaggelizō," *EWNT* II, 174; cf. P. Stuhlmacher, *Evangelium*, 218-44).

13. In this connection, cf. Becker, *Jesus*, 111.

14. J. Becker, *Jesus*, 107-8.

15. Compare with Mark 5:1-20 as a particularly poignant example.

16. The story of the healing of the lame man in Mark 2:1-11 demonstrates in an exemplary manner that this is true also of fellowship with God, not just with society. Scholars continue to contest whether the connection between healing and forgiveness of sin was originally intended to be embedded in this story since, after all, no causal relationship between guilt and sickness is construed here. O. Hofius ("Vergebungszuspruch") concurs, while many, including J. Becker (*Jesus*, 137-38), disagree.

17. Compare O. Hofius, *Jesu Tischgemeinschaft*; Becker, *Jesus*, 155-69.

18. Some expositors consider the first part of Jesus' response as a later, clarifying addition that disrupts the harshness of the scene and softens the hardness of the confrontation (thus Becker, op. cit., 165-66). It seems significant to me that both parts of the response fit seamlessly into Jesus' message.

19. Compare O. Michel, "telōnēs," *ThWNT* 8, 101f.

20. J. Jeremias, *New Testament Theology*, 112.

21. But compare also Ps 25:7ff.

22. F. Herrenbrück, Wer waren die "Zöllner"?

23. This is L. Schottroff and W. Stegemann's argument in *Jesus*, 7-13.

24. H. Merklein, "Umkehrpredigt," 123. Expositors contest whether the idea of "repentance" found in 15:7, 10, doesn't, in fact, alter or even falsify the basic thoughts of Jesus, since the parables speak only of a passive "being found" and the anger over Jesus' actions arose precisely because he did not first wait for signs of repentance and penance before taking sinners into fellowship with him. What seems to be decisive for Jesus is not what a person does but what is done to him. But since a person is neither a sheep nor a coin, Jesus shows some of his intentions for humans by the parable of the lost son. The way Jesus intended it, repentance is defined by persons allowing themselves to be found and being prepared to live out of the salvation bestowed upon them (cf. W. Klaiber, *Call and Response*, 102).

25. Beyond Luke 15, cf. also Ezek 34:16; Matt 10:6; 15:24.

26. Compare John 3:15ff.; 1 Cor 1:18, but also Mark 10:45.

27. On this, see J. Becker, *Jesus*, 53-58.

28. Such an understanding of the story might invoke for Jesus the reproach of Lutheran theologians. It can be seen to be an exemplary illumination of what the Council of Trent meant by "prevenient grace." The son's decision is certainly no "work" (Weder, *Gleichnisse*, 258, A. 69). But it does describe metaphorically that a person is not passive in the salvific act.

29. Compare J. Jeremias, *Parables*, 104-5; R. Pesch, "Zur Exegese Gottes," 163.

30. Pesch, op. cit., 167.

31. Ibid., 173.

32. Ibid., 167.

33. Literally, "God, let yourself be reconciled to me even though I am a sinner."

34. On the translation, compare *Parables*, 113-14.

35. God's actions are described through the passive phrase "as one justified." Perhaps there is in this story still a reminiscence of the priestly announcement of justification in the temple, as deduced from Ezek 18:9; Ps 24:4ff.

36. Thus Pesch, op. cit., 175, continuing the aforementioned quotation.

37. H. Weder, *Gleichnisse*, 260ff.

38. E. Jüngel, *Paulus und Jesus*, 283.

39. Regarding the connection between the acceptance and the commissioning of a

sinner, compare also the exemplary story of Simon Peter's catch of fish (Luke 5:8-10). Therefore it is no contradiction when Jesus, in answering the question about eternal life, points to the twofold love commandment and says to a person: "Do this, and you will live" (Luke 10:25-28). For a person is invited aside from all attempts "to justify himself" (v. 29!) and to distinguish himself by so doing, to live simply by the merciful love of God (v. 33!).

40. Arguments against a derivation of this saying of Jesus are found in J. Roloff, "Anfänge der soteriologischen Deutung," those in favor in P. Stuhlmacher "Vicariously Giving His Life," and in *Biblische Theologie I*, 130, which says: "One can therefore tell from Mark 9:31 (Luke 9:44); Luke 22:37; and Mark 10:45 and parallels that the ancient Christian and Pauline doctrine of justification has taken up Jesus' own interpretation of his sacrificial act with the help of Isa 53 and further promulgated it from a post-Easter perspective."

41. For example, 1 Cor 1:30; 6:11; Rom 4:25; cf. Kertelge, *TRE 28*, 1997, 289f.

42. W. Wrede, *Paulus*, 67; A. Schweitzer, *Mysticism of Paul*, 205-26; K. Stendahl, *Paul among Jews*, 1f, 24-26.

43. Thus E. P. Sanders, *Paul and Palestinian Judaism*; ibid., *Paul and the Law*; and, in a more modified fashion, J. D. G. Dunn, *Theology*, 335ff.; cf. Niebuhr, "Rechtfertigungslehre, Westerholm, *Perspectives*."

44. The probable chronological order of the undoubtedly genuine letters is likely 1 Thessalonians, 1 and 2 Corinthians, Galatians, Philippians, Romans—though 2 Corinthians and Galatians were written very close to each other. On this compare J. Becker, *Paul*, 17-32.

45. Thus G. Strecker, "Befreiung"; *Theology of the New Testament*, 138-40.

46. H. J. Thilo, "Paulus—pschoanalytisch gesehen," 14.

47. Thus F. Hahn in "Entwicklung," which also address the methodological question.

48. Thus T. Söding, "Kreuzestheologie."

49. This is the tendency described in Stendahl, *Paul among Jews*.

50. Compare Ch. Dietzfelbinger, *Berufung*; S. Kim, *Origin*.

51. Compare also the self-representation in Phil 3:5ff.

52. Compare Acts 7 and 11:20, and on this, see Ch. Dietzfelbinger, op. cit., 15-42.

53. On this, see H. Merklein, "Bedeutung des Kreuzestodes Christi," 5-7.

54. E. Lohse, *Paulus*, 58f.

55. W. G. Kümmel's *Römer 7* remains foundational to a rebuttal of an autobiographical reading of Rom 7. Whether or not an unconscious rift becomes evident in Romans 7, a rift that Paul could only express after his conversion to Christ is another question. On this, see G. Theissen, *Psychological Aspects*, 228-50.

56. On this, see H. Merklein, op. cit., 1-106.

57. T. Holtz, "*apokalyptō*," *EWNT*, 314.

58. M. Hengel, *Son of God*, 63; compare also Rom 1:3ff. with 1:16ff. and with the connection of the terms "righteousness" and "Son of God"; D. Lührmann, "Christologie und Rechtfertigung," 356f.

59. Compare on this M. Hengel and A. Schwemer, *Paul*, 47-50, 91-98.

60. Compare W. Schrage, "Heiligung als Prozess."

61. Compare T. Söding, "Der Erste Thessalonicherbrief."

62. Compare H. Weder, *Das Kreuz Jesu*, 126-37.

63. Compare C. Wolff, *1 Kor*, 35ff., to this translation.

64. Compare with the detailed exposition of Rom 1:20ff.

65. The *Hellenes*, who spoke Greek and had been integrated into Hellenistic culture, are here being contrasted with the Jews who continued the traditions of their own people.

66. Compare with the demands for signs in the Gospels (Mark 8:11).

67. See G. Theissen, *Social Reality and the Early Christians*, for a sociological analysis of the Corinthian church. He shows that members of the upper class were represented in the congregation. This heightens the theological weight of Paul's argument, cf. W. Klaiber, *Rechtfertigung und Gemeinde*, 92.

68. W. Schrage, *1 Kor. 1*, 212, with reference to Rom 4:17.

69. Thus Wolff, *1 Kor*, 45. For it would also not be appropriate to say: "Through Christ we became wise." For our purposes, the question of whether there is a pre-Pauline formulaic expression behind this phrasing can remain unresolved.

70. Schrage, op. cit., 216, with reference to 2 Cor 5:21, where exactly the opposite expression occurs: "in him we might become the righteousness of God."

71. R. Bultmann argues that this marks the intersection between a theology of the cross and the doctrine of justification (*Theology of the New Testament Vol. 1*, 242ff.; cf. Rom 3:27). Compare generally S. Gathercole, *Boasting*.

72. Here too "sanctification" is first of all what happens to people through Christ and, through this makes them committed to sanctification (Rom 6:18, 19, 22; 15:16).

73. Compare with U. Schnelle, *Gerechtigkeit*, 37ff. It is a matter of definition whether the genuine Pauline teaching on justification is already evident in this pre-Pauline formulation (and its Pauline usage). This can be questionable if one only acknowledges it where a "fundamental critique of the Law as a path to salvation" is practiced (thus G. Strecker, "Befreiung," 254; Schnelle, op. cit., 100ff.). But a critique of the Law is already present in 1 Cor 9:20ff.; 15:56).

74. The teaching on the charisms (1 Cor 12–14) very positively shows how the lives of even the weak and the simple are gifted so richly by God that everyone is important and valuable for others and for the community.

75. Thus F. Hahn, "Entwicklung," 356.

76. Thus. T. Söding, "Kreuzestheologie," 180.

77. Thus F. Hahn, "Entwicklung," 365.

78. W. Kraus, *Volk Gottes*, 216; W. Klaiber, *Rechtfertigung und Gemeinde*, 149ff.

79. On this, see J. D. G. Dunn, "Works of the Law"; ibid., "Yet Once More"; ibid., "Justice of God," who in this context also speaks of "boundary markers" or "badges" and points to interesting parallels in the contemporary confessional landscape. (For more on this discussion see H. Hübner, "Werke des Gesetzes.")

80. E. P. Sanders speaks of "covenantal nomism" (*Paul and Palestinian Judaism*, 422ff.).

81. F. Mussner, "Das Wesen des Christentums"; D. Lührmann, "Abendmahlsgemeinschaft."

82. It is unclear whether he still has in mind the situation in Antioch or to what extent the problems in Galatia are already determining how he expresses things.

83. Thus J. Becker, *Paul*, 96, who therefore paraphrases: "God accepts people through baptism because of their belief in Jesus Christ, not because of legalistic lifestyle, that is, on the basis on circumcision and observance of the law."

84. On this, see the works of Dunn (above, note 79) who sees an important support for his theory in the Qumran texts and especially in 4QMMT, a text that has recently been made public (Dunn, "4QMMT and Galatians"; similarly see M. Bachmann, "4QMMT und Galaterbrief"; for a different perspective see H. W. Kuhn, "Bedeutung," 209ff.).

85. E. P. Sanders, *Paul and the Law*, 10, 159ff., is a particular proponent of this view.

86. M. Theobald, "Der Kanon," 144, 156; J. Becker, op. cit.

87. F. Vouga, *Gal*, 58, sees in this "meaning-making function of the prepositions" the decisive indication that 4QMMT= 4Q398 14 II, 3, presents "no factual parallels to the Pauline formulations."

88. See on this, Theobald, op. cit., 160ff.

89. Now compare Theobald, op. cit., 134ff. to this interpretation.

90. F. Vouga, *Gal*, 39.

91. Thus also H. Merklein, "Bedeutung des Kreuzestodes," 4-14.

92. Contemporary exegesis of this matter in Judaism points in totally the opposite direction and is determined by 1 Macc 2:52 (cf. also 4QMMT); on this see F. Hahn, "Gen 15:6," 94ff.; Dunn, "4QMMT," 151ff.

93. Interpretive camps are evenly divided on the question of whether, according to Paul, justification through the law fails because the goal is "quantitatively" unsuccessful (i.e., because the entire law is never fulfilled) or "qualitatively" unsuccessful (because the law is wrongly considered the way of salvation). Here, Paul seems to vacillate between the two. The debate between J. Blank (Catholic) in his "Warum sagt Paulus," who represents the traditionally "Protestant" solution and U. Wilckens (Lutheran) in his "Was heisst bei Paulus," who represents the traditionally "Catholic" position, is classic.

94. For Paul, the translation, "The one righteous by faith will live," cf. Vouga, *Gal*, 75.

95. Paul seeks to firm up this idea in what follows through further salvation historical considerations of the role of the law in the history of the people of God. He explains that the law took on a kind of vigilante role and had to keep the people in a kind of protective custody until faith came (3:24ff.), which leads to righteousness and thus into fellowship with God.

96. On this, see W. Klaiber, *Rechtfertigung und Gemeinde*, 92-94.

97. Compare Hübner, *Law in Paul's Thought*, 33-36; by way of contrast see Sanders, *Paul, the Law*, 158.

98. Vouga.

99. Dunn "Justice of God" sees in this the enduring significance of the doctrine of justification.

100. Vouga, *Gal*, 39.

101. Ibid., 92, on 3:28.

102. On this, see K. Donfrieded., *The Romans Debate*.

103. E. Käsemann, *Romans*, 404.

104. Compare with M. A. Seifrid (*Justification*, 187-210) who has examined these connections under the rubric of the meaning of the doctrine of justification.

105. In so doing, Paul uses a familiar, probably Jewish-Christian formula (1:3ff.) that confesses Jesus as the promised Messiah, the descendant of David, and the Son of God. Compare U. Wilckens, *Röm I*, 56-61; however, K. Haacker (*Röm*, 25ff.) is skeptical about the existence of a pre-Pauline formula.

106. K. Haacker, ibid., 38.

107. U. Wilckens, *Röm I*, 83f.

108. Thus also K. Haacker, *Röm*, 38. Everyone who believes is "primarily intended in an inviting and inclusive way, not in a restrictive say!"

109. The connection between God's salvation and righteousness and their revelation to all the world is characteristic of this tradition; cf. Ps 98:2; Isa 56:1 (also 46:13; 51:5), Mal 4:2, and in the Qumran writings 1QH 14:15ff.; CD 20:20; 1Q27 I, 6. E. Käsemann

in particular has explored what these mean for the interpretation of the genitive construction "the righteousness of God"; cf. E. Käsemann, *Gottes Gerechtigkeit*; and, dependent on him, P. Stuhlmacher, *Gerechtigkeit Gottes*; ibid., "Apostle Paul's View of Righteousness"; similarly, K. Kertelge, "Rechtfertigung;" a critical response to this is R. Bultmann, DIKAIOSYNE THEOU; E. Lohse, "Gerechtigkeit Gottes."

110. Compare CD 20:20ff. (Vermes, "Damascus Document," 127-43); 1 QH 14:15ff., Vermes 247-49), and for a different emphasis see 1Q27 I, 6ff. (Vermes, 389-90).

111. Käsemann, *Romans*, 30-31, with reference to Jer 9:2; 2 Cor 2:16; 3:18.

112. U. Wilckens, *Röm I*, 88.

113. In contrast to the more usual translation, "The one who is righteous by faith will live," I will consider this translation to be more appropriate not only for the Hebrew text in Hab 2:4 but also for Gal 3:10 and Rom 1:17 (as does Haacker, *Röm*, 44, in contrast to Käsemann, *Romans*, 30f.).

114. Compare 1:15. This is true despite the contradiction to 15:20ff. Compare with Wilckens, *Röm I*, 80.

115. Käsemann, *Romans*, 390-92; W. Kraus, *Volk Gottes*, 326-33.

116. N. A. Dahl, *The One God* (in a discussion with Käsemann, *Romans*, 102 ff.)

117. Dahl, op. cit., 191.

118. Haacker, in *Röm*, 45, thus fittingly translates *asebeia* and *adikia*.

119. The futuristic explanation that H. J. Eckstein suggests in "Gottes Zorn" does not correspond to the context—or at least only in the sense that Haacker proposes: God rather "breaks in."

120. Compare W. Klaiber, *Call and Response*, 102-4.

121. See G. Bornkamm, "Die Offenbarung des Zornes Gottes"; W. Pannenberg, *Systematic Theology* I, 185-87.

122. Käsemann, *Romans*, 38. This is not the context in which to discuss whether Paul rightly sees same-sex love as an expression of a fateful narcissism.

123. Compare Wis 13-15.

124. Here, "Righteousness in God's sight" or "to be justified" signifies recognition through God's word of judgment. Paul is arguing from the standpoint of the common Jewish conviction and only appears to oppose his teaching on justification (in contrast to E. Sanders, *Paul, the Law*, 125ff.).

125. Here Paul is taking up a common idea of the Old Testament and Judaism; cf. Jer 4:4; Deut 10:16; 30:6, and especially *Jub* 1:23.

126. What is meant here is God's being right (Haacker, *Röm*, 78; cf. Neh 9:33; Dan 9:5, 7); most pointed of all is Psalm of Solomon 9:2: "The dispersion of Israel (was) among every nation, according to the saying of God; that your righteousness might be proven right, O God, in our lawless actions. For you are a righteous judge over all the peoples of the earth" (Wright, "Psalms of Solomon," 660).

127. Paul argues on two levels. He demonstrates that the Scripture's judgment concerns Jews and that no one's life, neither Jew nor Greek, can stand before God (cf. with Dunn ["Once More"] who argues differently).

128. Schlatter vehemently counters this view in *Romans*, 87-91.

129. In contrast to Haacker (*Röm*, 83f.), who follows Dunn on this point.

130. Compare, on the one hand, U. Wilckens, *Römer I*, 177-79, and on the other, O. Hofius, "Das Gesetz des Mose," 54-56.

131. Käsemann shows this particularly well, *Romans*, 65-68.

132. E. Käsemann, *Romans*, 203, following Bultmann, "Römer 7."

133. Wilckens points this out in *Röm II*, 88 n358.

134. See O. Hofius, "Gesetz und Evangelium," 84f.

135. Compare G. Theissen, *Psychological Aspects*, 208-11.

136. O. Hofius, "Gesetz der Mose," 54. Compare the positive parallels in Gal 2:19ff.: Christ becomes the center of one's life.

137. The wording of 9:31 is noteworthy because here the "law" almost takes the place of righteousness.

138. This is true despite the connection with the tradition of Phineas; cf. Num 25:6-13; Ps 106:30ff.; 1 Macc 2:54; in contrast, see Dunn, *Theology*, 350-53.

139. Compare the rejection of one's "own righteousness" (Deut 9:4-6). That one's "own" righteousness is not the same as "self-righteousness" (E. P. Sanders, *Paul, the Law*, 115ff.) to me does not seem to fit for Paul in light of Phil 3:9.

140. Wilckens, *Röm II*, 221, who, however, doesn't fundamentally see these statements as being targeted against a righteousness from the law but rather only on condition that Israel is now also a sinner. In contrast, see Westerholm, *Paul*, 234ff.

141. Käsemann, *Romans*, 282.

142. Compare Rom 1:18ff. with 3:21ff.; 7:7ff. with 8:1ff., and 9:1–10:3 with 10:4ff.

143. Despite continuing attempts to interpret the genitive *pistis Iesou Christou* as "faith" or "faithfulness of Jesus Christ," there are reasons to hold on to the translation "faith in Jesus Christ," as Gal 2:16 clearly shows; cf. Dunn, *Theology*, 379ff.

144. As Wilckens properly says, *Römer II*, 215.

145. The perfect-tense *pephanerōtai* expresses what happened once and for all in Christ and is valid still today (Haacker [*Röm*, 85] translates it as: "Become reality"). What is revealed today in the proclamation of the gospel has its foundation in the historical revelation of Jesus Christ.

146. According to the LXX, *Doxa theou* (the glory of God) is a technical term for the divine presence. According to Jewish tradition, Adam participated in God's glory and lost it in the fall. *The Apocalypse of Moses*, 20, names righteousness and glory as Adam's original clothing (M. D. Johnson, "The Life of Adam and Eve," 298).

147. God is the logical subject of the passive "they were justified by his grace."

148. *Apolytrōsis* occurs rarely in Paul; see Rom 8:23 (used futuristically there); 1 Cor 1:30; cf. further Col 1:14; Eph 1:7, 14; 4:30; for the range of interpretation, compare Kertelge, "*apolytrōsis*," EWNT I, 331-36, and W. Haubeck, *Loskauf*.

149. Some of the terms do not otherwise occur in Paul, and the parallel texts of vv. 25 and 26 can also be explained by this. On this, compare E. Käsemann [*Römer 3:24-26*], who considers this piece of tradition to begin with v. 24; further, see P. Stuhlmacher, "Recent Exegesis on Romans," and R. Baumann, *Gottes Gerechtigkeit*, 188ff.

150. J. Roloff, "*hilastērion*," EWNT II, 456; some exegetes prefer to translate *hilastērion* broadly as "atonement" or "expiation." Compare to Haacker, *Röm*, 90f.

151. In the Old Testament, these are only linked in one place, in Isa 53:11. Apart from this, the hope for justification and substitutionary or atonement ideas remain unconnected. In contrast to Paul, see H. Merklein, "Sühnetod Jesu"; O. Hofius, "Sühne und Versöhnung"; C. Breytenbach, "Versöhnung, Stellvertretung und Sühne"; H. Hübner, "Rechtfertigung und Sühne."

152. Here I am indebted to C. Breytenbach's basic thesis in *Versöhnung*, in contrast to

O. Hofius ("Erwägungen"), who attempts to link the Pauline ideas on reconciliation with the Old Testament sayings on atonement found mainly in cultic contexts. Paul links reconciliation and atonement by way of the notion of substitution.

153. Compare also 5:1 where justification and peace with God are linked.

154. With regard to the translation, cf. Klaiber, *Call and Response*, 55.

155. Compare Breytenbach, 140; Klaiber, *Rechtfertigung und Gemeinde*, 99f.

156. "Being in Christ" and justification have the same theological weight; Sanders (*Paul and Palestinian Judaism*, 504) thinks otherwise.

157. No doubt Paul is here thinking of the love commandment, that summarizes the law of God, such as is found in Gal 5:14 and Rom 13:8, and toward whose fulfillment the Spirit of God moves and leads.

158. Compare with this text, P. Fiedler, *Röm 8:31-39*.

159. Paul, or rather the Pauline tradition, depends on Isa 50:8.

160. Compare Isa 53:4-12; Rom 4:25.

161. The allusion to Gen 22:16 is intended to underscore what this costs God and his love. There is, however, no allusion to an expiatory meaning to the sacrifice of Isaac (cf. J. Fitzmyer, "Romans," 531f.). Anywhere Paul speaks of the love of God or of Christ, it is linked to reference to his giving of himself and his being sent to death (cf. Rom 5:5ff.; Gal 2:20; also Eph 5:2, 25; John 3:16; 1 John 4:9ff.).

162. Käsemann, *Romans*, 252: "the sum of Paul's theology."

163. In contrast to Dunn (*Theology*, 363), cf. Hübner, *Law in Paul's Thought*, 101-24, and S. Gathercole, *Boasting*, 200ff.

164. Nowadays there is consensus in both Protestant and Catholic exegesis that in his translation Luther rightly inserted the word "alone," which is not literally to be found in the Greek text. Compare with Fitzmyer (*Romans*, 360-62), who referred way back to Thomas Aquinas and K. Kertelge, "Paulus zur Rechtfertigung allein aus Glauber."

165. Here, Paul does not quite mean by "works" what Dunn otherwise identifies as "Works of the law" (for example, circumcision); but cf. Dunn, *Romans*, 200ff.; and further, E. Käsemann, *Perspectives on Paul*, 79-101.

166. U. Wilckens (*Röm I*, 263), who rebels against such a tradition therefore suggests: "*ho mē ergazomenos* can only mean: The one who is guilty of not having done the works of the law will not be able to regain righteousness for himself." This is not basically un-Pauline, yet it completely misses the point of how Rom 4:5 and v. 4 are connected.

167. Compare G. Delling, "Partizipiale Gottesprädikationen."

168. Exodus 23:7; Prov 17:15; 24:24; Isa 5:23.

169. Compare 1 Macc 2:52; Jas 2:23ff.; Heb 11:17ff. (cf. Hahn, "Gen 15:6," 94ff.).

170. This aspect of grace of "reckoning" Paul also notes in Ps 32:3: When God "forgives the unrighteous and does not count sin against them," positively stated this means that God reckons righteousness to a person without a person being able to give evidence of "works" (4:6-12).

171. Romans 10:17. The Greek word for "proclamation," *akoē*, actually means "what is heard," (cf. NRSV) and only then that which is proclaimed.

172. Galatians 3:2, 5, where not only faith but also the "proclamation of faith" is very consciously set in opposition to "works of the law." It is the gospel, and not our faith, that gifts us with the Spirit.

173. Compare Rom 8:10ff.; cf. also 2 Cor 3:6-9 where Paul describes his task as being in service of the "new Covenant" and therefore in service of the Spirit of righteousness and life.

174. *Extra nos*= beyond ourselves; cf. O. Michel, *Röm*, 254: "The Doctrine of the Spirit of God preserves the message of justification '*extra nos*,' but makes it present in concrete, earthly life."

175. Compare Gal 4:1-7; Rom 8:13-17. There are extraordinary parallels here to the story of the lost son in Luke 15.

176. This is the basic thrust of Rom 8:18-30.

177. C. Wolff, *1 Cor*, 311. Here the question of "who is something" and "who is worth something" is again treated, this time from a totally new perspective.

178. On this, see 1 Thess 1:3.

179. Compare F. Neugebauer, *In Christus*.

180. U. Wilckens, *Römer I*, 288.

181. Compare Gal 6:14 and esp. 2 Cor 11:30–12:10.

182. Compare H. D. Betz, *Gal*, 465.

183. The differing choice of words shows how Paul judges the difference between the works done in the flesh and those "grown" from the Spirit.

184. W. Schrage, *1 Cor 1*, 433.

185. Compare Rom 6:1-11; 1 Cor 6:11; Gal 3:26ff., and F. Hahn, "Taufe."

186. Thus, on the one hand, E. P. Sanders is right when he suggests that it's a matter of "getting in" in the justification event, but he is wrong in limiting his meaning to this question (*Paul, the Law*, 4-10). Strangely enough, Paul never systematizes this connection between faith, baptism, and justification to an *ordo salutis* (on this, compare with Dunn, *Theology*, 455ff.).

187. It is for this reason that throughout this section Paul plays with the terms "freedom" and "servitude."

188. Paul also describes the goal of fellowship with God, to which righteousness leads, with the key word "sanctification."

189. Compare H. Umbach, *In Christus getauft: "Gemeinde als sündenfreier Raum."*

190. On this, cf. W. Joest, *Paulus and das luthersche simul iustus et peccator*; U. Wilckens, "Gemeinsame Erklärung," 47ff.

191. Compare W. Klaiber, *Rechtfertigung und Gemeinde;* ibid., "Rechtfertigung und Kirche."

192. O. Hofius, "Herrenmahl," 239.

193. 1 Cor 12:12ff. links the image of the body with the christological idea of *sōma*, and therefore anticipates 12:27 as regards content even if not terminologically; this is an idea to be upheld despite what A. Lindemann says in "Die Kirche als Leib Christi," 148.

194. Compare to Lindemann, op. cit.: by "democratic" is meant the mutual interdependence and fundamentally equal value of the members of the body, not the way in which decisions are reached.

195. E. Käsemann, "Amt und Gemeinde," 119.

196. Compare 3:1-3; 10:12-18, and on this see S. Hafemann, "'Self-Commendation'"; U. Heckel, *Kraft in Schwachheit*, 144-214.

197. E. Käsemann, "Die Legitimität des Apostels."

198. G. Barth, "Die Eignung des Verkündigers," 269ff.: "That the salvific action experienced in the cross and resurrection of Christ is epitomized in the justification of the ungodly is for Paul...also the criterion and norm for the understanding of ecclesial office."

199. Compare F. Mussner, *Theologie der Freiheit*, 42ff.

200. J. Blank, *Paulus und Jesus*, 314.

201. The close connection between a Christian's way of life and the apostolic task, neither of which are nevertheless identified, is the reason that the distinction between the general Christian and apostolic "we" in 2 Cor is so hard to discern.

202. Compare E. Jüngel, "Die Autorität des bittenden Christus."

203. Compare O. Hofius, "Wort der Versöhnung," 29ff.

204. On this, see Heckel, *Kraft in Schwachheit*, 121-42. He correctly points out that 13:3 is the real high point of Paul's argument.

205. Compare M. Seifrid, *Justification*, 256.

206. Compare Rom 4:24; 5:19; Gal 5:5.

207. Romans 5:9ff.; 8:23; 1 Thess 1:9ff.; cf. Wolter, *Rechtfertigung*, 217ff.

208. F. Vouga, *Gal*, 143.

209. "The many" (Rom 5:19), seen in light of Hebrew linguistics and the parallels to v. 18, are considered to be the "totality" of humanity. The future tense of v. 19 is presumably meant eschatologically (as Käsemann, but not Wilckens, sees it).

210. On the issue of translating this as either "to accept" or as "to receive," see Klaiber, *Call and Response*, 154.

211. I agree with the consensus in New Testament research that these letters originated in the "school of Paul" and that, with varying emphases and development of the Pauline tradition, were written sometime between A.D. 80 (Ephesians) and A.D. 100 (Pastoral Epistles) (U. Schnelle, *History*, 352, 383ff.).

212. Compare U. Luz, "Rechtfertigung bei den Paulusschülern"; H. Merklein, "Paulinische Theologie in der Rezeption des Kolosser- und Epheserbriefes"; G. Lohfink, "Paulinische Theologie in der Rezeption der Pastoralbriefe"; M. Wolter, *Die Pastoralbriefe als Paulustradition*; A. Lindemann, *Paulus im ältesten Christentum*; M. Gese, *Das Vermächtnis des Paulus*.

213. However, there Paul does not speak of Christians also being raised and ascending, but rather keeps the eschatological proviso.

214. Although the parallels to Rom 6 make it likely that Eph 2:4-7 is making an allusion to the baptism event, baptism is not spoken of expressly. In contrast to what Hahn says in "Taufe," 103, this seems to demonstrate a tightly connected development of the respective Pauline texts.

215. Compare 1 Cor 1:29; 3:21; Rom 3:27; Gal 6:14.

216. M. Gese, *Vermächtnis*, 166; the negative assessment of this text by many exegetes he rightly declines, for v. 10b describes "the goal of God's creative activity, an achievement that humans cannot accomplish."

217. This section shows the christological fulfillment of Isa 57:19. Compare with P. Stuhlmacher, "He Is Our Peace," 191.

218. F. Mussner, "Eph 2," 332: "In Eph 2:11-22 the church is seen as the fruit of the justification event, *sola fide et gratia.*"

219. In 2:16, "the cross is forcefully shown as...the source of reconciliation and peace" and in 2:18 also, the "role of Christ as the conveyor of salvation" remains pronounced; J. Gnilka, *Eph*, 145, 147.

220. Compare H. Lips, "Ordination," III, *TRE*, 25, 1995, 340-43.

221. L. Oberlinner, *2 Tim*, 30.

222. Compare to U. Luz, "Rechtfertigung," 378ff.

223. The exact content of this *parathēkē* is debated. Compare the varying interpretations of G. Lohfink, "Paulinische Theologie," 97-105; J. Roloff, *1 Tim*, 373; M. Wolter, *Die Pastoralbriefe*, 118-30; and L. Oberlinner, *2 Tim*, 47-51.

224. H. Merkel, *Pastoralbriefe*, 101.

225. This connection of baptism and justification was already part of the pre-Pauline tradition (cf. 1 Cor 6:11) that Paul reinterpreted through the connection to faith; cf. F. Hahn, "Taufe," 104. Post-Pauline tradition once again more strongly emphasizes this connection with baptism.

226. Brox, *Pastoralbriefe*, 306.

227. On this, cf. the parallel thought process in Titus 2:11-14.

228. Merkel, Pastoralbrief, 104. Luz ("Rechtfertigung," 377) emphasizes the differences more strongly, whereas A. Lindemann, in *Paulus im ältesten Christentum* (141-47), defends against an anachronistic critique of these letters.

229. The two articles by P. G. Müller and K. Löning, "Zum 'Paulinismus' in der Apostelgeschichte," have a differentiated description.

230. Compare 10:22, 35. Yet here too the discussion is not about the fact that one can achieve salvation through "deeds of righteousness" (cf. also Rom 2:10). "The point is overstepping the boundary of Jewish folk customs" (G. Schille, *Apostelgeschichte*, 248); cf. also how the phrase has been reinterpreted through the subject of faith in 10:43!

231. Compare Luz, "Rechtfertigung," 379.

232. For example, that the Letter to the Ephesians no longer discusses the topic of the law.

233. *LW* 34, 112.

234. H. Küng, "Der Frühkatholizismus in Neuen Testament."

235. Thus also T. Söding, "Kriterium der Wahrheit?"; F. Hahn, "Gerechtigkeit Gottes."

236. Compare E. Lohse, "Glaube und Werke"; R. Walker, "Allein aus Werken"; Ch. Burchard, "Zu Jakobus 2," 14-26.

237. Compare 1 Cor 1:26ff.; Luke 6:20.

238. It is worth noting how closely James's argument in 1:22-25 mirrors that of Paul in Rom 2:13ff.

239. The term in Matt 21:32 could at the very earliest have been part of the pre-Matthean tradition. On the term "righteousness" in Matthew, see G. Strecker, *Weg*; M. J. Fiedler, *Begriff*; ibid., "Gerechtigkeit"; H. Giesen, *Christliches Handel*.

240. G. Strecker, *Weg*, 157ff., does so, but also Luz, *Matthew 1-7*, 237-38.

241. Matthew gives the same emphasis in composing his gospel by adding the materials of the *Logienquelle* to both the tradition and shape of Mark's gospel, inserting parenthetical material "into the story of God and his Son, Jesus, which discloses a new, deep dimension of grace for the hearers of the ethical gospel." U. Luz, *Matthew 1-7*, 76.

242. Compare the framing in 4:23 and 9:35 of the first extended section of the Gospel, which tells of Jesus as the Messiah in both word and deed.

243. 1 QH 6:3; 1 QH 6:7.

244. Parallel to the term "lowly in spirit" in 1 QM 14:7, is found the designation "those perfect in the Way."

245. For me, the meaning of the third Beatitude is open to interpretation. Are the "meek" or "friendly" ones meant (such an interpretation would correspond fairly closely with the use of the term elsewhere in Matthew) or are the "lowly" or "powerless" ones meant, which is what the background to Ps 37 and the paradoxical promise that they will inherit the earth seems to indicate.

246. U. Luz's examples in *Matthew 1-7*, 237-38, of "hunger and thirst" contradict his

own understanding that what the text is talking about is the striving for an appropriate behavior before God. Compare M. J. Fiedler, *Begriff*, 115-18.

247. Fiedler, *Gerechtigkeit*, 69ff.

248. U. Luz, *Matthew 1–7*, 246.

249. On this, compare G. Bornkamm, "Der Auferstandene," 310.

250. Regarding the following, compare with W. Klaiber, "Die Aufgabe einer theologischen Interpretation des 4. Evangeliums."

251. The connection to the miracles of Jesus has again and again led to the revelation of the glory of Jesus being connected to the Hellenistic conceptions of epiphany (see U. B. Müller, *Geschichte der Christologie*, 36ff.). But this is not tenable.

252. Compare H. Gese, "The Prologue to John's Gospel," 205-9.

253. In the Old Testament, cf. with Exod 14:4, 17ff., and Exod 15.

254. On the connections between this text and 2 Cor 3:1–4:6, see M. Hooker, "The Johannine Prologue," 56ff.; further, see Müller, *Christologie*, 40.

255. On the history of interpretation of the connection between *doxa* and *dikaiosynē*, cf. P. Stuhlmacher, *Gerechtigkeit Gottes*, 196ff.

256. Compare H. Wildberger, "mn" *THAT I*, 202-8.

257. L. Goppelt, "Wahrheit als Befreiung," 83.

258. Y. Ibuki, *Die Wahrheit im Johannesevangelium*, 356ff.

259. Further examples can be found in Stuhlmacher, *Gottes Gerechtigkeit*, 196.

260. Compare G. Barth, "pistis," *EWNT III*, 226ff.

261. Bultmann, *Theology of the New Testament*, Vol. 2, 75.

262. Compare E. Käsemann, *New Testament als Kanon*; W, Schrage, "Frage nach der Mitte"; J. Reumann, *Righteousness*, 181 ff.; T. Söding, "Kriterium der Wahrheit?"

263. As, for example, the prioritizing of Christology over the doctrine of justification by W. Pannenberg in *Systematic Theology* Vol. 3, 213-14; W. Haubeck, "Rechtfertigung und Sühne" 103; T. Söding, *op. cit.*, 241-46.

264. As W. Härle proposes in *Dogmatik*, 135-38.

265. G. Gloege, *Rechtfertigungslehre als hermeneutische Kategorie*.

266. Compare E. Käsemann, *New Testament als Kanon*, 405.

267. Compare W. Schrage, "Frage nach der Mitte," 439ff.

268. Compare F. Crüsemann, "Jahwes Gerechtigkeit," 450; Söding, op. cit., 232ff.

269. H. Gese, "The Atonement," 114.

270. H. Seebass, *Genesis I*, 95.

271. Compare W. Zimmerli, "Heiligkeit."

272. H. Seebass, "Innere Einheit," 139 (analogous to Jer 16:14ff.).

273. H. Gese, "The Law," 92. Compare Jüngel, *Justification*, 229n186; E. Käsemann, *Perspectives on Paul*, 155-56.

Chapter 4: Everything Is Grace: Divergent Positions in the Tradition

1. Compare A. McGrath, *Iustitia Dei*; O. H. Pesch and A. Peters, *Einführung*; W. Dettloff and G. Sauter, "Rechtfertigung III-V," *TRE 28*, 1997, 308-52.

2. O. H. Pesch in Pesch and Peters, *Einführung*, 11.

3. O. H. Pesch, 12ff.

4. Irenaeus, *Against Heresies* Book III, 19.1 (281-82).

5. Athanasius, *The Incarnation*, 54, 93.

6. Pesch, ibid., 13.

7. For a discussion on this question, cf. Felmy, op. cit., 134-40; E. Mauer, *Rechtfertigung*, 59-69, 106-18; A Kallis, "Rechtfertigung II, *theosis*," 1983, 1005-1007.

8. D. Stainloae, *Orthodoxe Dogmatik II*, 260.

9. Op. cit., 258.

10. Compare E. Mühlenberg in C. Andresen, ed., *Handbuch, I*, 459.

11. Compare W. Dettloff, *TRE* 28, 1997, 308-15, and Pesch, op. cit., 55-107.

12. O. H. Pesch, ibid., 89 (but notice the similarities to and differences from Rom 5:5!).

13. M. A. Schmidt, in C. Andresen, *Handbuch I*, 670.

14. M. A. Schmidt, op. cit., 671; O. H. Pesch, op. cit., 105.

15. With reference to Gal 5:5 (though with a noted differentiation to its intended sense), in Catholic theology since the age of scholasticism *fides caritate formata* describes "the virtue of faith formed by love" in contrast to the "empty, loveless factual belief of nominal Christians and demons, which is useless for salvation" (E. Gössmann, "Glaube, V," *TRE 13*, 1984, 310).

16. Compare O. H. Pesch, *Theologie*, 746; Jüngel, *Justification*, 249-51.

17. Compare W. Dettloff, *TRE* 28, 1997, 313ff.

18. G. Sauter, *TRE* 28, 1997, 315.

19. Compare G. Sauter's take on the text in *Rechtfertigung* 32-35 (*Luther's Works*, Vol. 34, "Preface to the Complete Edition," 327-38); and E. Jüngel's more recent interpretation in *Justification*, 70-75.

20. A. Peters, *Rechtfertigung*, 39.

21. K. Holl, "Rechtfertigungslehre," 123.

22. Holl, op. cit., 122. G. Sauter's emphasis is quite different in *TRE* 28, 1997, 319: "Justification therefore occurs not as a transformation but rather calls the ungodly one to forsake himself."

23. This would seem to be the more apt formulation in contrast to the earlier and more usual one that speaks of a "synthetic judgment" in justification. On this, cf. Holl, "Rechtfertigungslehre," 123ff.; W. Härle, *Analytische und synthetische Urteile*.

24. On this, cf. W. Joest, *Gesetz und Freiheit*, 65ff.; in contrast to this Sauter proposes that *simul iustus et peccator* permits neither a quantitative nor a qualitative division" (*TRE* 28, 318).

25. *Luther's Works*, Vol. 25, 260. This section of the text has been much discussed; cf. K. Holl, "Zur Verständigung,"155ff.; Jüngel, *Justification*, 214-24.

26. For me it is questionable whether one can therefore talk so unequivocally of the "inability to observe justification," as G. Sauter does (*TRE* 27, 319).

27. W. Joest, *Dogmatik 2*, 440ff.

28. CR 21, 421, cited by Pesch and Peters, *Einführung*, 132.

29. On this, cf. W. Joest, *Dogmatik 2*, 443.

30. McNeill, *Calvin: Institutes*, 797-98 (III, 16:1.).

31. Despite criticisms of particular details, the following see the result of the Council of Trent as predominantly positive: A. von Harnack, *History of Dogma*, vol. 7, 57; P. Brunner, *Rechtfertigungslehre*; among those who evaluate it more negatively are W. Joest, "Die tridentinische Rechtfertigungslehre"; K. Barth, *Church Dogmatics* Vol. 4, Pt. 1, 624-26 (despite H. Küng, *Rechtfertigung*!); V. Subilia, *Rechtfertigung*, 72-89.

32. Compare Pesch and Peters, *Einführung*, 182ff.; W. Joest, *Dogmatik II*, 444ff.

33. Compare Joest, op. cit., 446; Pesch and Peters, op. cit., 191ff. and in the decree on justification in chs. 7–9 (Schroeder, "Council of Trent," 33-34. Justification *sola fide* is expressly discarded as an option [canon 9, 11f., 14; "Council of Trent," 43]).

34. This is why Subilia summarily dismisses it in *Rechtfertigung*, 269ff!

35. For this part of my argument, I follow the plan Wesley himself suggests in Sermon 85, II, 1 for the way of salvation (cf. Klaiber and Marquardt, *Living Grace*, 228).

36. Sermon 85, II, 1 (*Works of J. Wesley*, Vol. 3, 204).

37. A. Outler, *Theologische Akzente*, 97.

38. For Wesley Rom 5:5 describes the "Character of a Methodist" (and every real Christian) *Works of J. Wesley*, Vol. 9, 34-46.

39. Sermon 5, II, 1 (*Works of J. Wesley*, Vol. 1, 187).

40. Compare Sermon 43, III, 3 (*Works of J. Wesley*, Vol. 2, 63); 45, III, 1 (*Works of J. Wesley*, Vol. 2, 184).

41. Compare the thoughtful conversation on this matter between Zinzendorf and Wesley, documented, among others, by J. Moltmann in *The Spirit of Life*, 163-72.

42. Sermon 20, 12f. (*Works of J. Wesley*, Vol. 1, 458).

43. Ibid.

44. Compare K. Holl, *Gesammelte Aufsätze I*, Luther, 1948.

45. Compare K. Barth, *Church Dogmatics* Vol. 4, Pt. 1, 514-642; A. Peters, *Rechtfertigung*, 128-70 (citation on 166); E. Jüngel, *Justification*, 18-31.

46. Tillich speaks of the "justification, not of the sinner, but of him who doubts" (228) (cf. P. Tillich, *Systematic Theology Vol. 3*, 222-28; A. Peters, *Rechtfertigung*, 107-27); R. Bultmann on the demythology as the "logical implementation" of the doctrine of justification "for the area of recognition" (ibid., "Zum Problem der Entmythologisierung," 207).

47. Elsa Tamez, *The Amnesty of Grace* (Nashville: Abingdon, 1993).

48. On this, now also compare U. Wilckens, "Gemeinsame Erklärung."

49. Luther, *Luther's Works*, Vol. 33, 157.

50. Even Calvin took up this term, see McNeill, *Calvin: Institutes*, 768 (III, 13, 5).

51. Schroeder, "Council of Trent," Canon 4, 42-43.

52. Schroeder, "Council of Trent," ch. 5, 31-32.

53. "Formula of Concord," 525-26.

54. Ibid., 532.

55. J. Wesley, *Works of J. Wesley*, Vol. 3, 203f. (Sermon 85, II, 1). Compare Klaiber and Marquardt, *Living Grace*, 228-41.

56. Compare W. Klaiber, *Call and Response*, 163-81.

57. K. Lehmann and W. Pannenberg, *Condemnations of the Reformation Era*, 47.

58. *Joint Declaration*, 4.20, 17.

59. E. Jüngel, *Justification*, 242.

60. *Joint Declaration*, 4.21, 17.

61. H. Weder, "Die Entdeckung des Glaubens im Neuen Testament," 58.

62. Compare items 25 and 26 of the *Joint Declaration*!

63. *Joint Declaration*, Annex 2.C., 45 (with a quotation from Thomas Aquinas!).

64. Schroeder, Council of Trent, Canons 9 and 12, 43.

65. On this, cf. G. Sauter, *TRE* 28, 1997, 362.

66. On this cf. with *Christsein gestalten*, 45; and also W. Klaiber, "Aus Glauben, damit aus Gnaden."

67. I. Dalferth, *Existenz Gottes*, 243, who radicalizes the notion of the "mere passive."

68. See G. Wainwright, "Rechtfertigung," 206.

69. See ch. 7 of the Council of Trent's Decree on Justification (Schroeder, 33-34).

70. *Joint Declaration*, Annex 2.C., 45.

71. "Preface to the Epistle of St. Paul to the Romans" (*Luther's Works* Vol. 35, 155).

72. "On the Bondage of the Will," *Luther's Works*, Vol. 33, 155; cf. E. Jüngel, "Amica exegesis," 268.

73. Tappert, "Formula of Concord," 534.

74. G. Barth, *Phil* 49; see also Wesley's exegesis in his sermon on this text, Sermon 85: "First. God worketh in you; therefore, you *can* work: Otherwise it would be impossible.... Secondly, God worketh in you; therefore, you *must* work: You must be 'workers together with him,' (they are the very words of the Apostle,) otherwise he will cease working." (*Works of J. Wesley*, Vol. 3, 206-08 [III, 3. 7.].

75. See K. Ch. Felmy, *Orthodoxe Theologie*, 140.

76. Felmy, op. cit., 140ff. This "participation" in which a person actively completes his orientation toward God is however described quite variously and can also be understood as a joining together of grace and human deeds, for example, in the image of the "two wings with which a person flies to heaven," but one can also lay the emphasis on the fact that everything that a person does with the freedom given him by God derives from God's grace.

77. Compare *Luther's Works*, Vol. 25, 260.

78. See G. Wainwright, "Rechtfertigung," 200.

79. Käsemann argues this way in *Romans*, 156; see in contrast, Wilckens, *Röm I*, 328.

80. See the history of interpretation on this passage in Wilckens, *Röm II*, 101ff. The fact that J. D. G. Dunn (*Theology*, 474-77) considers the description of the I in Rom 7 as also being the Christian's experience shows that this question continues to be current.

81. P. Althaus, *Paulus und Luther*, 94.

82. Klauck, *1 Johannes*, 189 (on 1 John 3:4-6); cf. John 8:34-36; Rom 5:17-7:6.

83. Jüngel, "Amica exegesis," 264; ibid., *Justification*, 221, where he also tries to show this disparity in the formula *simul iustus et peccator* and shows that it stands in service of a dynamic understanding of the justification event.

84. See U. Wilckens, "Gemeinsame Erklärung," 48-56; H. Hübner, "Rechtfertigungslehre," 94-103.

85. G. Maron, *Kirche und Rechtfertigung*, 267.

86. For a discussion on Maron and for a basic understanding of the issues see S. Pemsel-Maier, *Rechtfertigung durch Kirche?*

87. These differences have to do primarily with the ecclesial offices for the transmission of salvation, see *Kirche und Rechtfertigung*, paragraphs 198-204.

88. Thus the definition in *WA* 39, I, 205, 2.

89. C. F. von Weizsäcker, *Der Garten des Menschlichen*, 506 (of course Catholic teaching is represented rather crudely here!).

90. B.-J. Hilberath, in Th. Schneider, *Handbuch 2*, 43.

91. Of course it is intriguing to consider whether this is also true of Christian identity markers such as baptism. The nuanced formulation in Mark 16:16 points to the fact that people were aware of this problem in early Christianity.

92. See K. Stendahl, The Apostle Paul and the Introspective Conscience of the West"; see also, E. Käsemann, *Perspectives on Paul*.

93. See K. Nürnberger, "Wider die Verengung," 157.

94. See Elsa Tamez, *Amnesty of Grace*; and W. Altmann, "Rechtfertigung in einem Kontext der Ausgrenzung."

95. See W. Klaiber, "Missionarische Ökumene"; ibid., "Hintergrund und Ziele."

Chapter 5: What Is Justification? Summarizing Theses

1. On these theses, cf. W. Klaiber, "Ökumenische Verantwortung."

2. Jüngel, *Justification*, 46.

3. W. Härle, "Zur Gegenwartsbedeutung," 128ff.

4. The fact that there are renewed debates about whether justification of the sinner means the person is declared righteous or made righteous has no sound exegetical foundation. For Paul knows "*no* difference between imputed and effective justification." Justification is "a creative act of justice done by God"; P. Stuhlmacher, *Biblische Theologie* I, 334ff.

5. Here I am trying to broach the topic of *simul iustus et peccator*.

6. *Joint Declaration*, Annex 2.C, 45.

7. E. Jüngel, "Kirche als Sakrament," 326.

8. Klaiber and Marquardt, *Living Grace*, 256.

9. I. Schoberth, "Rechtfertigung und Schülersehnsucht," 56. "Justification reminds one of the creator, who desires to preserve his creation and gives it space to live, which people need. For in this space, one finds a life which remains under the care of God" (ibid., 55). Schoberth demonstrates the relevance of the message of justification for religious education (and, without knowing it, hints at Wesley's understanding of "holiness and happiness" as a gift of justification) by her decision to look at "holiness and happiness" [58] together.

10. W. Härle, "Zur Gegewartsbedeutung," 134.

11. Compare the dialectical passage in Phil 2:12-13.

12. Paul would not have been able to join in saying this sentence of Luther's: "Our deeds, even in the best of lives, are utterly worthless" (*Evangelisches Gesangbuch* 299, 2). It is an important matter to Paul that his ministry not be without purpose, that he not have worked "in vain," and that he not have received grace "for nothing."

13. See E. Jüngel, *Justification*, 272-77; W. Schlichting, ed., *Rechtfertigung und Weltverantwortung*.

14. K. Nürnberger, "Wider die Verengung der Rechtfertigungslehre," 157.

15. Compare J. Werbick, "Rechtfertigung des Sünders—Rechtfertigung Gottes," 50. He continues: "The question about who is ultimately responsible for this history of disaster and depravity can remain unanswered; for the believer, the certainty that this history of depravity cannot separate him from God's love (Rom 8:38ff.) is sufficient, since God endured it 'in his own body'—in our brother Jesus Christ."

BIBLIOGRAPHY

There is an almost limitless body of literature on the doctrine of justification. For this reason, this bibliography contains only the bibliographical information for the monographs and articles in journals and edited volumes mentioned in the notes. I have mentioned commentaries using the abbreviation for the particular biblical book in the notes. Dictionary articles are not included in this bibliography. Abbreviations for dictionaries, journals, and compilations, as well as for standard text editions follow the list of abbreviations in the *Theologische Realenzyklopädie* (2nd ed., edited by S. M. Schwertner [Berlin-New York: Walter de Gruyter, 1994]).

BIBLIOGRAPHY

Althaus, Paul. *Paulus und Luther über den Menschen: Eine Vergleich.* 4th ed. Studien zur Luther-Akademie 14. Gütersloh: Gütersloher Verlagshaus Gerd Mohn, 1963.

Altmann, Peter. *Rechtfertigung in einem Kontext der Ausgrenzung,* ÖR 48, 1999, 448-58.

Andresen, Carl, ed. *Handbuch der Dogmen- und Theologiegeschichte I.* Göttingen: Vandenhoeck & Ruprecht, 1982.

Assmann, Jan. Ma'at: *Gerechtigkeit und Unsterblichkeit im alten Ägypten.* 2nd ed. Munich: C. H. Beck, 1995.

Athanasius. *The Incarnation of the Word of God.* New York: Macmillan, 1951.

Avemarie, Friedrich. *Tora und Leben: Untersuchungen zur Heilsbedeutung der Tora in der frühen rabbinischen Literatur.* TSAJ 55. Tübingen: Mohr, 1996.

Bachmann, Michael. "4QMMT und Galaterbrief," ZNW 89, 1998, 91-113.

Barbiero, Gianni. "Das erste Psalmbuch als Einheit: eine synchrone Analyse von Psalm 1–41." ÖBS 16. Frankfurt: P. Lang, 1999.

Barth, Gerhard. *Der Brief an die Philipper.* ZBK NT 9. Zürich: Theologischer Verlag, 1979.

———. "Die Eignung des Verkündigers in 2 Kor 2:14–3:6." *Kirche: Festschrift für Günther Bornkamm zum 75. Geburtstag.* Edited by Dieter Lührmann and Georg Strecker. Tübingen: Mohr, 1980, 257-70.

Barth, Karl. *Church Dogmatics Volume 4: The Doctrine of Reconciliation.* Part 1. Translated by G. T. Thomson. Edinburgh: T&T Clark, 1956.

Baumann, Rolf. *Gottes Gerechtigkeit: Verheissung und Herausforderung für diese Welt.* Herder Taschenbuch 1643. Freiburg im Breisgau: Herder, 1989.

Becker Jürgen. *Das Heil Gottes: Heils- und Sündenbegriffe in den Qumrantexten und im Neuen Testament.* StUNT 3. Göttingen: Vandenhoeck & Ruprecht, 1964.

————. *Jesus of Nazareth.* Translated by James E. Crouch. New York: Walter de Gruyter, 1998.

————. *Johannes der Täufer und Jesus von Nazareth.* BSt 63. Neukirchen-Vluyn: Neukirchener, 1972.

————. *Paul: Apostle to the Gentiles.* Translated by O. C. Dean Jr. Louisville: Westminster/John Knox, 1993.

Betz, Hans Dieter. *Der Galaterbrief: Ein Kommentar zum Brief des Apostels Paulus an die Gemeinden in Galatien.* Hermeneia. Munich: Kaiser, 1988.

Betz, Otto. "Rechtfertigung in Qumran." *Rechtfertigung: Festschrift für Ernst Käsemann zum 70. Geburtstag.* Edited by Johannes Friedrich, Wolfgang Pöhlmann, and Peter Stuhlmacher. Tübingen: Mohr; Göttingen: Vandenhoeck & Ruprecht, 1976, 17-36.

Blank, Josef. "Der leidende Gottesknecht (Jes 53)." *Studien zur biblischen Theologie.* Edited by Robert Mahoney. SBA 13. Stuttgart: Katholisches Bibelwerk, 1992, 37-96.

————. *Paulus und Jesus: eine theologische Grundlegung.* StANT 18. Munich: Kösel, 1968.

————. "Warum sagt Paulus: 'Aus Werken des Gesetzes wird niemand gerecht'?" *Paulus: Von Jesus zum Christentum: Aspekte der paulinischen Lehre und Praxis.* Munich: Kösel, 1982, 42-68.

Boecker, Hans Jochen. *Law and the Administration of Justice in the Old Testament and Ancient East.* Translated by Jeremy Moiser. Minneapolis: Augsburg, 1980.

————. *Redeformen des Rechtslebens im AT.* WMANT 14. Neukirchen-Vluyn: Neukirchener, 1964.

Bornkamm, Günther. "Der Auferstandene und der Irdische, MT.28:16-20." *Überlieferung und Auslegung im Matthäusevangelium.* Edited by Günther Bornkamm, Gerhard Barth, and Heinz Joachim Held. 5th ed. WMANT 1. Neukirchen: Neukirchener, 1968, 289-310.

————. "Die Offenbarung des Zornes Gottes." *Das Ende des Gesetzes: Paulusstudien.* Gesammelte Aufsätze Vol. 1. BevTh 16. Munich: C. Kaiser, 1966, 9-33.

Braulik, Georg. "The Development of the Doctrine of Justification in the Redactional Strata of the Book of Deuteronomy: A Contribution to the Clarification of the Necessary Conditions for Pauline Theology." *The Theology of Deuteronomy: Collected Essays of Georg Braulik.* Translated by Ulrika Lindblad. N. Richland Hills, Tex.: BIBAL, 1994. 151-64.

————. "Gesetz als Evangelium. Rechtfertigung und Begnadung nach der deuteronomischen Thora," *ZThK* 79, 1982, 127-60.

Breytenbach, Cilliers. *Versöhnung: Eine Studie zur paulinischen Soteriologie.* WMANT 60. Neukirchen-Vluyn: Neukirchener, 1989.

————. "Versöhnung, Stellvertretung und Sühne," *NTS* 39, 1993, 59-79.

Brox, Norbert. *Die Pastoralbriefe: uebersetzt und erklaert.* RNT 7/2. Regensburg: Friedrich Pustet, 1969.

Brunner, Peter. "Die Rechtfertigungslehre des Konzils v. Trient." *Pro ecclesia: Gesammelte Aufsätze zur dogmatischen Theologie.* Vol. 2. Berlin: Lutherisches Verlagshaus, 1966, 141-69.

Bultmann, Rudolf. "DIKAIOSUNĒ THEOU" *Exegetica: Aufsätze zur Erforschung des Neuen Testaments.* Tübingen: Mohr (Siebeck), 1967, 470-75.

————. "Römer 7 und die Anthropologie des Paulus," ibid., 198-209.

———. *Theology of the New Testament*. Vols. 1 and 2. Translated by Kendrick Grobel. London: SCM, 1952.

———. "Zum Problem der Entmythologisierung," *KuM* 2, 179-208.

Burchard, Christoph. "Zu Jak 2, 14-26," *ZNW* 71, 1980, 27-45.

Calvin, Jean. *Calvin: Institutes of the Christian Religion. Vol 1.* edited by John T. McNeill. Translated by Ford Lewis Battles, LOC. Philadelphia: Westminster, 1960.

Camponovo, Odo. *Königtum, Königherrschaft und Reich Gottes in den frühjüdischen Schriften.* OBO 58. Freiburg, Schweiz: Universitätsverlag, 1984.

Carson, D. A.; O'Brien, Peter T.; Seifrid, Mark A. *Justification and Variegated Nomism. Vol. I: The Complexities of Second Temple Judaism; Vol. II: The Paradoxes of Paul.* WUNT II 140 and 181, Tübingen: Mohr Siebeck 2001 and 2004.

Christsein gestalten: Eine Studie zum Weg der Kirche. Kirchenamt im Auftrag des Rates der Evangelische Kirche in Deutschland. Gütersloh: Gütersloher Verlagshaus Mohn, 1986.

Cremer, Hermann. *Biblico-theological Lexicon of New Testament Greek.* 4th ed. Translated by William Urwick. Edinburgh: T&T Clark, 1962.

———. *Die paulinische Rechtfertigungslehre im Zusammenhange ihrer geschichtlichen Voraussetzungen.* 2nd ed. Gütersloh: C. Bertelsmann, 1900.

Crüsemann, Frank. "Jahwes Gerechtigkeit (sdaqa/sädäq) im Alten Testamenti," *EvTh* 36, 1979, 427-50.

Dahl, Nils Alstrup. "The Doctrine of Justification: Its Social Function and Implications." *Studies in Paul: Theology for the Early Christian Mission.* Minneapolis: Augsburg, 1977, 95-120.

———. "The Missionary Theology in the Epistle to the Romans." *Studies in Paul,* 70-94.

———. "The One God of Jews and Gentiles." *Studies in Paul,* 178-91.

Dalferth, Ingolf U. *Existenz Gottes und christlicher Glaube: Skizzen zu einer eschatolgischen Ontologie.* BEvT 93. Munich: C. Kaiser, 1984.

Delling, Gerhard. "Partizipiale Gottesprädikationen in den Briefen des NT," *StTh* 17, 1963, 1-59.

Dietzfelbinger, Christian. *Die Berufung des Paulus als Ursprung seiner Theologie.* 2nd ed. WMANT 58. Neukirchen-Vluyn: Neukirchener Verlas, 1989.

Dodd, C. H. *The Bible and the Greeks.* 3rd ed. London: Hodder & Staughton, 1964.

Donfried, Karl P., ed. *The Romans Debate.* Rev. and exp. Peabody, Mass.: Hendrickson, 1991.

Dunn, James D. G. "4 QMMT and Galatians," *NTS* 43, 1997, 147-53.

———. "The Justice of God," *JThSt NS* 43, 1992, 1-22.

———. *Romans.* WBC. Dallas: Word, 1988.

———. *The New Perspective on Paul. Collected Essays.* Tübingen: Mohr Siebeck, 2005.

———. *The Theology of Paul the Apostle.* Grand Rapids: Eerdmans, 1998.

———. "Works of the Law and the Curse of the Law (Galatians 3:10-14)." *Jesus, Paul, and the Law: Studies in Mark and Galations.* London: SPCK, 1990, 215-41.

———. "Yet once more—'The Works of the Law': A Response," *JStNT* 46, 1992, 99-117.

Ebach, Jürgen. *Streiten mit Gott: Hiob, Teil 1, Hiob 1-20.* Kleine Biblische Bibliothek. Neukirchen-Vluyn: Neukirchener, 1996.

Eckstein, Hans-Joachim. "'Denn Gottes Zorn wird vom Himmel her offenbar werden.' Exegetische Erwägungen zu Röm 1,18," *ZNW* 78, 1987, 74-89.

Elliger, Karl. *Deuterojesaja. Teilband 1. Jesaja 40,1–45,7.* 2nd ed. BK 11/1. Neukirchen-Vluyn: Neukirchener, 1989.

Fahlgren, Karl Hjalmar. *sedaka, nahestehende und entgegengesetzte Begriffe im Alten Testament.* Uppsala: Almqvist & Wilsell, 1932.

Felmy, Karl Christian. *Die orthodoxe Theologie der Gegenwart: Eine Einführung.* Darmstadt: Wissenschaftliche Buchgesellschaft, 1990.

Fiedler, M. J., *Der Begriff dikaiosyne im Matthäus-Evangelium,* Diss. Theol. (Halle, 1957).

———. "'Gerechtigkeit' im Matthäusevangelium." ThV 8, 1977, 63-75.

Fiedler, P. "Röm, 8, 31-39 als Brennpunkt paulinischer Botschaft," ZNW 68, 1977, 23-34.

Fitzmyer, Joseph A. "Romans." *AncB* 33. Edited by David Noel Freedman. New York: Doubleday, 1993.

Fohrer, Georg. *Das Buch Hiob.* 2nd ed. KAT 16. Gütersloh: Gütersloher Verlagshaus G. Mohn, 1989.

Gathercole, Simon J. *Where Is Boasting? Early Jewish Soteriology and Paul's Response in Romans 1-5.* Grand Rapids, Mich.: W. B. Eerdmans, 2002.

Gese, Hartmut. "The Atonement." *Essays on Biblical Theology,* Translated by Keith Crim. Minneapolis: Augsburg, 1981, 93-116.

———. "Death in the Old Testament." *Essays on Biblical Theology,* 34-59.

———. "Die Frage nach dem Lebenssinn: Hiob und die Folgen," ZThK 79, 1982, 162-79.

———. "The Law." *Essays on Biblical Theology.* Translated by Keith Crim. Minneapolis: Augsburg, 1981, 60-92.

———. "The Prologue to John's Gospel." *Essays on Biblical Theology.* 167-222.

Gese, Michael. *Das Vermächtnis des Apostels: Die Rezeption der paulinischen Theologie im Epheserbrief.* WUNT 2, 99. Tübingen: Mohr (Siebeck), 1997.

Giesen, Heinz. *Christliches Handeln: Eine redaktionskritische Untersuchung zum dikaiosyne-Begriff im Matthäus-Evangelium.* EHS.T 181. Frankfurt: P. Lang, 1982.

Gloege, Gerhard. "Die Rechtfertigungslehre also hermeneutische Kategorie," ThLZ 89, 1964, 161-76.

Gnilka, Joachim. *Der Epheserbrief.* HThK 10, 2. Freiburg: Herder, 1990.

Goppelt, Leonhard. "Wahrheit als Befreiung—Das Neutestamentliche Zeugnis von der Wahrheit nach dem Johannes-Evangelium." *Was ist Wahrheit?: Ringvorlesung der Evangelisch-Theologischen Fakultät der Universität Hamburg.* Edited by Hans-Rudolf Müller-Schwefe. Göttingen: Vandenhoeck & Ruprecht, 1965, 80-93.

Gross, Heinrich. "'Rechtfertigung' nach dem Alten Testament: Bibeltheologische Beobachtungen." *Kontinuität und Einheit. Für Franz Mussner.* Edited by Paul-Gerhard Müller and Werner Stenger. Freiburg, Basel, Vienna: Herder, 1981, 17-29.

Haacker, Klaus. *Der Brief des Paulus an die Römer.* ThHK NT 6. Leipzig: Evangelische Verlagsanstalt, 1999.

Hafemann, Scott. "'Self-Commendation' and Apostolic Legitimacy in 2 Corinthians: A Pauline Dialectic?" NTS 36, 1990, 66-88.

Hahn, Ferdinand. "Genesis 15:6 im Neuen Testament." *Probleme biblischer Theologie: Festschrift für Gerhard von Rad zum 70. Geburtstag.* Edited by Hans Walter Wolff. München: C. Kaiser, 1971, 90-107.

———. "Gerechtigkeit Gottes und Rechtfertigung des Menschen nach dem Zeugnis des Neuen Testaments." EvTh 59, 1999, 335-46.

———. "Gibt es eine Entwicklung in den Aussagen über die Rechtfertigung bei Paulus?" EvTh 53, 1993, 342-66.

———. "Taufe und Rechtfertigung." *Rechtfertigung: Festschrift für Ernst Käsemann zum 70. Geburtstag.* Edited by Johannes Friedrich, Wolfgang Pöhlmann, and Peter

Stuhlmacher. Tübingen: Mohr (Siebeck); Göttingen: Vandenhoeck & Ruprecht, 1976, 95-124.

Härle, Wilfried. "Analytische und synthetische Urteile in der Rechtfertigungslehre, *NZSTh* 16, 1974, 17-34.

———. *Dogmatik*. De Gruyter Lehrbuch. Berlin: de Gruyter, 1995.

———. "Zur Gegenwartsbedeutung der Rechtfertigungslehre," *ZThK* 95, 1998, 101-39.

Harnack, Adolf von. *History of Dogma*. Vol. 7. Translated by Neil Buchanan. New York: Russell & Russell, 1958.

Haubeck, Wilfrid. *Loskauf durch Christus: Herkunft, Gestalt und Bedeutung des paulinischen Loskaufmotivs*. Giessen: Brunnen, 1985.

———. "Rechtfertigung und Sühne bei Paulus," *JETh* 11, 1997, 93-104.

Heckel, Ulrich. *Kraft in Schwachheit: Untersuchungen zu 2. Kor 10-13*. WUNT 2, 56. Tübingen: Mohr (Siebeck), 1993.

Hengel, Martin. *The Son of God: The Origin of Christology and the History of Jewish-Hellenistic Religion*. Translated by John Bowden. Philadelphia: Fortress, 1976.

Hengel, Martin, and Anna Maria Schwemer. *Paul between Damascus and Antioch: The Unknown Years*. Translated by John Bowden. Louisville: Westminster/John Knox, 1997.

Hermisson, Hans-Jürgen. "Der Lohn des Knechts." *Die Botschaft und die Boten: Festschrift für Hans Walter Wolff zum 70. Geburtstag*. Edited by Jörg Jeremias und Lothar Perlitt. Neukirchen-Vluyn: Neukirchener, 1981, 269-87.

———. *Deuterojesaja BK XI/2 (Lfg 7-9; 45, 8–48, 11)*. Neukirchen-Vluyn: Neukirchener, 1991.

———. "Diskussionsworte bei Deuterojesaja," *EvTh* 31, 1971, 665-76.

Herrenbrück, Fritz. "Wer waren die 'Zöllner'?" *ZNW* 72, 1981, 178-94.

Hill, David. *Greek Words and Hebrew Meanings: Studies in the Semantics of Soteriological Terms*. NTS. MS 5. London: Cambridge University Press, 1967.

Hofius, Otfried. "Das Gesetz des Mose und das Gesetz Christi." *Paulusstudien* WUNT 51. Tübingen: Mohr, 1989, 50-74.

———. "Das vierte Gottesknechtslied in den Briefen des Neuen Testaments." *NTS* 39, 1993, 414-43.

———. "Erwägungen zur Gestalt und Herkunft des paulinischen Versöhnungsgedanken." *Paulusstudien*. WUNT 51. Tübingen: Mohr, 1989, 1-14.

———. "Gesetz und Evangelium nach 2. Korinther 3." *Paulusstudien*, 75-120.

———. "'Gott hat unter uns aufgerichtet das Wort der Versöhnung' (2. Kor 5,19), *Paulusstudien*, 15-32.

———. "Herrenmahl und Herrenmahlparadosis," ibid., 203-40.

———. *Jesu Tischgemeinschaft mit Sündern*. CwH 86. Stuttgart: Calwer, 1967.

———. "'Rechtfertigung des Gottlosen' als Thema biblischer Theologie," *Paulusstudien*, 121-47.

———. "Sühne und Versöhnung. Zum paulinischen Verständnis des Kreuzestodes Jesu." *Paulusstudien*, 33-49.

———. "Vergebungszuspruch und Vollmachtsfrage: Mk 2:1-12 und das Problem priesterlicher Absolution im antiken Judentum." *"Wenn nicht jetzt, wann dann?": Aufsätze für Hans-Joachim Kraus zum 65. Geburtstag*. Edited by Hans-Georg Geyer, et. al. Neukrichen-Vluyn: Neukirchener, 1983, 115-28.

Holl, Karl. "Die Rechtfertigungslehre in Luthers Vorlesung über den Römerbrief mit besonderer Rücksicht auf die Frage der Heilsgewissheit." *Gesammelte Aufsätze zur*

Kirchengeschichte. Volume I: Luther. 7th ed. Tübingen: Mohr (Siebeck), 1948, 111-54.

―――. "Zur Verständigung über Luthers Rechtfertigungslehre." *Rechtfertigung als Grundbegriff evangelischer Theologie: Eine Textsammlung.* Edited by Gerhard Sauter. *ThB* 78. Munich: C. Kaiser, 1989, 152-74.

Hooker, M. "The Johannine Prologue and the Messianic Secret." *NTS* 21. 1974, 40-58.

Hossfeld, Frank-Lothar. "Gedanken zum alttestamentlichen Vorfeld der Rechtfertigungslehre." *Worum geht es in der Rechtfertigungs-lehre?*: das Biblische Fundament der 'Gemeinsamen Erklärung' von katholischer Kirche und lutherischem Weltbund. Edited by Thomas Söding. QD 180. Freiburg: Herder, 1999, 13-26.

Hübner, Hans. "Die paulinische Rechtfertigungslehre als ökumenisch-hermeneutisches Problem," in *"Worum geht es in der Rechtfertigungslehre?"* Edited by T. Söding. *QD* 180, 1999, 76-105.

―――. *Law in Paul's Thought.* Translated by C. G. Greig. Edited by John Riches. Studies of the New Testament and Its World. Edinburgh: T&T Clark, 1984.

―――. "Rechtfertigung und Sühne bei Paulus." *Biblische Theologie als Hermeneutik: Gesammelte Aufsätze.* Göttingen: Vanderhoeck & Ruprecht, 1995, 272-85.

―――. "Was heisst bei Paulus 'Werke des Gesetzes?'" ibid,. 166-74.

Ibuki, Yu. *Die Wahrheit im Johannesevangelium.* BBB 39. Bonn: P. Hanstein, 1972.

Irenaeus. *Five Books of S. Irenaeus Against Heresies.* Translated by John Keble. Library of Fathers of the Holy Catholic Church. Oxford: James Parker and Co., 1872.

Janowski, Bernd. "Auslösung des verwirkten Lebens. Zur Geschichte und Struktur der biblischen Lösegeldvorstellung," *ZThK* 79, 1982, 25-59.

―――. "Die Tat kehrt zum Täter zurück. Offene Fragen im Umkreis des 'Tun-Ergehen-Zusammenhangs'." *ZThK* 91, 1994, 247-71.

―――. "Er trug unsere Sünden." Jesja 53 und die Dramatik der Stellvertretung. *ZThK* 90, 1993, 1-24.

―――. "JHWH der Richter—ein rettender Gott. Psalm 7 und das Motiv des Gottesgerichtes." *JBTh* 9, 1994, 53-86.

Jeremias, Joachim. *New Testament Theology: The Proclamation of Jesus.* Translated by John Bowden. New York: Scribner, 1971.

―――. *The Parables of Jesus.* 2nd rev. ed. New York: Scribner, 1972.

Joest, Wilfried. "Die tridentinische Rechtfertigungslehre." *KuD* 9, 1963, 41-69.

―――. *Dogmatik, Vol. 2: Der Weg Gottes mit dem Menschen.* UTB 1413. Göttingen: Vandenhoeck & Ruprecht, 1987.

―――. *Gesetz und Freiheit: Das Problem des Tertius usus legis bei Luther und die neutestamentliche Parainese.* 3rd ed. Göttingen: Vandenhoeck & Ruprecht, 1961.

―――. "Paulus und das Luthersche Simul Iustus et Peccator," *KuD* 1, 1995, 269-320.

Johnson, M. D. "Life of Adam and Eve: A New Translation and Introduction." *The Old Testament Pseudepigrapha.* Vol. 2. Edited by James H. Charlesworth. Anchor Bible Reference Library. New York: Doubleday, 1985, 249-95.

Jüngel, Eberhard. "Amica Exegesis einer römischen Note." *ZThK.B.* 10, 1998, 252-79.

―――. "Die Autorität des bittenden Christus." *Unterwegs zur Sache: theologische Bemerkungen.* BevTh 61. Munich: C. Kaiser, 1972, 179-88.

―――. "Die Kirche als Sakrament?" *Wertlose Wahrheit: Zur Identität und Relevanz des christlichen Glaubens.* BevTh 107. Munich: Kaiser, 1990, 311-34.

―――. *Justification: The Heart of the Christian Faith: A Theological Study with an Ecumenical Purpose.* Translated by Jeffrey F. Cayzer. Intro. by John Webster. Edinburgh: T&T Clark, 2001.

————. *Paulus und Jesus: eine Untersuchung zur Präzisierung der Frage nach dem Ursprung der Christologie.* HUTh 2. Tübingen: Mohr (Siebeck), 1979.

Käsemann, Ernst. "Amt und Gemeinde im Neuen Testament," in ibid., *Exegetische Versuche und Besinnungen* (EVB) I. 6th ed. Göttingen: Vandenhoeck & Ruprecht, 1970, 109-34.

————. *Commentary on Romans.* Translated and edited by Geoffrey W. Bromiley. Grand Rapids: Eerdmans, 1980.

————. *Das Neue Testament als Kanon: Dokumentation und kritische Analyse zur gegenwärten Diskussion.* Göttingen: Vandenhoeck & Ruprecht, 1970.

————. "Die Legitimität des Apostels. Eine Untersuchung zu II. Korinther 10-13 (*ZNW* 41, 1942, 33-71). *Paulusbild in der neueren deutschen Forschung.* WdF 24. Darmstadt: Wissenschaftliche Buchgesellschaft, 1964, 475-521.

————. *Essays on New Testament Themes.* Philadelphia: Fortress, 1982.

————. "Gottes Gerechtigkeit bei Paulus," *EVB* II, 1970:4, 181-93.

————. *Perspectives on Paul.* Translated by Margaret Kohl. Philadelphia: Fortress, 1971.

————. "Zum Verständnis von Römer 3,24-26, *EVB* 1, 96-100.

Kertelge, Karl. "Paulus zur Rechtfertigung allein aus Glauben," in *"Worum geht es in der Rechtfertigungslehre?* Edited by T. Söding. QD 180, 1999, 64-75.

————. *Rechtfertigung bei Paulus: Studien zur Struktur und zum Bedeutungsgehalt des paulinischen Rechtfertigungsbegriffs.* NTA NF 3. Münster: Aschendorff, 1972.

Kessler, R. " 'Ich weiss, dass mein Erlöser lebet.' Sozialgeschichtlicher Hintergrund und theologische Bedeutung der Löser-Vorstellung in Hiob 19, 25. *ZThK* 89, 1992, 139-58.

Kim, Seyoon. *The Origin of Paul's Gospel.* WUNT II, 4. Tübingen: Mohr, 1981.

Klaiber, Walter. "Aus Glauben, damit aus Gnaden. Der Grundsatz paulinischer Soteriologie und die Gnadenlehre John Wesleys," *ZThK* 88, 1991, 313-38.

————. *Call and Response: Biblical Foundations of a Theology of Evangelism.* Translated by Howard Perry-Trauthig and James A. Dwyer. Nashville: Abingdon, 1997.

————. "Die Aufgabe einer theologischen Interpretation des 4. Evangeliums," *ZThK* 82, 1985, 300-24.

————. "Hintergrund und Ziele der ACK-Konsultationsprozesses," in *Aufbruch zu einer missionarischen Ökumene.* Hamburg: EMW, 1991), 115-34.

————. "Ökumenische Verantwortung für die Rechtfertigungsbotschaft heute," *Ökumene vor neuen Zeiten: FS Theodor Schneider.* Edited by Konrad Raiser und Dorothea Sattler. Freiburg, Basel, Wien: Herder, 2000, 209-24.

————. "Missionarische Ökumene—Ökumenische Mission, *ÖR* 47, 1998, 291-306.

————. *Rechtfertigung und Gemeinde: Eine Untersuchung zum paulinischen Kirchenverständnis.* FRLANT 127. Göttingen: Vandenhoeck & Ruprecht, 1982.

————. "Rechtfertigung und Kirche. Exegetische Anmerkungen zum aktuellen ökumenischen Gespräch." *KuD* 42, 1996, 285-317.

Klaiber, Walter, and Manfred Marquardt. *Living Grace: An Outline of United Methodist Theology.* Translated by J. Steven O'Malley and Ulrike R. M. Guthrie. Nashville: Abingdon, 2001.

Klauck, Hans-Josef. *Der erste Johannesbrief.* EKK 23/1. Zürich and Neukirchen-Vluyn: Neukirchener, 1991.

Koch, Klaus. "Die Entstehung der sozialen Kritik bei den Profeten,": in *Spuren des hebräischen Denkens* (GA vol.1). Neukirchen-Vluyn: Neukirchener, 1991, 146-66.

————. "Die hebräische Sprache zwischen Polytheismus und Monotheismus." in ibid, 25-64.

————. "Gibt es ein Vergeltungsdogma im AT?" ibid., 65-105.

————. "Sädäq und Maat. Konnektive Gerechtigkeit in Israel und Ägypten?" *Gerechtigkeit: Richten und Retten in der abendländischen Tradition und ihren altorientalischen Ursprüngen.* Edited by Jan Assmann, Bernd Janowski, and Michael Welker. Reihe Kulte/Kulturen. Munich: Fink, 1998, 37-64.

————. sdq *im Alten Testament*, Theol. diss., Heidelberg, 1953.

————. "Tempeleinlassliturgien und Dekaloge," in *Spuren*, 169-83.

————. "Wesen und Ursprung der "Gemeinschaftstreue" im Israel der Königszeit," in *Spuren*, 107-27.

Köhler, Ludwig. *Hebrew Man*. Translated by Peter R. Ackroyd. Nashville: Abingdon, 1956.

Kraus, Hans-Joachim. *Das Evangelium der unbekannten Propheten. Jesaja 40-66.* Neukirchen-Vluyn: Neukirchener, 1990.

————. *Psalms 1-59: A Continental Commentary*, Translated by Hilton C. Oswald, Minneapolis: Fortress, 1978.

————. *Theology of the Psalms*. Translated by Keith Crim. Minneapolis: Augsburg, 1986.

Kraus, Wolfgang. *Das Volk Gottes: Zur Grundlegung der Ekklesiologie bei Paulus*. WUNT 85. Tübingen: Mohr, 1996.

Kuhn, W. "Die Bedeutung der Qumrantexte für das Verständnis des Galaterbriefes." *New Qumran Texts and Studies*. Edited by George J. Brooke with Florentino García Martínez. StTDJ 15. Leiden: Brill, 1994, 169-222.

Kümmel, Werner Georg. "Römer 7 und die Bekehrung des Paulus." *Römer 7 und das Bild des Menschen im Neuen Testament*. ThB 53. Munich: C. Kaiser, 1974, IX-160.

Küng, Hans. "Der Frühkatholizismus im Neuen Testament als kontroverstheologisches Problem." *Das Neue Testament als Kanon: Dokumentation und kritische Analyse zur gegenwärtigen Diskussion*. Edited by Ernst Käsemann. Göttingen: Vandenhoeck & Ruprecht, 1970, 165-204.

————. *Justification: The Doctrine of Karl Barth and a Catholic Reflection*. 40th Anniversary edition with new foreword by Hermann Häring. Louisville: Westminster/John Knox, 2004.

Lehmann, Karl, and Wolfhart Pannenberg, eds. *The Condemnations of the Reformation Era: Do They Still Divide?* Translated by Margaret Kohl. Minneapolis: Fortress, 1990.

Levin, Christoph. "Altes Testament und Rechtfertigung." *ZThK* 96, 1999, 161-76.

Lindemann, Andreas. "Die Kirche als Leib Christi," *ZThK* 92, 1995, 140-65.

————. *Paulus im ältesten Christentum: das Bild des Apostels und die Rezeption der paulinischen Theologie in der frühchristlichen Literatur bis Marcion*. BHTh 58. Tübingen: Mohr (Siebeck), 1976.

Lohfink, Gerhard. "Paulinische Theologie in der Rezeption der Pastoralbriefe," in *Paulus in den neutestamentlichen Spätschriften: zur Paulusrezeption im Neuen Testament*. Edited by Karl Kertelge. QD 89. Freiburg: Herder, 1981, 70-121.

Lohse, Eduard. "Die Gerechtigkeit Gottes in der paulinischen Theologie," in ibid., *Die Einheit des Neuen Testaments: Exegetische Studien zur Theologie des Neuen Testaments*. 2nd ed. Göttingen: Vandenhoeck & Ruprecht, 1973, 209-27.

————. *Die Texte aus Qumran*. Fourth ed. München: Kösel 1986.

————. "Glaube und Werke. Zur Theologie des Jakobusbriefes," *Einheit des NT*, 285-306.

————. *Paulus. Eine Biographie*. Munich: C. H. Beck, 1996.

Löning, K. "Paulinismus in der Apostelgeschichte." *Paulus in den neutestamentlichen Spätschriften: zur Paulusrezeption im Neuen Testament.* Edited by Karl Kertelge. QD 89. Freiburg: Herder, 1981, 202-34.

Lührmann, Dieter. "Abendmahlgemeinschaft? Gal 2:11ff." *Kirche: Festschrift für Günther Bornkamm zum 75. Geburtstag.* Edited by Dieter Lührmann and Georg Strecker. Tübingen: Mohr, 1980, 271-86.

———. "Christologie und Rechtfertigung." *Rechtfertigung: Festschrift für Ernst Käsemann zum 70. Geburtstag.* Edited by Johannes Friedrich, Wolfgang Pöhlmann, and Peter Stuhlmacher. Tübingen: Mohr; Göttingen: Vandenhoeck & Ruprecht, 1976, 351-63.

Luther, Martin. "Bondage of the Will." Translated by Philip S. Watson. *Luther's Works,* Vol. 33.

———. "Lectures on Romans." Translated by Jacob A. O. Preus. *Luther's Works,* Vol. 25.

———. *Luther's Works.* Gen. ed. Helmut T. Lehmann. Philadelphia: Fortress, 1972.

———. "Preface to the Complete Edition of Luther's Writings." Translated by Lewis W. Spitz. *Luther's Works,* Vol. 34, 327-38.

———. "Theses Concerning Faith and Law." Translated by Lewis W. Spitz. *Luther's Works,* Vol. 34, 109-32.

Lutheran World Federation and the Roman Catholic Church. *Joint Declaration on the Doctrine of Justification.* English language edition. Grand Rapids: Eerdmans, 2000.

Luz, Ulrich. *Matthew: A Commentary.* Translated by Wilhelm C. Linss. Minneapolis: Augsburg, 1989.

———. "Rechtfertigung bei den Paulusschülern." *Rechtfertigung, FS E. Käsemann.* Tübingen: Mohr; Göttingen: Vandenhoeck & Ruprecht, 1976, 365-83.

Maier, Johann, and Kurt Schubert. *Die Qumran-Essener: Die Texte vom Toten Meer.* Vol. 2. UTB 1863. Munich and Basel: E. Reinhardt, 1995.

Maron, Gottfried. *Kirche und Rechtfertigung: Eine kontroverstheologische Untersuchung, ausgehend von den Texten des Zweiten Vatikanischen Konzils.* KiKonf 15. Göttingen: Vandenhoeck & Ruprecht, 1969.

Maurer, Ernstpeter. *"Rechtfertigung": Konfessionstrennend oder konfessionsverbindend.* BensH 87. Göttingen: Vandenhoeck & Ruprecht, 1998.

McGrath, Alister E. *Iustitia Dei: A History of the Christian Doctrine of Justification.* 2 vols; Cambridge: Cambridge University, 1986.

Merkel, Helmut. *Die Pastoralbriefe: Übersetzt und erklärt.* NTD 9/1. Göttingen: Vandenhoeck & Ruprecht, 1991.

Merklein, Helmut. "Der Sühnetod Jesu nach dem Zeugnis des Neuen Testaments." *Studien zu Jesus und Paulus. II.* WUNT 105. Tübingen: Mohr, 1998, 31-59.

———. "Die Bedeutung des Kreuzestodes Christi für den paulinischen Gerechtigkeits- und Gesetzesthematik." *Studien zu Jesus und Paulus.* WUNT 43. Tübingen: Mohr (Siebeck), 1987, 1-106.

———. "Die Umkehrpredigt bei Johannes dem Täufer und Jesus von Nazaret," *Studien I,* 109-26.

———. *Jesu Botschaft von der Gottesherrschaft: eine Skizze.* SBS 111. Stuttgart: Katholisches Bibelwerk, 1989.

———. "Paulinische Theologie in der Rezeption des Kolosser- und Epheserbriefes," in *Studien I,* 409-53.

Michel, D. "Das Ansehen des Glaubens als Gerechtigkeitstat: Gen 15, 6" in *Recht und Ethos im AT: Gestalt und Wirkung. Festschrift für Horst Seebass.* Edited by Stefan Beyerle et al. Neukirchen-Vluyn: Neukirchener, 1999, 103-13.

Michel, Otto. *Der Brief an die Römer*. 14th ed. KEK 4. Göttingen: Vandenhoeck & Ruprecht, 1978.

Moltmann, Jürgen. *The Spirit of Life: A Universal Affirmation*. Translated by Margaret Kohl. Minneapolis: Fortress, 1992.

Mosis, Rudolf. "'Glauben' und 'Gerechtigkeit' zu Gen 15:6." *Die Väter Israels: Beiträge zur Theologie der Patriarchenüberlieferungen im AT*. Edited by Manfred Görg. Stuttgart: Katholisches Bibelwerk, 1989, 225-57.

Müller, Paul Gerhard. "Der 'Paulinismus' in der Apostelgeschichte," in *Paulus in den neutestamentlichen Spätschriften*. Edited by K. Kertelge. QD 89. Freiburg: Herder, 1981, 157-201.

Müller, Ulrich B. *Die Geschichte der Christologie in der johanneischen Gemeinde*. SBS 77. Stuttgart: KBW, 1975.

Mussner, Franz. "Das Wesen des Christentums ist synesthiein." *Mysterium der Gnade: Festschrift für Johann Auer*. Edited by Heribert Rossmann and Joseph Ratzinger. Regensburg: F. Pustet, 1975, 92-102.

————"Eph 2 als ökumenisches Modell." *Neues Testament und Kirche: für Rudolf Schnackenburg*. Edited by Joachim Gnilka. Freiburg, Basel, Vienna: Herder, 1974, 325-36.

————. *Theologie der Freiheit nach Paulus*. QD 75. Freiburg im Breisgau; Basel; Vienna: Herder, 1976.

Neugebauer, Fritz. *In Christus=En Christoi: eine Untersuchung zum Paulinischen Glaubensverständnis*. Göttingen: Vandenhoeck & Ruprecht, 1961.

Niebuhr, Karl-Wilhelm. "Die paulinische Rechtfertigungslehre in der gegenwärtigen exegetischen Diskussion." *Worum geht es in der Rechtfertigungs-lehre?: das biblische Fundament der 'Gemeinsamen Erklärung' von katholischer Kirche und lutherischem Weltbund*. Edited by Thomas Söding. QD 180. Freiburg: Herder, 1999, 106-30.

Niehr, Herbert. *Rechtsprechung in Israel: Untersuchungen zur Geschichte der Gerichtsorganisation im Alten Testament*. SBS 130. Stuttgart: Katholisches Bibelwerk, 1987.

Nürnberger, Klaus. "Wider die Verengung der Rechtfertigungslehre," *JbM* 25, 1993, 141-71.

Oberlinner, Lorenz. *Die Pastoralbriefe, zweite Folge: Kommentar zum zweiten Timotheusbrief: Auslegung*. HThK 11/2. Freiburg: Herder, 1995.

Oeming, Manfred. "Ist Genesis 15:6 ein Beleg für die Anrechnung des Glaubens zur Gerechtigkeit?" *ZAW* 95, 1983, 182-97.

Outler, Albert Cook. "Theologische Akzente." *Der Methodismus*. Edited by C. Ernst Sommer. KW 6. Stuttgart: Evangelisches Verlagswerk, 1968, 84-102.

Pannenberg, Wolfhart. *Systematic Theology*. Vols 1-3. Translated by Geoffrey W. Bromiley. Grand Rapids: Eerdmans, 1991.

Pemsel-Maier, Sabine. *Rechtfertigung durch Kirche?: Das Verhältnis von Kirche und Rechtfertigung in Entwürfen der neueren katholischen und evangelischen Theologie*. SSTh 5. Würzburg: Echter, 1991.

Perlitt, Lothar. "Anklage und Freispruch Gottes. Theologische Motive in der Zeit des Exils," *ZThK* 69, 1972, 290-303.

Pesch, Otto Hermann. *Theologie der Rechtfertigung bei Martin Luther und Thomas von Aquin: Versuch eines systematisch-theologischen Dialogs*. Walberberger Studien der Albertus-Magnus-Akademie. Theologische Reihe 4. Mainz: Matthias-Grünewald-Verlag, 1967.

Pesch, Otto Hermann, and Albrecht Peters. *Einführung in die Lehre von Gnade und Rechtfertigung*. 2nd ed. Darmstadt: Wissenschaftliche Buchgesellscaft, 1989.

Pesch, Rudolf. "Zur Exegese Gottes durch Jesus von Nazaret. Eine Auslegung des Gleichnisses vom Vater und seinen beiden Söhnen." *Jesus, Ort der Erfahrung Gottes*. Edited by Bernhard Casper, et al. Freiburg: Herder, 1976, 140-89.

Peters, Albrecht. *Rechtfertigung*. HST 12. Gütersloh: Gütersloher Verlagshaus Mohn, 1990.

Preuss, Horst Dietrich. *Old Testament Theology*. Vol. 2. OTL. Louisville: Westminster/John Knox, 1995.

Rad, Gerhard von, "Anrechnung des Glaubens zur Gerechtigkeit," in *Gesammelte Studien zum AT, ThB* 8. Munich: C. Kaiser 1958, 130-35.

———. " 'Gerechtigkeit' und 'Leben' in der Kultsprache der Psalmen," in ibid., 225-47.

———. *Old Testament Theology*. Vol. 1: *The Theology of Israel's Historical Traditions*. Translated by D. M. G. Stalker. Intro. Walter Brueggemann. OTL. Louisville: Westminster/John Knox, 2001.

Reumann, John Henry Paul. *Righteousness in the New Testament: Justification in the Lutheran-Catholic Dialogue*. With responses by Joseph A. Fitzmeyer and Jerome D. Quinn. Philadelphia: Fortress, 1982.

Reventlow, Henning, Graf. *Rechtfertigung im Horizont des Alten Testaments*. BevTh 58. Munich: C. Kaiser, 1971.

Roloff, Jürgen. "Anfänge der soteriologischen Deutung des Todes Jesus (Mk X.45 und Lk XXII.27)," *NTS* 19, 1972/73, 38-64.

———. *Der erste Brief an Timotheus*. EKK 15. Zürich: Benziger, 1988.

Sanders, E. P. *Paul and Palestinian Judaism: A Comparison of Patterns of Religion*. London: SCM, 1972.

———. *Paul, the Law, and the Jewish People*. Philadelphia: Fortress, 1983.

Sauter, Gerhard, ed. *Rechtfertigung als Grundbegriff evangelischer Theologie: Eine Textsammlung*. ThB 78. Munich: C. Kaiser, 1989.

Schille, Gottfried. *Die Apostelgeschichte des Lukas*. ThHK 5. Berlin: Evangelische Verlagsanstalt, 1983.

Schlatter, Adolf *Romans: The Righteousness of God*. Translated by Siegfried S. Schatzmann. Foreword by Peter Stuhlmacher. Peabody, Mass.: Hendrickson, 1995.

Schlichting, Wolfhart, ed. *Rechtfertigung und Weltverantwortung*: Internationale Konsultation, Neuendettelsau, 9-12. September 1991: Bericht und Referate. Neuendettelsau: Freimund-Verlag, 1993.

Schmid, Hans Heinrich. *Gerechtigkeit als Weltordnung: Hintergrund und Geschichte der alttestamentlichen Gerechtigkeitsbegriffes*. BHTh 40. Tübingen: Mohr (Siebeck), 1968.

———. "Gerechtigkeit und Glaube. Genesis 15, 1-6 und sein biblisch-theologischer Kontext," *EvTh* 40, 1980, 396-419.

Schmidt, Werner H. "Rechtfertigung des Gottlosen." *Die Botschaft und die Boten. FS H.W. Wolff*. Edited by Jörg Jeremias und Lothar Perlitt. Neukirchen-Vluyn: Neukirchener, 1981, 157-68.

———. "Werk Gottes und Tun des Menschen. Ansätze zur Unterscheidung von 'Gesetz und Evangelium' in Alten Testament, *JBTh* 4, 1989, 11-28.

Schneider, Theodor, ed. *Handbuch der Dogmatik*, vol 2. Düsseldorf: Patmos, 1992.

Schnelle, Udo. *Gerechtigkeit und Christusgegenwart: Vorpaulinische und paulinische Tauftheologie*. GTA 24. Göttingen: Vandenhoeck & Ruprecht, 1983.

————. *The History and Theology of the New Testament Writings.* Translated by M. Eugene Boring. Minneapolis: Fortress, 1998.

Schniewind, Julius. *Das Evangelium nach Matthäus.* 9th ed. NTD 2. Göttingen: Vandenhoeck & Ruprecht, 1960.

Schoberth, Ingrid. "Rechtfertigung und Schülersehnsucht," *EvTh* 59, 1999, 49-61.

Schottroff, Luise, and Wolfgang Stegemann. *Jesus and the Hope of the Poor.* Translated by Matthew J. O'Connell. Maryknoll, N.Y.: Orbis, 1986.

Schrage, Wolfgang. *Der erste Brief an die Korinther.* Vol. 1. (1. Kor 1, 1-6, 11), EKK 7:1. Zürich: Braunschweig Neukirchener, 1991.

————. "Die Frage nach der Mitte und dem Kanon im Kanon des neuen Testaments in der neueren Diskussion," in *Rechtfertigung. FS. E.* Käsemann. Edited by J. Friedrich et al. Tübingen: Göttingen, 1976, 415-42.

————. "Heiligung als Prozess bei Paulus." *Jesu Rede von Gott und ihre Nachgeschichte im frühen Christentum: Festschrift für Willi Marxsen zum 70. Geburtstag.* Edited by Dietrich-Alex Koch, Gerhard Sellin, and Andreas Lindemann. Gütersloh: Güterloher Verlagshaus G. Mohn, 1989, 222-34.

Schreiner, J. " 'Deklatorische Formel' und rechtsgültige Feststellung in AT," in ibid., *Leben nach der Weisung Gottes,* Würzburg: Echter, 1992, 282-300.

Schroeder, H. J. *Canons and Decrees of the Council of Trent.* Original Text with English Translation. St. Louis: Herder, 1941.

Schweitzer, Albert. *The Mysticism of Paul the Apostle.* Translated by William Montgomery. New York: Macmillan, 1960.

Seebass, Horst. "Über die innere Einheit vom Altem und Neuem Testament." *Eine Bibel, zwei Testamente: Positionen biblischer Theologie.* Edited by Christoph Dohmen and Thomas Söding. UTB 1893. Paderborn: Ferdinand Schöningh, 1995, 131-42.

————. *Genesis 1, Urgeschichte (1,1—11,26).* Neukirchen-Vluyn: Neukirchener, 1996.

Seifrid, Mark A. *Christ, our Righteousness, Paul's theology of justification.* NSBT 5, Downers Grove, IL: InterVarsity, 2000.

————. *Justification by Faith: The Origin and Development of a Central Pauline Theme.* NT.S 68. Leiden: Brill, 1992.

Söding, Thomas. "Der Erste Thessalonicherbrief und die frühe paulinische Evangeliumsverkündigung." *Das Wort vom Kreuz: Studien zur paulinischen Theologie.* WUNT 93. Tübingen: Mohr, 1997, 31-56.

————. "Kreuzestheologie und Rechtfertigungslehre," in ibid., 153-84.

————. "Kriterium der Wahrheit? Zum theologischen Stellenwert der paulinischen Rechtfertigungslehre," in *Worum geht es in der Rechtfertigungslehre? Das biblische Fundament der "Gemeinsamen Erklärung" von Katholischer Kirche und Lutherischem Weltbund,* QD 180, 1999, 193-246.

Spieckermann, H. *Heilsgegenwart. Eine Theologie der Psalmen,* FRLANT 148. Göttingen: Vandenhoeck & Ruprecht, 1989.

Stahl, R. "Die glaubenden Gerechten. Rechtfertigung im Alten Testament." *Gedenkt an das Wort: Festschrift für Werner Vogler zum 65. Geburtslag.* Edited by Christoph Kähler, Martina Böhm, and Christfried Böttrich. Leipzig: Evangelische Verlagsanstalt, 1999, 243-51.

Staniloae, Dumitru. *Orthodoxe Dogmatik Volume 2.* Ökumenische Theologie 15. Zürich: Gütersloher Verlagshaus G. Mohn, 1990.

Stendahl, Krister. *Paul among Jews and Gentiles, and Other Essays.* Philadelphia: Fortress, 1976.

———. "The Apostle Paul and the 'Introspective' Conscience of the West. In *Paul among Jews*, 78-96.

Strecker, Georg. *Der Weg der Gerechtigkeit: Untersuchung zur Theologie des Matthäus.* FRLANT 82. 3rd ed. Göttingen: Vandenhoeck & Ruprecht, 1971.

———. "Befreiung und Rechtfertigung. Zur Stellung der Rechtfertigungslehre in der Theologie des Paulus." *Eschaton und Historie: Aufsätze.* Göttingen: Vandenhoeck & Ruprecht, 1979, 229-256.

———. *Theology of the New Testament.* Translated by M. Eugene Boring. New York: W. de Gruyter, 2000.

Stuhlmacher, Peter. "The Apostle Paul's View of Righteousness," *Reconciliation, Law, and Righteousness: Essays in Biblical Theology.* Translaed by Everett R. Kalin. Philadelphia: Fortress, 1981, 68-93.

———. *Biblische Theologie des Neuen Testaments*, Vol. 1. Grundlegung. Von Jesus zu Paulus. Göttingen: Vandenhoeck & Ruprecht, 1992.

———. *Das paulinische Evangelium.* FRLANT 95. Göttingen: Vandenhoeck & Ruprecht, 1968.

———. *Gerechtigkeit Gottes bei Paulus.* FRLANT 87. Göttingen: Vandenhoeck & Ruprecht, 1965.

———. "'He is Our Peace' (Eph. 2:14): On the Exegesis and Significance of Ephesians 2:14-18." *Reconciliation, Law, and Righteousness*, 182-200.

———. "Recent Exegesis on Romans 3:24-26" in ibid., 94-109.

———. "Vicariously Giving His Life for Many, Mark 10:45 (Matt. 20:28)." Ibid. 16-29.

Subilia, Vittorio. *Die Rechtfertigung aus Glauben: Gestalt und Wirkung vom Neuen Testament bis heute.* Göttingen: Vandenhoeck & Ruprecht, 1981.

Tamez, Elsa. *The Amnesty of Grace: Justification by Faith from a Latin American Perspective.* Translated by Sharon H. Ringe. Nashville: Abingdon, 1993.

Tappert, Theodore G., ed. "Formula of Concord (1577)." *The Book of Concord: The Confessions of the Evangelical Lutheran Church.* In collaboration with Jaroslav Pelikan, Robert H. Fischer, and Arthur C. Piepkorn. Philadelphia: Fortress, 1959, 463-636.

Theissen, Gerd. *Psychological Aspects of Pauline Theology.* Translated by John P. Calvin. Philadelphia: Fortress, 1986.

———. *Social Reality and the Early Christians: Theology, Ethics, and the World of the New Testament.* Translated by Margaret Kohl. Minneapolis: Fortress, 1992.

Theobald, Michael. "Der Kanon von der Rechtfertigung (Gal 2,16; Röm 3,28)—Eigentum des Paulus oder Gemeingut der Kirche?" in *Worum geht es in der Rechtfertigungslehre?* Edited by T. Söding. QD 180, 1999, 131-92.

Thilo, Hans-Joachim. "Paulus—Die Geschichte einer Entwicklung psychoanalytisch gesehen." *WzM* 37, 1985, 2-14.

Tillich, Paul. *Systematic Theology.* Three volumes in one. Chicago: University of Chicago Press, 1967.

Umbach, Helmut. *In Christus getauft, von der Sünde befreit: Die Gemeinde als sündenfreier Raum bei Paulus.* FRLANT 181. Göttingen: Vandenhoeck & Ruprecht, 1999, 182-206.

Vermez, Geza. *The Complete Dead Sea Scrolls in English.* New York: Penguin, 1997.

Vouga, François. *An die Galater.* Handbuch zum Neuen Testament 10. Tübingen: Mohr (Siebeck), 1998.

Walker, R. "Allein aus Werken. Zur Auslegung von Jak 2:14-26," *ZThK* 61, 1964, 155-92.

Weder, Hans. *Das Kreuz Jesu bei Paulus: Ein Versuch, über den Geschichtsbezug des christlichen Glaubens nachzudenken.* FRLANT 125. Göttingen: Vandenhoeck & Ruprecht, 1981.

———. "Die Entdeckung des Glaubens im Neuen Testament," in *Glauben heute. Christ warden—Christ bleiben.* Gütersloh: Publisher, 1988, 52-64.

———. *Die Gleichnisse Jesu als Metaphern: Traditions- und redaktionsgeschichtliche Analysen und Interpretationen.* FRLANT 120. Göttingen: Vandenhoeck & Ruprecht, 1980.

———. *Die "Rede der Reden": Eine Auslegung der Bergpredigt heute.* Zürich: Theologischer, 1985.

Weizsäcker, Carl Friedrich von. *Der Garten des Menschlichen.* 5th ed. Munich: C. Hanser, 1978.

Wellhausen, Julius. *Israelitische und jüdische Geschichte.* 7th ed. Berlin: G. Reimer, 1914.

Werbick, Jurgen. "Rechtfertigung des Sünders—Rechtfertigung Gottes," *KuD* 27, 1981, 45-57.

Wesley, John. *The Works of John Wesley.* (Bicentennial Edition), Vol. 1-4: Sermons I-IV (ed. Albert Outler), Nashville: Abingdon, 1984-87. Vol. 9: The Methodist Societies (ed. Rupert E. Davies), Nashville: Abingdon, 1989.

Westerholm, Stephen. "Paul and the Law in Romans 9-11." *Paul and the Mosaic Law.* Edited by James D. G. Dunn. WUNT 89. Tübingen: Mohr (Siebeck), 1996, 215-37.

———. *Perspectives Old and New on Paul. The "Lutheran" Paul and His Critics.* Grand Rapids, Mich.: W. B. Eerdmans, 2004.

Westermann, Claus. "Boten des Zornes: Der Begriff des Zornes Gottes in der Prophetie." *Die Botschaft und die Boten, Festschrift für Hans Walter Wolff zum 70.* Neukirchen-Vluyn: Neukirchener, 1981. Edited by Jörg Jeremias und Lothar Perlitt. 147-56.

———. "Das Buch Jesaja: Kap 40-66," *ATD* 19, 1986:5.

Wilckens, Ulrich. *Der Brief an die Römer.* Vols 1 and 2 (Röm 1-5/6-11). EKK 6. Neukirchen-Vluyn: Neukirchener, 1987.

———. "Die 'Gemeinsame Erklärung zur Rechtfertigungslehre'(GE) und ihre biblische Grundlage." *Worum geht es in der Rechtfertigungs-lehre?: Das biblische Fundament der 'Gemeinsamen Erklärung' von katholischer Kirche und lutherischem Weltbund. Edited by Thomas Söding.* QD 180. Freiburg: Herder, 1999, 27-63.

———. "Was heisst bei Paulus: 'Aus Werken des Gesetzes wird kein Mensch gerecht'?" *Rechtfertigung als Freiheit. Paulusstudien.* Neukirchen-Vluyn: Neukirchener, 1974, 77-109.

Wildberger, Hans. *Isaiah 1-12: A Commentary.* Translated by Thomas H. Trapp. Minneapolis: Fortress, 1991.

———. *Isaiah 28–39: A Continental Commentary.* Translated by Thomas H. Trapp. Minneapolis: Fortress, 2002.

Wilkens, E., ed. *Helsinki 1963.* Berlin and Hamburg: Luther Verlagshaus, 1964.

Wintermute, O. S. "Jubilees: A New Translation and Introduction." *The Old Testament Pseudepigrapha.* Vol. 2. Edited by James H. Charlesworth. ABRL. New York: Doubleday, 1985, 35-142.

Wolff, Christian. *Der erste Brief des Paulus an die Korinther.* ThHK 7. Leipzig: Evangelische Verlagsanstalt, 1996.

Wolff, Hanna. *Neuer Wein, Alte Schläuche: das Identitätsproblem des Christentums im Lichte der Tiefenpsychologie.* Radius-Bücher. Stuttgart: Radius, 1981.

Wolff, Hans Walter. *Dodekapropheton. 2, Joel und Amos.* 3rd ed. BK 14/2. Neukirchen-Vluyn: Neukirchener, 1985.

Wolter, Michael. *Die Pastoralbriefe als Paulustradition*. FRLANT 146. Göttingen: Vandenhoeck & Ruprecht, 1988.

―――. Rechtfertigung und zukünftiges Heil: Untersuchung zu Röm 5,1-11. BZNW 43. Berlin: de Gruyter, 1978.

Wrede, William. "Paulus." *Das Paulusbild in der neueren deutschen Forschung*. Hg. von Karl Heinrich Rengstorf, WdF 24. Darmstadt: Wissenschaftliche Buchgesellschaft. 1964, 1-97.

Wright, R. B. "Psalms of Solomon: A New Translation and Introduction." *The Old Testament Pseudepigrapha*. Vol. 2. Edited by James H. Charlesworth. ABRL. New York: Doubleday, 1985, 639-70.

Ziesler, J. A. *The Meaning of Righteousness in Paul: A Linguistic and Theological Enquiry*. NTS.MS 20. Cambridge: Cambridge University Press, 1972.

Zimmerli, Walther. "Alttestamentliche Prophetie und Apocaklyptik auf dem Wege zur 'Rechtfertigung des Gottlosen.'" *Rechtfertigung: Festschrift für Ernst Käsemann zum 70. Geburtstag*. hrsg. Johannes Friedrich, Wolfgang Pöhlmann and Peter Stuhlmacher. Tübingen: Mohr; Göttingen: Vandenhoeck & Ruprecht, 1976, 575-92.

―――. "'Heiligkeit' nach dem sogenannten Heiligkeitsgesetz," *VT* 30, 1980, 493-512.

―――. "'Leben' und 'Tod' im Buch des Propheten Ezechiel," in *Gottes Offenbarung. Gesammelte Aufsätze zum AT*. 2nd ed. ThB 19. Munich: C. Kaiser, 1963, 178-91.

―――. *Old Testament Theology in Outline*. Translated by David E. Green. Atlanta: John Knox, 1978.

INDEX OF SCRIPTURE AND OTHER ANCIENT TEXTS